For Michael,

on the day

placing of the

on the these,

in memory of several

years of pleasant association,

Ted.

21 March 1974

THE SECOND GIFT

A STUDY OF GRACE

THE SECOND GIFT

A Study of Grace

SARUM LECTURES

by

Edward Yarnold, S.J.

 St Paul Publications

ST PAUL PUBLICATIONS
SLOUGH SL3 6BT ENGLAND

Copyright © 1974 St Paul Publications

Nihil obstat: G.E. Roberts
Imprimatur: + Charles Grant, Bishop of Northampton
            20 June 1974

First published November 1974

Printed in Great Britain by the Society of St Paul, Slough

SBN 85439 103 7

To John and Jenny Halliburton

CONTENTS

ACKNOWLEDGEMENTS

The Scripture quotations in this book are taken from the Revised Standard Version Common Bible, copyrighted 1973 by the Division of Christian Education of the National Council of the Churches of Christ in the U.S.A. and used by kind permission.

My thanks are also due to the following publishers for their courteous permission to quote from copyright sources: Messrs T. and T. Clark (K. Barth: *Church Dogmatics*); Darton, Longman and Todd (O. Casel: *The Mystery of Christian Worship;* B. Lonergan: *Collection;* K. Rahner: *Theological Investigations*); Eyre and Spottiswoode (C. Ernst: *Summa Theologiae,* vol. 30); Sheed and Ward (A. Hulsbosch: *God's Creation;* K. Rahner: *Nature and Grace;* P. Schoonenberg: *The Christ*); A. and C. Black (J.N.D. Kelly: *Early Christian Doctrines*); Burns and Oates Ltd. (E. Allison Peers: *The Complete Works of St John of the Cross*); Geoffrey Chapman (H. de Lubac: *The Mystery of the Supernatural;* J.L. McKenzie: *Myths and Realities*); Gill-Macmillan (J.P. Mackey: *Life and Grace;* O. Semmelroth: *Church and Sacrament*); the Longman Group (E.L. Mascall: *Christ, the Christian and the Church* and *Via Media*); Faith Press (J. Meyendorff: *A Study of Gregory Palamas*); Mowbrays (C. Moeller and G. Philips: *The Theology of Grace and the Ecumenical Movement*); Collins (C.F. Mooney: *Teilhard de Chardin and the Mystery of Christ;* P. Teilhard de Chardin: *Christianity and Evolution, The Future of Man, Le Milieu Divin* and *The Phenomenon of Man*); The Mercier Press (J.J. Scullion: *The Theology of Inspiration*); T. Nelson (J. Stierli: *Heart of the Saviour*); *The Way* (J. Ashton: 'The Consciousness of Christ'); Doubleday (R.M. Grant, ed.: *The Secret Sayings of Jesus*); the English Province of the Society of Jesus (G.M. Hopkins: *Collected Poems*).

For God is good, or rather he is the source of goodness. Being good, he cannot be grudging in anything. Accordingly he has not grudged existence to anything, but made all things out of nothing by his own Word, our Lord Jesus Christ. Among these things he took pity on the human race before everything on the earth, and saw that, by reason of its origin, it could not last for ever. So he gave men a further gift (pleon ti charizomenos), *and did not simply create them as he created all the irrational living creatures on earth. He made them according to his own image, giving them also a share in the power of his own Word, so that, possessing, so to speak, shadows of his Word and becoming rational, they might be able to remain for ever in blessedness, living the true life which belongs to the saints in paradise.*

(St Athanasius, *De Incarnatione*)

ABBREVIATIONS

CC   *Corpus Christianorum.* Turnhout, 1953

DS   *Enchiridion Symbolorum, Definitionum et Declarationum de Rebus Fidei et Morum* (ed. H. Denzinger and A. Schönmetzer). Herder, Barcelona etc., 33rd ed., 1965.

Dict. Spir. *Dictionnaire de Spiritualité.* Beauchesne, Paris, 1937

DTC   *Dictionnaire de Théologie Catholique.* Paris, 1903-50.

ET   English translation.

GCS   *Die Griechischen Christlichen Schriftsteller der Ersten Drei Jahrhunderte.* Leipzig and Berlin, 1897

JBC   *The Jerome Bible Commentary* (ed. R.E. Brown, J.A. Fitzmyer, R.E. Murphy). G. Chapman, London, 1969.

PG   *Patrologia Graeca* (ed. J.P. Migne). Paris, 1857-66.

PL   *Patrologia Latina* (ed. J.P. Migne). Paris, 1844-64.

SC   *Sources Chrétiennes.* Paris, 1940

ST   *Summa Theologiae.*

INTRODUCTION

These lectures were delivered thanks to the munificence of John Bampton, sometime of Trinity College, Oxford, whose will provided in 1751 for the establishment of a fund to endow the preaching of an annual series of 'eight divinity lecture sermons'. About the turn of the present century the fund seems to have fallen on hard times, so that a lecturer was now appointed only in alternate years. Happily, however, the good stewardship of the trustees, allied with the propensity of money to expand in the economic conditions of today, has made possible the establishment of a series of Sarum Lectures, to be delivered in the years in which there are no Bamptons. The first of these was given in the year 1954-5 by that great scholar, still happily flourishing among us as his ninetieth year approaches, Charles Harold Dodd. [1]

The subject prescribed for the Sarum Lectures is compendious: they are to be 'in support of the Christian faith'. However, the principle of *epieikeia* suggests that the Founder's original wishes should if possible be respected. Bampton had drawn up a longer list of subjects, the last of which was 'the Articles of the Christian faith, as comprehended in the Apostles' and Nicene Creeds'. The subject I have chosen is grace — a choice, be it said, which owes nothing to the fact that last year the best-selling gramophone-record was of the hymn 'Amazing Grace', performed upon bagpipes. This theme falls readily

---

[1] Dodd's very fruitful life came to an end a few months after these lines were written and delivered.

under Bampton's last subject; for any study of grace is a commentary on the article of the Creed: 'I believe in the Holy Spirit, the Lord and giver of life'.

The subject could be expressed also in the words of another who loved to frequent Bampton's graceful cathedral at Salisbury, George Herbert, Rector of Fugglestone with Bemerton on the outskirts of that city. In his unselfconscious, though highly-wrought lyric entitled *Easter* he writes:

> Rise, heart, thy Lord is risen. Sing His praise
> Without delays,
> Who takes thee by the hand, that thou likewise
> With Him mayst rise;
> That, as His death calcinèd thee to dust,
> His life may make thee gold, and much more, just. . .
>
> I got me flowers to strew Thy way;
> I got me boughs off many a tree;
> But Thou wast up by break of day,
> And brought'st Thy sweets along with Thee.

My subject, like Herbert's, is grace: the sweets brought by the risen Lord, man's share in his resurrection, the life that makes us gold and just.

*   *   *

Many books have been written about grace, and the reader may well wonder whether there is anything new in this one. Accordingly it may be helpful if I try to sum up the argument of the whole book in a single paragraph. Those who would like a fuller summary can turn at once to the Conclusion.

My purpose is not to write a history or an exhaustive dogmatic treatise of the doctrine of grace. My purpose can in fact be stated in one sentence: it is to discuss the practical implications of the doctrine of habitual grace. I begin with two fundamental principles, which I try to justify in the first three chapters. They are: (1) that God's grace is not something apart from us, not only his mercy, his favour or his love; it is all of these, but it is much more; it is a mercy and favour and love which transforms us, makes us new creatures, endows us with an abiding power to know and love him which is infinitely above our natural powers; (2) that this new life of grace is not realized in experiences which are distinguishable from natural human experiences; for whenever we reflect or choose as moral beings, we are under the influence of grace; the reflection and the choice are our experiences of grace. In the remaining chapters I indicate areas of this experience of grace, and try to show that it is the realization of habitual grace, the new potentiality with which God's loving presence endows us.

What I have called the two fundamental principles are commonly held today, at least by Roman Catholic theologians; what is perhaps new is the weight I have allowed to the first principle in working out the practical implications.

In discussing these implications I am inevitably taken into the field of psychology; nevertheless this book is an essay in systematic theology rather than in the psychology of religion. The difference is one of starting-point. One could begin with the psychological data, and try to discern in them the pattern of grace; or one can begin with the Gospel, and try to show how the truths of revelation relate to particular experiences. My interests and training determined me to adopt the second course.

This book contains the lectures substantially as I delivered them. I have, however, tried to tighten the expression and remove obscurities and inaccuracies, and I have included several passages which I had to omit from the lectures for lack of time.

My thanks are due to a great many friends for their help and encouragement: especially my friends and colleagues at Campion Hall and Heythrop College, Anthony Meredith, Brian Daley, Ian Brayley, Gerard Diamond, Robert Butterworth and Joseph Laishley; there have been many besides, too many to name. I would also like to thank Mrs Gilda Punshon, Mrs Cathie Cipolla and Mrs Barbara Cleary, who contrived to produce an intelligible typescript from my much-corrected draft; and Miss Margaret Pellow for her acute help with the proofs.

CHAPTER 1

THE SECOND GIFT

In this first chapter I wish to consider the scriptural and patristic teaching about grace. Immediately one comes up against a problem of method. One possible line of procedure would be simply to follow concordances and lexicons, and so to catalogue and systematize the passages in which the biblical authors and the Fathers use the word 'grace', (*charis, gratia*). But such a method of investigation would distort our vision from the start. For I am concerned rather with what the Church has come with time to understand by the word 'grace', which may not be exactly the same thing as the ancient writers meant. Later expressions of faith, if they are to be legitimate, must have grown out of the scriptural teaching; but this teaching may have been conveyed in the Bible not only by the word 'grace', but by other individual words and phrases, sometimes merely by implication.

Grace is by no means the only area in which the literal use of concordances would be misleading. The same is all too evidently true about the divinity of Christ. It would be quite erroneous to maintain that the sum total of the scriptural grounds for belief in his divinity consists of a list of passages in which the name 'God' is applied to him. We have also to consider other titles: Son of God, Son of Man, Word, Lord, and so on. And one cannot rest content with the investigation of titles: the claims that he made, the things that he did, the worship that was paid to him, and the powers attributed to him, all constitute part of the New Testament evidence for Christ's divinity.

In order to gather and assess the evidence it is necessary to impose a pattern on the New Testament material, just as a scientist needs to construct hypotheses before testing them (for hypotheses are not part of his observed data), and the historian, in R.G. Collingwood's phrase, needs to read his sources 'with a question in his mind, having taken the initiative by deciding for himself what he wants to find out from them.'[1] But to speak of 'imposing' a pattern is not quite accurate, for that suggests that some violence is done to the original. Rather one has to *perceive* a pattern in the material, and then to plot its shape in detail, tracing lines where the pattern is hidden by other superimposed forms, without however ever twisting the data to fit the pattern.

One can take courage from the fact that to have used the concordance method would itself have been to impose a pattern, which could falsify the evidence both by omission and addition. By omission, because there may be relevant passages where the word under discussion is not used: by addition, because, in the passages which Cruden or Lampe so conveniently gather, the word may not always have the same meaning.

When we examine the scriptural and patristic writings on the subject I have chosen, a very simple pattern meets the eye. It stands out sharply in St Athanasius' work *De Incarnatione*. After rejecting false Epicurean, Platonic and gnostic theories of creation, he proceeds to expound the Christian view:

> For God is good, or rather he is the source of goodness. Being good, he cannot be grudging in anything. Accordingly he has not grudged existence to anything, but made all things out of nothing by his own Word, our Lord Jesus Christ. Among these things he took pity on the human race before everything on the earth, and saw that, by reason of its origin, it could not last for ever. So he *gave men a further gift* (*pleon ti charizomenos*), and did not simply create them as he created all the irrational living creatures

[1] *The Idea of History* (Clarendon Press, Oxford, 1946), p. 269.

on earth. He made them according to his own image,
giving them also a share in the power of his own Word,
so that, possessing, so to speak, shadows of his Word and
becoming rational, they might be able to remain for ever
in blessedness, living the true life which belongs to the
saints in paradise. [2]

Creation is a gift, says St Athanasius; but God did not 'simply
create' men; he 'gave them a further gift' in addition to creation.
This saying provides the pattern that I shall trace in the Bible
and the Fathers. It is not the only pattern; but it seems to me
to include everything which theologians mean when they speak
of grace, and at the same time it has a clear connection with the
New Testament word *charis*, which literally means 'favour'.

(a) *The Old Testament*

Throughout the Old Testament there is one constantly
recurring theme which expresses the special favour and promises
of God, the theme of covenant. The covenant with Abraham,
the covenant on Sinai and the covenant with David are given
different emphases and connected in different ways at different
points of the nation's history. [3] Deuteronomy stresses the Sinaitic
covenant, which is God's choice of the Israelites as his people.
They are to be dedicated to his service, and are promised his
protection. This covenant is therefore a second gift which God
gave freely to those whom he favoured; the Israelites had done
nothing to deserve it.

For you are a people holy to the Lord your God; the
Lord your God has chosen you to be a people for his own
possession, out of all the peoples that are on the face of
the earth. It was not because you were more in number
than any other people that the Lord set his love upon
you and chose you, for you were the fewest of all peoples;

---

[2] *De Incarnatione* (Cross) iii.3. 'Rational' translates *logikos*, the ad-
jective derived from *logos* ('word').

[3] Cf. R.E. Clements, *Abraham and David* (SCM, London, 1967),
chapter 6.

B

but it is because the Lord loves you, and is keeping the
oath which he swore to your fathers, that the Lord has
brought you out with a mighty hand, and redeemed you
from the house of bondage, from the hand of Pharaoh
king of Egypt (Deut 7.6-8).

The Old Testament writers express the privileged intimacy
of the covenant-relationship in a variety of images. In a primitive account of the Sinaitic covenant in Exodus, the relationship
is expressed in terms of worship:

> Now therefore, if you will obey my voice and keep my
> covenant, you shall be my own possession among all
> peoples; for all the earth is mine, and you shall be to me
> a kingdom of priests and a holy nation (Ex 19.5-6).

A whole range of personal relationships is called upon to illustrate God's love for his chosen people. In Deuteronomy the
song of Moses asks:

> Is he not your father, who created you,
>   who made you and established you? (Deut 32.6)

Second Isaiah compares Yahweh's love with a mother's:

> 'Can a woman forget her sucking child,
>   that she should have no compassion on the son of
>   her womb?'
> Even these may forget,
>   yet I will not forget you (Is 49.15).

The image recurs in the last chapter of Isaiah:

> As one whom his mother comforts,
>   so I will comfort you (Is 66.13).

The Lord is also the husband of his people. Linking together
and at the same time distinguishing the first and the second
gifts, Second Isaiah declares:

> Your Maker is your husband,
>   the Lord of hosts is his name. . .
> For the Lord has called you
>   like a wife forsaken and grieved in spirit,
> like a wife of youth when she is cast off (Is 54.5-6).

This analogy between sinful Israel and an unfaithful wife is a common theme in the prophets; the infidelity is compounded in the comparison by the fact that the wife owes all to the husband. It has been suggested that the covenant formula, 'You shall be my people, and I will be your God', [4] is in fact borrowed from the marriage formula, 'She is my wife and I her husband from this day for ever'. [5]

There are many other images which express the covenant-relationship which is Israel's privilege. Israel is the Lord's possession, which is his by right of conquest. [6] Israel is the vineyard which the Lord has taken from the desert and cultivated. [7] Israel is the Lord's flock; for want of good shepherds, he himself will be the shepherd:

> ... I myself will search for my sheep, and will seek them out. As a shepherd seeks out his flock when some of his sheep have been scattered abroad, so I will seek out my sheep... And I will bring them out from the peoples, and gather them from the countries, and will bring them into their own land (Ezek 34.11-13; cf. 2-16).

The prophets link God's favour for his chosen people with the gift of the Spirit. Ezekiel assures the exiles in Babylon that God will make them once more a free nation, and then the covenant will be restored and even enhanced, and their hearts renewed by the gift of the Spirit.

> For I will take you from the nations, and gather you from all the countries, and bring you into your own land. I will sprinkle clean water upon you, and you shall be clean from all your uncleannesses, and from all your idols I will cleanse you. A new heart I will give you, and a new spirit I will put within you; and I will take out of your flesh the heart of stone and give you a heart of flesh. And I will put my spirit within you, and cause you to walk

[4] Cf. for example Ezek 36.28.
[5] A. Cowley, *Aramaic Papyri of the Fifth Century B.C.* (Clarendon Press, Oxford, 1923), no. 15, line 4.
[6] Cf. Deut 7.6-8, quoted above.
Cf. Is 5.1-7.

in my statutes and be careful to observe my ordinances.
You shall dwell in the land which I gave to your fathers;
and you shall be my people, and I will be your God
(Ezek 36.24-28).

But the Israelites are not allowed to think that they have any
claim on these blessings, for they are nothing but a gift:

It is not for your sake that I will act, says the Lord God;
let that be known to you. Be ashamed and confounded
for your ways, O house of Israel (Ezek 36.32).

Jeremiah foretells with even more clarity the restoration of
Israel and Judah to the Lord's favour, which will set them in
a position of even greater privilege than they enjoyed before:

Behold, the days are coming, says the Lord, when I will
make a new covenant with the house of Israel and the
house of Judah, not like the covenant which I made with
their fathers when I took them by the hand to bring
them out of the land of Egypt, my covenant which they
broke, though I was their husband, says the Lord. But
this is the covenant which I will make with the house of
Israel after those days, says the Lord: I will put my law
within them, and I will write it upon their hearts; and I
will be their God, and they shall be my people. And no
longer shall each man teach his neighbour and each his
brother, saying, 'Know the Lord,' for they shall know me,
from the least of them to the greatest, says the Lord; for
I will forgive their iniquity, and I will remember their
sin no more (Jer 31.31-4).

The prophets repeatedly state that this restoration of the
old covenant, or institution of the new, will effect a conversion
in the hearts of the people, so that they reject their evil ways.
The description of the Lord as Israel's husband is, as we have
noticed, frequently associated with a parable of the forgiveness
and restoration to favour of an erring or divorced wife:

For the Lord has called you
    like a wife forsaken and grieved in spirit,
like a wife of youth when she is cast off,
    says your God (Is 54.6).

In various books of the Old Testament a distinction is
clearly drawn between the Lord's original generosity in raising
up Israel from the common lot of mankind to a place of privilege,
and his second gift in restoring Israel to favour (and in some
passages even to greater favour) after their sin. The prophets
are not alone in writing on this theme: the point is vividly
expressed throughout the song of Moses already quoted:

> He found him in a desert land,
>> and in the howling waste of the wilderness;
> he encircled him, he cared for him,
>> he kept him as the apple of his eye.
> Like an eagle that stirs up its nest,
>> that flutters over its young,
> spreading out its wings, catching them,
>> bearing them on its pinions,
> the Lord alone did lead him. . .
>
> But Jeshurun waxed fat, and kicked,
>> you waxed fat, you grew thick, you became sleek;
> then he forsook God who made him,
>> and scoffed at the Rock of his salvation. . .
> You were unmindful of the Rock that begot you,
>> and you forgot the God who gave you birth.
>
> The Lord saw it, and spurned them,
>> because of the provocation of his sons and daughters.
> And he said, 'I will hide my face from them,
>> I will see what their end will be. . .
> And I will heap evils upon them;
>> I will spend my arrows upon them;
> They shall be wasted with hunger,
>> and devoured with burning heat
>> and poisonous pestilence. . .'
>
> For the Lord will vindicate his people
>> and have compassion on his servants,
> when he sees that their power is gone,
>> and there is none remaining, bond or free. . .
>
> 'See now that I, even I, am he,
>> and there is no god beside me;
> I kill and I make alive;

> I wound and I heal;
> and there is none that can deliver out of my hand.'
>   (Deut 32.10-39)

In the Old Testament, then, and especially in Deuteronomy
and the prophets, God gives his covenant to his people simply
as a gift, not only insofar as he was free to choose them from
all the people of the earth, but also insofar as the covenant is
still offered to them despite their infidelities. The restored gift
is often said to be greater than the original. It is offered to
them corporately, as a people, not as a collection of individuals,
although responsibility still rests upon individuals, at least in
Jeremiah and Ezekiel:

> In those days they shall no longer say:
> 'The fathers have eaten sour grapes,
>   and the children's teeth are set on edge.'
> But everyone shall die for his own sin; each man who
> eats sour grapes, his teeth shall be set on edge (Jer
> 31. 29-30; cf. Ezek 18.2-4).

(b) *The New Testament*

Like the Old Testament writers, the writers of the New
make the idea of a second gift central in their theology of man.
Thus, God's love for his people is expressed throughout the
Johannine and Pauline writings even more explicitly than in
the Old Testament; love is even God's definition. [8] This love is
sometimes expressed in terms of God's choice of those who are
to be dedicated to him.

> Blessed be the God and Father of our Lord Jesus Christ,
> who has blessed us in Christ with every spiritual blessing
> in the heavenly places, even as he chose us in him before
> the foundation of the world, that we should be holy and
> blameless before him (Eph 1.3-4).

In Romans St Paul turns to Exodus 33.19 for a statement of
God's freedom of choice: 'I will be gracious to whom I will be

[8] 'God is love' (1 Jn 4.16).

gracious, and will show mercy on whom I will show mercy'
(Rom 9.15); and John expresses the same point in words that
were destined to affect St Augustine so profoundly: 'No one
can come to me unless the Father who sent me draws him'
(Jn 6.44). [9]

Both the corporate and the individual dimensions of this call
are spelt out in much more detail than in the Old Testament.
The account of Pentecost in Acts is designed to show how God's
call unifies the human race. The story of the Tower of Babel had
shown that the consequence of man's rebellion against God was
the loss of unity, a loss which is symbolized in men's inability to
'understand one another's speech', and in their 'scattering' over
the face of the earth (Gen 11.7, 9). [10] Now at Pentecost Parthians
and Medes and people from many parts of the world hear the
apostles preach, 'each of us in his own native language' (Acts
2.8). For *glossolalia,* the usual sign of the Spirit, Luke substitutes
the understanding of foreign tongues; in this way he shows that
the division caused by the sin at Babel is ended.

In St Paul's mind the most important thing about the unity
of the people of the new covenant is that it is a unity 'in Christ'.

> For as many of you as were baptized into Christ have put
> on Christ. There is neither Jew nor Greek, there is neither
> slave nor free, there is neither male nor female; for you
> are all one in Christ Jesus (Gal 3.27-8; cf. Eph. 1.3-4,
> quoted above).

The favourite Pauline image of this unity is the body. The
Stoic precedents for the use of this image are well-known; [11]
and Paul in his earlier writings perhaps does not do much more
than put in a Christian context the Roman ideal that citizens of
all classes in a state should co-operate for the common good like
the various organs of a body. So it is in Romans:

---

[9] *Tract. in Jo.* xxvi.4. (CC 36.261-2; PL 35.1608).

[10] Such a list of nations was a conventional expression of universality.
Cf. *JBC* 45:17.

[11] Cf. E. Schweizer, *TWNT, sōma* A4, ET vii.1038-9. Paul, however,
was probably influenced by rabbinic sources; cf. p. 118.

> For by the grace given to me I bid every one among you
> not to think of himself more highly than he ought to
> think, but to think with sober judgment, each according
> to the measure of faith which God has assigned him. For
> as in one body we have many members, and all the mem-
> bers do not have the same function, so we, though many,
> are one body in Christ, and individually members one of
> another. Having gifts that differ according to the grace
> given to us, let us use them (Rom 12.3-6).

The emphasis in 1 Corinthians 12 is similar. In Colossians and
Ephesians, however, a new dimension is added to the image: the
emphasis is not on the mutual help of the members, but on their
relationship to Christ the Head, who is the source of the unity,
life and growth of the whole body.

> Let no one disqualify you, insisting on self-abasement and
> worship of angels, taking his stand on visions, puffed up
> without reason by his sensuous mind, and not holding fast
> to the Head, from whom the whole body, nourished and
> knit together through its joints and ligaments, grows with
> a growth that is from God (Col 2.18-19).

In Ephesians the unity of the body is linked with the Spirit, who
is the source of unity: the people of Ephesus are urged to be

> eager to maintain the unity of the Spirit in the bond of
> peace. There is one body and one Spirit, just as you were
> called to the one hope that belongs to your call, one Lord,
> one faith, one baptism, one God and Father of us all, who
> is above all and through all and in all (Eph 4.3-6).

The author then goes on to speak of the different gifts of
Christ in terms which are reminiscent of Romans and 1 Corinthians:

> But grace was given to each of us according to the measure
> of Christ's gift... And his gifts were that some should
> be apostles, some prophets, some evangelists, some pastors
> and teachers, for the equipment of the saints, for the work
> of ministry, for building up the body of Christ (Eph 4.
> 7, 11-12).

All this is familiar enough; we are not far from the well-trodden ground of Livy and Plutarch. But another note has been sounded: the Ascension has been introduced. Psalm 68 is quoted in this connection: 'When he ascended on high he led a host of captives, and he gave gifts to men' (Eph 4.8, following the Septuagint version of Ps 68.18). In St Luke's theology the Ascension is the necessary prelude to the outpouring of the Spirit:

> Being therefore exalted at the right hand of God, and having received from the Father the promise of the Holy Spirit, he has poured out this which you see and hear (Acts 2.33; cf. Lk 24.49).

So too, in this chapter of Ephesians, the Ascension is the preparation for the giving of the gifts, which at the beginning of the chapter have been associated with the Holy Spirit; their effect, it is constantly repeated, like the effect of the Spirit at Pentecost, is to produce unity.

There is another advance in the thought at this point. The unity spoken of is not now simply co-operation and mutual respect, but a unity of shared faith and even shared life:

> . . . until we all attain to the unity of the faith and of the knowledge of the Son of God, to mature manhood, to the measure of the structure of the fullness of Christ. . . We are to grow up in every way into him who is the head, into Christ, from whom the whole body, joined and knit together by every joint with which it is supplied, when each part is working properly, makes bodily growth and upbuilds itself in love (Eph 4.13-16).

This unity of Christ's chosen people in him is described in several other metaphors: the vine (Jn 15.1-10), the living stones of a temple built on Christ the cornerstone (1 Pet 2.5-7; Eph 2.20-22), wild oliveshoots grafted on to the cultivated olive (Rom 11.17-24); the kingdom of priests of Exodus (Rev 1.6; 5.10; 1 Pet 2.9; cf. Ex 19.6). The new Jerusalem is Christ's Bride (Rev 21.2). We have already seen Paul's claim that this unity implies the healing of all divisions (Gal 3.28); the point is made again in similar language in Colossians (3.11), and in strikingly new terms in Ephesians:

> For he is our peace, who has made us both one, and has broken down the dividing wall of hostility, by abolishing in his flesh the law of commandments and ordinances, that he might create in himself one new man in place of the two, so making peace, and might reconcile us both to God in one body through the cross, thereby bringing the hostility to an end (Eph 2.14-16).

The last part of this passage links the reconciliation of men with one another to the reconciliation of men with God. We shall return to this point in Chapter Five.

It is not only the corporate dimensions of election which are developed in the New Testament; the implications for the individual are also explored at much greater depth than in the Old. In Matthew's account of the Judgment each individual answers separately for himself (Mt 25.31-46). The Good Shepherd calls the sheep by name (Jn 10.3). In the church of Pergamum he who conquers is promised 'a white stone, with a new name written on the stone which no one knows except him who receives it' (Rev 2.17). The believer experiences nothing less than a birth *anōthen* (from above, or anew) (Jn 3.3), a birth by water and Spirit (Jn 3.5), a birth 'not of blood nor of the will of the flesh nor of the will of man, but of God' (Jn 1.13). 'That which is born of the flesh' is sharply distinguished from 'that which is born of the Spirit' (Jn 3.6). St Paul sees the Christian as a 'new creation' (2 Cor 5.17); his 'inner nature is being renewed every day' (2 Cor 4.16). Paul regards the process as an adoption by God (e.g. Rom 8.23), a concept which in John's eyes implies much more than an external dignity, or even than the assurance of God's loving protection:

> See what love the Father has given us, that we should be called children of God; and so we are... Beloved, we are God's children now; it does not yet appear what we shall be, but we know that when he appears we shall be like him, for we shall see him as he is (1 Jn 3.1-2).

In St Paul's thought this adoption is the work of the Spirit. The eighth chapter of Romans explains in great detail the practical effects of the Spirit's action. 'The law of the Spirit of

life in Christ Jesus has set me free from the law of sin and death'
(8.2). 'Those who live according to the Spirit set their minds on
the things of the Spirit', and to do this is 'life and peace' (8.5, 6).
'The Spirit of God dwells in you', so that you are 'in the Spirit',
and 'have the Spirit of Christ', 'the Spirit of him who raised
Jesus from the dead', who 'will give life to your mortal bodies
also through his Spirit who dwells in you' (8.9-11). 'All who
are led by the Spirit of God are sons of God', for the Spirit is
'the Spirit of sonship', who enables us to address God in Jesus'
own words 'Abba! Father!', and who so bears 'witness with
our spirit that we are children of God, and if children, then heirs,
heirs of God and fellow heirs with Christ' (8.14-17).

One can detect in this chapter a tension between the given
and the conditional, between the present and the future. 'You
have received the Spirit of sonship' (8.15), but 'we wait for
adoption as sons, the redemption of our bodies' (8.23); 'you
will live', we are 'heirs', but with a proviso — 'if [you live] by
the Spirit', 'provided we suffer with him in order that we may
also be glorified by him' (8.13, 17). For the Spirit dwelling in
us is only the 'first fruits' (8.23), an idea which St Paul expresses
elsewhere by the word 'guarantee' (arrabōn, 2 Cor 1.22), thus
anticipating St John's contrast between what we are 'now', and
'what we shall be' (1 Jn 3.2). Meanwhile St Paul points to the
presence of the Spirit even now, praying within our hearts 'with
sighs too deep for words' (Rom 8.26).

Later in the same chapter of Romans, though without
immediate reference to the Spirit, St Paul describes this transformation of the adopted in another way when he speaks of those
predestined by God 'to be conformed to the image of his son'
(8.29). In 2 Corinthians he attributes this resemblance to the
action of the Spirit, and compare it with the glory of God
reflected on the face of Moses:

> And we all, with unveiled face, reflecting [or beholding,
> katoptrizomenoi] the glory of the Lord, are being changed
> into his likeness from one degree of glory to another; for
> this comes from the Lord who is the Spirit (2 Cor 3.18).

In some of these statements it is hard to decide whether
the writer is speaking of the present or the future age. A
distinction may not in fact be possible, for the future grows
from the present; the Holy Spirit is not only the Spirit of
promise and the guarantee of what is to come, [12] but is already
the first fruits (Rom 8.23); our growth is 'from one degree of
glory to another' (2 Cor 3.18). So too in the great declaration
of hope at the beginning of 2 Peter, there is no clear dividing-
line between this life and the next:

> His divine power *has granted* to us all things that pertain
> to life and godliness, through the knowledge of him who
> called us to his own glory and excellence, by which he has
> granted to us his precious and very great promises, that
> through these you may escape from the corruption that is
> in the world because of passion, and become partakers of
> the divine nature (2 Pet 1.3-4).

This transforming gift of the Spirit of sonship can also be
described in other terms. 'Do you not know that you are God's
temple and that God's Spirit dwells in you?', St Paul asks the
Corinthians (1 Cor 3.16; cf. 6.19). The Fourth Gospel speaks
of the 'gift', the 'sending' and the 'coming' of the Holy Spirit
(14.16, 26; 15.26); the Father and Son are also said to come
to the Christian: 'If a man loves me, he will keep my word, and
my Father will love him, and we will come to him and make
our home with him' (14.23).

The New Testament writers use many images to express
God's gift of himself to man. In the Fourth Gospel, Jesus is
life (11.25; 14.6), light (1.9; 8.12), the source of living water
(4.10; cf. 7.37-9), the bread of life. St Paul uses the metaphor
of perfume: 'We are the aroma of Christ in God' (2 Cor
2.15).

The beginning of the transforming gift is baptism, when
the Christian is 'baptized into his death', so that 'we shall
certainly be united with him in a resurrection like his' (Rom

[12] Cf. Gal 3.14; 4.28-9 and Eph 1.13-14.

6.3, 5). 'As many of you as were baptized into Christ have put on Christ' (Gal 3.27).

So far I have been searching the New Testament for the implications of the fact that we are chosen or called by God. The election is a grace, that is, a privilege. But it is also a grace in another sense: it is a pardon. St Paul states this with great emphasis:

> While we were still weak, at the right time Christ died for the ungodly. Why, one will hardly die for a righteous man — though perhaps for a good man one will dare even to die. But God shows his love for us in that while we were yet sinners Christ died for us (Rom 5.6-8).

The 'good news of a great joy' announced to the shepherds was simply the birth of a *Saviour* (Lk 2.10-11). The name Jesus, to which Luke attaches so much importance (1.31; 2.21), is explained in Matthew: 'You shall call his name Jesus, for he will save his people from their sins' (1.21). As in the Old Testament parables of the unfaithful wife, what we have received from God is mercy as well as bounty.

Both the Old Testament, then, and the New, especially the Pauline and Johannine writings, present us with the fact of God's choice. God has chosen certain people to receive his promises, and no one has any right to be chosen, especially as 'all have sinned and fall short of the glory of God' (Rom 3.23).

These, then, are some of the ways in which the New Testament writers develop the idea of a 'second gift'. A passage in the eighth chapter of Romans, which has already proved so rich a quarry, draws many of these themes together:

> We know that in everything God works for good with those who love him, who are called according to his purpose. For those whom he foreknew he also predestined to be conformed to the image of his Son, in order that he might be the first-born among many brethren. And those whom he predestined he also called; and those whom he called

he also justified; and those whom he justified he also glorified (Rom 8.28-30).

(c) *The Fathers*

The idea that God has given men a second gift after creation appears in the Fathers in many forms. Sometimes they discuss this gift explicitly; at others they take it as a firm presupposition on which they can base further arguments. From the variety of material available I shall simply select some examples which illustrate the importance of this concept in patristic thinking.

One of the earliest ways in which this point is made is in terms of the *logos*. The word 'logos' was used in several schools of Greek thought, and with various meanings. Thus, in the Stoic system, which was a form of spiritual materialism, God's logos or word is diffused throughout the universe as a fiery substance which is immanent in all things as the principle of their order and energy. This diffusion of God's own stuff is called the 'seed-words' (*logoi spermatikoi*); and in man it is particularly concentrated to form his reason. Word, order and reason are all denoted by the term 'logos'. The Middle Platonists did not accept the Stoic materialism, but like the Stoics understood by 'logos' man's reason. They also believed in a world-soul, or principle of order in the universe; but they preferred to call it Mind (*nous, psuchē*), rather than Word. In the Old Testament God's word was his instrument in creation (e.g. Ps 33.6); and the book of Proverbs, perhaps under the influence of Platonic thought, hypostasized this concept into the figure of Wisdom, which was the power God fashioned to be 'beside him, like a master workman' in creating the world (Prov 8.22-31). In the first century B.C. the book of Wisdom uses the terms 'wisdom' and 'word' indifferently to refer to this agent of God in the work of creation (Wis 9.1-2); God's word is also the means by which he heals (16.12) and judges (18.15). In the following century the Jewish philosopher Philo synthesized Greek and Hebrew thought still further, and applied the term 'logos', not only to God's creative intermediary, but also to the Jewish Law. [13] The Johannine writings also use the concept of *logos*, though scholars are not agreed whether they were influenced in this matter by Hellenistic sources.

The Greek Apologists of the second century, in their efforts to explain Christian belief in Christ to outsiders, likewise turned to the concept of *logos*. [14] The Logos is the Son, the rational power by which God orders his creatures. He is also immanent in all men; all who live by reason (*meta logou*) are Christians, 'even though they have been regarded as atheists'; [15] there is planted within them 'the seed of reason' (*sperma tou logou*). [16] They are what some modern theologians have called 'anonymous Christians'. [17] This is why even pagan philosophers could reach some degree of religious truth; there was no need to suppose, as Justin did, that Plato and other Greeks had plagiarized Moses. [18]

Man, then, of his nature, shares in the divine, the *logos*. Yet at this point there is an ambiguity. On the one hand, the *logos* can be conceived as a faculty on the pre-moral level, a psychological power which a man preserves whether he be good or bad: his power to think and speak, the mental powers that make even a bad man superior to an animal. In this sense the

[13] On the role of logos in Stoic philosophy see F.C. Copleston, *A History of Philosophy*, vol. i (Burns and Oates, London, 1946) chap. 36. Chap. 43 of the same work gives a concise account of Middle Platonism. On Philo, see H. Chadwick in *The Cambridge History of Later Greek and Early Medieval Philosophy* (CUP, Cambridge, 1967), chap. 8. On the logos-theology of Clement of Alexandria and Origen, see C. Bigg, *The Christian Platonists of Alexandria* (Clarendon Press, Oxford, 1913) and S.R.C. Lilla, *Clement of Alexandria* (OUP, London, 1971).

[14] L.W. Barnard, *Justin Martyr, His Life and Thought* (CUP, Cambridge, 1967), pp. 91-9, following C. Andresen, argues that Justin is influenced by Platonist rather than Stoic theories.

[15] Justin, 1 *Apol.*, 46 (PG 6.397); 2 *Apol.*, 10, 13 (461, 465).

[16] 2 *Apol.*, 8 (457).

[17] Cf. K. Rahner, 'Christianity and the Non-Christian Religions', *Theological Investigations*, vol. v (ET Darton, Longman & Todd, London, and Helicon, Baltimore, 1966) ch. 6.

[18] 1 *Apol.*, 60, 64 (417, 425).

logos in man cannot be described as a *second* gift, as it is an essential part of his being. Sometimes the Apologists, especially Justin, seem to be thinking along these lines. [19] On the other hand, the *logos* can be considered as something which raises man above himself, which he can forfeit or stifle by his refusal to respond to its promptings. [20] This second interpretation implies a distinction between a first and a second gift.

The distinction between the two gifts is often made by the Apologists in terms of immortality. They could learn from both Testaments that immortality is not simply a matter of prolonged or renewed earthly life; it is a transformation of man's whole being, a share in God's own life. [21] For Justin, man is not of himself immortal, because only what has no beginning can have no end; nevertheless, those who have appeared worthy of God do not die. [22] For his pupil Tatian, 'the soul of itself is not immortal but mortal; but it is capable of not dying.' [23] It was Theophilus of Antioch however who hit upon the explanation which for some time remained classical: 'For man had been made a middle nature, neither wholly mortal nor altogether immortal, but capable of either (*dektikos de hekaterōn*).' [24]

> . . . so that if he were to turn to the things of immortality by keeping the commandment of God, he would win immortality as a reward from him and would become a

---

[19] Justin (1 *Apol.*, 10; PG 341) links the 'rational faculties' (*logikai dunameis*) with the gift of the Logos.

[20] Cf. Tatian, *Or. adv. Gr.*, 13; PG 6. 833; he maintains that the soul is of itself (*kath' heautēn*) darkness, but is illuminated by the Logos.

[21] Cf. Rom 7.9: 'I was once alive apart from the law, but when the commandment came, sin revived and I died.' The connection between death and sin is already apparent in Wis 2.23-4: 'For God created man for incorruption, and made him in the image of his eternity, but through the devil's envy death entered the world, and those who belong to his party experience it.'

[22] *Dial.*, 5 (PG 6.485-8).

[23] *Or. adv. Gr.*, 13 (PG 6.833).

[24] *Ad Autol.*, ii.24 (PG 6. 1089). The phrase 'capable of either' became a classical formulation of man's ambivalence. Pelagius spoke of man's 'utrius partis possibilitatem' (*Ep. ad Dem.*, 3; PL 30.18A).

God; but if he turned to deeds of death, disobeying God, he would be responsible for his own death. . . . What man did not acquire for himself through his neglect and disobedience, God now freely bestows on him through his love and mercy, when men obey him. [25]

In those days before the Pelagian controversy had brought the problem of grace and free will into sharp focus, the Apologists tended to overemphasise the power of man's unaided moral efforts. Nevertheless, when due correction has been made in this respect, the essential point for our purposes still remains: man has a capacity for immortality, but immortality remains in God's free gift.

The same point is made by the early Fathers in two other ways: in terms of the Spirit and of the image of God in man. Tatian combines the two terminologies. He distinguishes the soul (*psuchē*) from the higher spirit (*pneuma*) in man, which is the image and likeness of God. [26] It is this spirit which keeps the soul alive; without it the soul

tends downwards towards matter and dies with the flesh. But when it is coupled with the divine Spirit, it is not helpless, but ascends to the regions to which the Spirit leads it. For the home of the Spirit is above, but the origin of the soul is below. [27]

If this nature and condition of man can be compared to a temple, God is pleased to dwell in it by his representative,

---

[25] *Ad Autol.*, ii.27 (1096). I have quoted the translation made by R.M. Grant, *Theophilus of Antioch, ad Autolycum* (Clarendon Press, Oxford, 1970) with certain modifications; chief among them is Nolte's reading of *ouk* for *oun* in the last sentence. Cf. R. Butterworth, 'A New Edition of Theophilus of Antioch', *Heythrop Journal*, 12 (1971), pp. 428-9.

[26] Some Fathers, such as Tatian and Gregory of Nyssa, do not distinguish between the image and the likeness; others follow Irenaeus in making a distinction between the two, though they explain the difference in a number of ways. Cf. for the Greek Fathers J. Kirchmeyer, DS vi.813-22, s.v. 'Grecque (Eglise)'; for the Latin Fathers A. Solignac, DS vii.1406-25, s.v. 'Image & Ressemblance'. For Tatian, cf. *Or. adv. Gr.*, 12 (PG 6.829).

[27] *Ibid.*, 13 (833).

C

the Spirit. But if man is not a tabernacle like this, he is no better than wild beasts, except for his power of speech. [28]

We have here clearly stated the theory of the second gift. He continues:

> For the perfect Spirit was the wings of the soul; but when the soul cast it off through sin, the soul fluttered like a fledgling and fell to the ground; having abandoned its heavenly intercourse, it craved the company of inferior beings. [29]

Irenaeus also linked the image and likeness of God with the Holy Spirit. Adam, the first representative man, lost the image and likeness for all the race; Christ, the second representative man, recovered it for all. What is important for the present argument is that Irenaeus believes that man is in some sense complete without the gifts of incorruptibility, the Spirit, the Logos, and the full likeness to God. He makes this point in three ways.

(1) In temporal categories: 'it was necessary *first* (*primo*) that nature should appear, *then* (*post deinde*) that the mortal should be overcome and swallowed up by immortality, the corruptible by incorruptibility, and that man should be made in the image and likeness of God, receiving knowledge of good and evil'. [30] In another passage he says that man has to be first created, and *then* receive the Spirit. [31]

(2) He makes the point in another way, by recourse to the concept of the 'natural'. Incorruptibility and the likeness to God are not 'natural' (*propriam naturaliter*) to man. [32]

(3) By means of a distinction between the image and the likeness Irenaeus finds another way of expressing the fact that the Spirit is a further gift of God to man. Man can remain just

[28] *Ibid.*, 15 (837-40).
[29] *Ibid.*, 20 (852).
[30] *Adv. Haer.*, iv.38.4 (Harvey ii.297).
[31] *Ibid.*, v.12.2 (Harvey ii.351).
[32] *Ibid.*, iii.20.1 (Harvey ii.106).

body and soul, 'animal, carnal, imperfect', endowed with the
image of God and not the likeness. But by virtue of the likeness, 'when this Spirit is mingled and united with the created
stuff of the soul, man becomes spiritual and perfect on account
of the pouring out of the Spirit'. [33] Despite Irenaeus' repeated
emphasis on man's moral growth in the Spirit, [34] it is clear that
the likeness is not simply natural virtue, but is God's own Spirit
freely given.

I took as the starting-point of this chapter a passage in St
Athanasius' *de Incarnatione* in which he explains man's share
in the Word as a further gift, which he calls *charis, grace*. In this
work and in its companion-piece the *Contra Gentes*, Athanasius
seems to share in the uncertainty of the Greek Apologists concerning the nature of the *logos* in man. He appears to have at
least three criteria in mind. First, *logos* is the mark that
distinguishes men from irrational beings (*aloga zōa* — presumably animals). [35] Secondly, it is freedom from the corruption
which is natural to man (*hē kata phusin phthora*), and *a fortiori*
from sin, which involves a corruption 'to more than the natural
extent' (*kai pleion tou kata phusin*). [36] Thirdly, it is the power
to live according to God (*to kata Theon zēn*). [37]

Athanasius in these works seems not to notice that the three
criteria are distinct and separable: it is possible for a person to
be set apart from animals by his power of thought, but through
sin to fail to live according to God. But in the second *Oration
against the Arians* Athanasius defines his thought much more
clearly. By nature (*phusei*) man is created by God; by grace
(*kata charin*), the grace of the Spirit, by God's kindness (*philan-
thrōpia*), by God's decree (*thesis*), *after* creation man receives
the Word. By *nature* God is his Maker; by *grace* and by adoption
God becomes his Father. [38]

[33] *Ibid.*, v.6.1 (Harvey ii.334).
[34] For example, *ibid.*, v.8.1 (Harvey ii.339-40).
[35] *De Incarn.*, iii.3.
[36] *Ibid.*, v.2.
[37] *Ibid.*, v.1.
[38] *Or. adv. Arian.*, ii.59 (PG 26.272-3).

Gregory of Nyssa uses his terms differently. There is an affinity to the divine in man's very nature; this is the image and likeness of God (he does not distinguish between the two). [39] Man is a mean between God and brute beasts, having on the one hand an element that is divine, rational and sexless, and on the other hand an element which is irrational, corporeal and sexual. He is like a statue of Janus with two faces. [40] But although Gregory holds that the image and likeness belongs to human nature, it is God's added gift bestowed upon nature. [41] So once more we have the theory of the second gift.

There are other ways in which the Fathers explain this further gift. Most startling is the claim that through the Son men become gods, which occurs as early as Theophilus, Clement of Alexandria [42] and Origen. [43] St Athanasius, following Clement, links this belief explicitly with the Incarnation: 'the Word became flesh so that he might make man capable of receiving divinity'. [44] This belief in man's divinisation is so strong among the Fathers that, paradox though it is, it can be used as an agreed premiss in an argument. Athanasius himself deduces from it a refutation of Arianism:

> He who is the Father's means of conferring divinity and light, he in whom all is made divine and alive, is not of a different substance from the Father, but is of the same substance. For by receiving a share in him we receive a share in the Father, because he is the Father's own Word. [45]

Gregory of Nazianzus, in his polemic against the Macedonians, bases on the same axiom an argument for the divinity of

[39] *Or. Cat.*, 5 (PG 45.21).
[40] *De Hom. Opif.*, 16.9; 18.3 (PG 44.181;192). There is in Gregory, as in some of the Apologists and in Athanasius, a tendency to regard reason as part of the second gift.
[41] *De Virg.*, 12 (Jaeger viii (1).300; PG 46.372).
[42] Theophilus, *Ad Autol.*, ii.27 (PG 6.1096). Clement, *Protrept.*, 1.8 (GCS p.9; PG 8.64).
[43] *In Jo.*, ii.2 (GCS pp. 54-5; PG 14.109).
[44] *Or. adv. Arian.*, ii.59 (PG 26.273).
[45] *De Syn.*, 51.1 (Opitz, p. 274; PG 26.784).

the Holy Spirit: 'If the Holy Spirit is not God, let him first become divine, and then make me divine as an equal', [46] he exclaims ironically. He uses the premiss also against Apollinarius, who held that Christ had no human mind, as that mind is necessarily corrupt. Man is redeemed from sin, Gregory argues, by the union in Christ of complete manhood and divinity, so that the image of God in man was 'leavened and mingled with God, *being deified by the godhead*'. [47] There must then have been a human mind in the incarnate Christ, or else the corresponding part of man would not have been divinised; and as sin is primarily in the mind, man would consequently have remained unredeemed. 'What he has not assumed, he has not healed' (*to gar aproslēpton atherapeuton*). [48]

St Augustine also thinks of grace as a second gift. Together with his fellow-members of the Council of Carthage 416, in a letter addressed to Pope Innocent I, he criticized Pelagius and his followers for limiting the use of the word 'grace' to the gift of creation:

> But, to judge by what we have learnt from our brothers who have also read their books, they [the Pelagians] maintain that God's grace is to be identified with his conception and creation of man's nature so that he has the power to fulfil God's law by his own free will, whether this law is inscribed by nature in man's heart or given to him in written form. This law also, they hold, is due to God's grace, for God gave it to men in order to help them. [49]

The saint admits that it is proper to speak of man's existence, and his possession of life, sensation and understanding, as a grace; nevertheless it is distinct from the grace of predestination, vocation, justification and glory. Pelagius must be made to confess that there is the grace Christian doctrine speaks of which

[46] *Orat.*, 34.12 (PG 36.252).
[47] Ep. 101 (*Contr. Apoll.*, 1) (PG 37.185C).
[48] *Ibid.*, 181C.
[49] Ep. 175.2 (PL 33.760).

'is not our nature, but is the means by which our nature is saved'. [50]

Augustine distinguishes the two gifts very clearly:

> We were something before we were the sons of God, and received the favour of becoming what we were not; just as an adopted son was not the son of the man who adopts him before he was adopted, but was someone who could be adopted... We too by his grace became what we were not, namely sons of God; but we were something, something much lower, namely sons of men. [51]

The same distinction is made in another context. In his work on the Trinity, he points out that the Holy Spirit is our spirit as well as God's: 'Spiritus ergo et dei qui dedit et noster qui accepimus'. For since it is the characteristic of the Holy Spirit to be God's gift, when the Spirit is given to us he becomes our spirit as well as that of the Father and the Son. But he is not our spirit merely in the sense in which the principle of our natural lives is called our spirit:

> the spirit which we have received as the principle of our being is different from the Spirit which we have received as the principle of our holiness (aliud est quod accepimus ut essemus, aliud quod accepimus ut sancti essemus). [52]

In this chapter I have tried to trace a pattern which recurs throughout the Old and New Testaments and in many of the Fathers. There it is said in a great variety of ways that over and above God's gift of creation he has given man a second gift — election, rebirth, renewal, resurrection; a share in the divine nature; the indwelling of the Holy Spirit; life in Christ, in his body, in the true vine; a share in the Word, in the image and likeness of God; immortality, divinisation, reconciliation. The purpose of this book is to study that second gift.

---

[50] Ep. 177.7 (767-8).
[51] Ep. 140 (Ad Honoratum), iv.10 (541-2).
[52] De Trin., v.14 (CC 50.223; PL 42.921).

CHAPTER 2

THE SUPERNATURAL,
THE COVENANT AND EVOLUTION

Among the many devices employed by psychologists to uncover the dark secrets of our subconscious, there is one which is called a 'thematic apperception test'. In this procedure a victim is confronted with an indeterminate pattern and is requested to state what it makes him think of: whatever he says is taken down and used as evidence of his character. Now there exists a refined version of this treatment, according to which the investigator plants suggestions in the pattern. For example, the vague shape may be so contrived as to be capable of suggesting a man attacking another; the theory being that the subject will respond to the suggestion only if he has violent or aggressive tendencies within himself.

This refined form of the thematic apperception test provides an analogy for what I was trying to do in the last chapter. I was seeking a definition of grace, and began by selecting one of the many patterns that emerge from the Bible's account of God's dealings with men. The motif of the pattern I chose was God's second gift to man. But it is not a pattern that we read into an incoherent jumble of data; the pattern is there in the data. Other motifs are there too, such as God's forgiveness, or his fidelity to his promises; but the motif I chose is important, and, I would say, dominant to such an extent that all other

patterns fall into place around it. I then went on to consider
how the Fathers of the Church observed this theme in the Old
and New Testaments, and themselves developed it.

In this chapter I wish to consider three models or categories
which have at various times been called into service in an
attempt to elucidate the second gift: the supernatural, the
covenant and evolution.

(a) *The Supernatural*

The terminology of the supernatural has become so deeply
rooted, in Roman Catholic theology at least, that to suggest that
it was an imperfect way of expressing the truth, which might
for some purposes be replaced by other expressions, would until
recently have been generally considered dangerously close to
modernism. However, J.P. Kenny began a recent study of the
theory of the supernatural with an even bolder statement. After
pointing out that 'younger thinkers' disapprove of this 'technical
term that scholasticism uses to cover the sublime reality of
man's divinisation and of his insertion into the mystery of
Christ', he continues:

> At present *supernatural* still enjoys the prestige of being
> an indispensable code-word of Roman Catholic theology.
> However, it is unlikely that it will long survive the eclipse
> of the system that begot it. Some other term (perhaps
> *Mystery of Christ?*) will perhaps supplant it. [1]

Even Henri de Lubac, for all his authoritative and pioneering
work in the study of the supernatural, permitted himself certain
discreet hints to the same effect. [2]

---

[1] *The Supernatural* (Alba House, Staten Island, 1972) p. xiii.

[2] 'The author does not himself want either to open fresh perspectives,
or to take fresh material from more up-to-date problems, or to
make use of categories not considered previously. He has purposely
set himself a more basic and more modest task. Starting from the
classic question of the relationship between nature and the supernatural, he has restricted his theological reflections to the sphere of
formal ontology where they are normally carried out, without any

In considering the supernatural it is necessary to begin by drawing some distinctions. [3] The word is commonly used to describe abnormal phenomena which are not only inexplicable by known scientific laws, but are considered to be in principle inexplicable by any conceivable scientific laws. Here lies the difference between science fiction and ghost-stories. Science fiction does not deal with the 'supernatural' but the unexplored; even though it tells stories about visitors from other worlds, or intelligent plants, or of processes for converting the metaphysical into the physical and thought into matter, the whole interest of the genre lies in the fact that there is said to be a scientific explanation for what is happening, however unfamiliar or bogus the explanation may be. Ghost stories, on the other hand, tell of events caused by spirits or the dead, and such events are popularly called supernatural. It is not, however, in this sense that the word is used by theologians, though there may be some popular confusion on this point. A recent study of the history of the theological term 'supernatural', a sober work dealing with men like Lombard and Aquinas, [4] has been dressed up in a dust-jacket carrying in no less than three places what looks like a photograph of a statue of the hideous lion-headed god (said variously to be Ahriman the god of darkness, or Aion the god of time) associated with the worship of Mithras.

However, even among theologians the word is used in various senses and with varying degrees of precision. Some writers take the term to refer to what they vaguely call a 'superior realm', 'set apart' from our 'natural world'. This is the target swiftly set up, and knocked down with a few sweeping blows in a recent Saturday religious article in *The Times*, which

---

attempt to make them more concrete; he has not therefore made use either of the "covenant" vocabulary, or of that of the "Christian mystery".' (*The Mystery of the Supernatural*, ET G. Chapman, London, 1967, pp. ix-x).

[3] On the various meanings of the word "supernatural", cf. I.F. Sagüés, 'De Deo Creante et Elevante' in *Sacrae Theologiae Summa*, vol. ii (Biblioteca de Autores Cristianos, Madrid, 1958), pp. 743-9.

[4] J.P. Kenny's book mentioned above.

appeared under the uncharacteristically trendy headline 'What's
so super about the supernatural?'[5] Not content with criticizing
the identification of the supernatural with the occult, and with
attacking 'the God of the gaps' (for whom, however, there is
more to be said than most secularists allow), the author also
tilts at the more respectable theologies of Whitehead and
Heidegger, both of whom 'fall into the supernaturalist pattern
of distinguishing the natural and the divine "more" beyond
or above the natural'. They are wrong, he claims, in regarding
'God and the things of God' as 'qualitatively different from
the natural'.

I am not quoting Alistair Kee in order to point out fallacies
in his arguments; it is, in any event, an article less prolific in
argument than in assertion. I quote him simply to illustrate one
interpretation of the word supernatural. A more illuminating
view of the supernatural was taken by Charles Gore in his
Bampton Lectures of 1891. For Gore, the moral spirit in man
is supernatural, as it is 'a new kind of life, working by new
laws of its own, the laws of conscience and of choice, and
exhibiting phenomena . . . which the merely physical world cannot, considered by itself, explain or account for'; so too Christ
is supernatural, because God 'here assumes humanity, spirit
and body, as the instrument through which to exhibit with
a new completeness and in a new intensity His own personality
and character'.[6] 'Christ is supernatural, if you mean by this
that He transcends all the manifested natures, and is not expli-
cable out of their elements. But if He is supernatural He is
also natural.'[7]

Most Roman Catholic theologians would feel a certain
awkwardness about using the word in this way. But whereas
Gore speaks of a supernatural person, they are accustomed to
speak of a supernatural grace or gift received by a person, or

[5] The Times, 19 August 1972.
[6] The Incarnation of the Son of God (John Murray, London, 1891),
    p. 35.
[7] Ibid., p. 39.

of a supernatural action performed by him. The difference here is one of syntax as much as of meaning, but it is sufficient to give a reader the sense of being in unfamiliar territory. There is, however, a more important difference. Gore insisted that the supernatural is always relative to a *particular* nature. [8] He could quote with approval Bishop Joseph Butler's opinion that

> there may be beings in the universe, whose capacities and knowledge and views may be so extensive as that the whole Christian dispensation may to them appear natural (Op. cit., p. 39, quoting *Analogy*, Pt. I, ch. i, conc.).

But in the Roman Catholic tradition it is possible to speak of the supernatural in the sense of something above any possible created nature.

One of the longest entries in the index of Evelyn Waugh's unfinished autobiography is devoted to a school-friend at Lancing who is referred to solely by his nick-name 'Preters'. He was so called 'because in his first term, when asked if he were interested in politics, he had answered "praeternaturally so" '. [9] The precocious schoolboy's use of the term was accurate, though pedantic. The word is used by theologians to describe what is beyond the natural capacities of man as we know him, but is not necessarily above the capacities of any creature God might choose to create. In this sense, some of the privileges which are traditionally ascribed to Adam and Eve before the Fall, such as immortality, infused knowledge and freedom from concupiscence and pain, were rightly said to be praeternatural. By this two distinct but closely related things would be meant: first, that these perfections were enhancements or extensions of man's natural powers, and did not involve completely new potentialities; secondly, that, though beyond the natural endowment of man, these gifts did not elevate him above the status of a creature *vis-à-vis* his Creator. Now the word 'supernatural'

---

[8] *Ibid.*, p. 35.
[9] *A Little Learning: the First Volume of an Autobiography* (Chapman & Hall, London, 1964), p. 127.

is sometimes used in this sense; but for our purposes the word will not be applied to endowments which, while heightening man's natural powers so as to make him a super-man, would leave him altogether on the creaturely side of the division between God and man; I shall limit the use of the term to those gifts by which God in sheer love raises men to a relationship with himself which is above the unaided capacity of any actual or possible creature.

There is one last distinction to be made. When God works a miracle, he chooses to endow one of his creatures with powers or properties beyond its nature: when water is changed into wine, for example, or when a man walks on water. These wonders are only *praeter*natural, for, although I should be surprised if the water in my glass changed into Veuve Cliquot, or if I found I could walk from one bank of the Cherwell to the other without getting my feet wet, it is conceivable that in another world these things might happen every day. However, there can be miracles which are praeternatural from one point of view, supernatural from another. This is clearly true of any miracle which involves creation or the raising of the dead. The effect itself is no more than praeternatural, as the creature is not raised above its creaturehood; but the cause must be supernatural, as only God can create out of nothing, or breathe into matter a human soul.

God's second gift, which is the subject of this book, is supernatural in the fullest sense: not praeternatural, leaving man a more fully-endowed man, as if a master were to shower gifts on a slave, but leave him in his servitude; not even a praeternatural gift produced in a supernatural way, as if the master were to confer on the slave privileges which only the master could give (such as permission to marry) but were still not to emancipate him; but a gift which makes us not only more than men, but more than creatures, 'partakers of the divine nature' (2 Pet 1.4), as if the master were to give the slave his freedom.

Those who are familiar with John Oman's work *The Natural*

and the Supernatural [10] will have noticed that his treatment of the subject is different from mine. For one thing, he does not distinguish between the supernatural and the praeternatural: for him 'the Supernatural means the world which manifests more than natural values, the world which has values which stir the sense of the holy and demand to be esteemed as sacred.' [11] Besides this, we are working from opposite ends: I am taking for granted the fact of God's second gift, and proceeding from there to examine different aspects of Christian life in search of traces of this gift; he begins from experience, and seeks to show that 'part of what we experience is natural, in the sense that its values are comparative and to be judged as they serve our needs; and part of it supernatural, in the sense that its values are absolute, to which our needs must submit.' [12]

The Latin word *supernaturalis* appears to have been coined by Christian translators from the Greek. [13] After an early instance ascribed to the sixth century, [14] there appear to be no other examples before the translations of, and commentaries on, the works of Pseudo-Dionysius in the ninth. [15] The Greek word to which it corresponded most closely was *huperphuēs* (from *huper*, above, and *phunai*, to be born or to grow), a term which was not originally theological, but simply meant 'overgrown, monstrous, extraordinary'; it then came to be used to describe the qualities of God which transcend their human analogues: his generosity, for example, or his majesty, or his simplicity. Other compound adjectives prefixed by *huper-* were also used in this sense: *huperouranios* (above the heavens), *huperkosmios*

[10] Cambridge University Press, 1931.

[11] *Ibid.*, p. 71.

[12] *Ibid.*, p. 72.

[13] The origin of the term is discussed at great length and with many references by H. de Lubac, *Surnaturel* (Aubier, Paris, 1946), pp. 325-428.

[14] *Ibid.*, pp. 327, 369. In this early instance *supernaturalis* is used to translate *huperphuēs* in a Latin version of a letter written by Isidore of Pelusium (Book 4, Ep. 166; PG 78.1260). For the early history of the word cf. J.P. Kenny, *op. cit.*, pp. 91-5.

[15] Cf. de Lubac, *Surnaturel*, pp. 327, 369.

32 THE SECOND GIFT

(above the world), *huperousios* (above being); the prepositional phrase *huper phusin* (above nature) also occurs frequently. Cyril of Alexandria used this last phrase to describe God's gifts to man: commenting on John 1.12 ('to all who received him, who believed in his name, he gave power to become children of God'), he wrote:

> By a free concession the Son made generally available what belonged to himself alone properly and by nature (*kata phusin*)... So we are raised through Christ to a dignity above our nature (*huper phusin*)... For a creature, created and servant though it is, is called to what is above its nature by the sheer good pleasure and will of the Father. [16]

Despite the early examples of it, it was not until the thirteenth century that the Latin word found an established place in the theologian's vocabulary. Aquinas found it particularly useful, and applied it not only to God himself, but to God's gifts which exceed the potentialities of man's nature. [17] It is therefore somewhat surprising that the word does not occur at all in the decrees of the Council of Trent, even in the decree on justification. Within four years of the end of the Council, however, it is to be found in Pius V's condemnation of Baius (Michael de Bay), where it is applied to man's share in the divine nature. [18] It soon became an everyday term of Roman Catholic theology, and occurred several times in the decrees of the first Vatican Council. [19]

The post-Tridentine theologians found the word very serviceable to express the distinction between God's first and his second gift. The first gift is nature; grace, the second gift, is above the powers and claims of any conceivable nature, and is therefore fittingly described as supernatural. The first gift is God's creative act, by which he not only brought man from

[16] *In Jo.*, 1.12 (PG 73.153).
[17] Cf. de Lubac, *Surnaturel*, pp. 393-9; Kenny, *op. cit.*, pp. 94-5.
[18] DS 1921, 1923.
[19] DS 3004-6, 3008.

nothingness into being, but brought him into being *as a man* with human capabilities. God's continuing work of sustaining us in being and action, although it might be considered a further stage of generosity distinct from his original gift of creation, follows from his act of creation, and is therefore to be included under the head of nature, the first gift. The second gift is of a totally different order: God makes us not servants but friends, adopted sons; he calls us his children, and so we are; he gives us his own Spirit, so that we may share in the life of his Son, with whom we die and rise; our creator becomes our bridegroom; we are not only made, we are chosen and called; in a word, we become partakers of the divine nature.

The model of the supernatural has the great advantage of emphasizing the fact that all this loving and self-giving activity of God is truly a second gift, distinct from the first in two ways. First, the supernatural is unattainable by human nature: 'no one can say, "Jesus is Lord", except by the Holy Spirit' (1 Cor 12.3); 'when we cry "Abba! Father!" it is the Spirit himself bearing witness with our spirit that we are children of God' (Rom 8.15-16). Secondly, the second gift is a second *gift;* man cannot *claim* it from God as something due to him. Of course, we have God's promises, and God must be faithful to them; but what he promises is in no way the fulfilment of an obligation to us. If God left us without the second gift, we would have no right to accuse him of neglecting us, as a child could accuse his parents of neglect if they imagined that their obligations ceased once they had brought him into the world. Nor can we earn a right to the second gift by our faithfulness in God's service. All this is implied by the use of the word 'supernatural'.

Here we come up against a problem which, as Henri de Lubac has shown in two magisterial and decisive works, [20] con-fused Roman Catholic theology for four centuries, and which

[20] *The Mystery of the Supernatural* (ET G. Chapman, London, 1967); *Augustinianism and Modern Theology* (ET G. Chapman, London, 1969). My great debt to the first of these works will be apparent to anyone who has read it.

provoked a convulsive but shortlived heresy-hunt as recently as 1950. What connection is there between the first and second gifts? In the sixteenth century the great Dominican cardinal Thomas de Vio, better known after Gaeta, his birthplace, as Cajetan, the most influential of the expositors of the thought of Aquinas, gave an answer that, though not wholly original, laid down the lines along which, with a very few exceptions, the whole of Roman Catholic thought was to run for four hundred years; and he was disastrously wrong.

St Thomas had written of man's natural desire (*desiderium naturale*) for the vision of God. [21] The term 'natural desire' denotes something much deeper than a conscious wish; it is a fundamental urge in the nature of a being. Thus a stone could be said to have a natural desire to fall; an animal, to preserve life; a human being to acquire knowledge and to communicate. Now it would be contradiction in terms, Cajetan argued, to say that man had a natural desire for the supernatural. [22] What Aquinas must have meant, then, was that man in grace is miraculously transformed [23] so that he begins to seek the vision

[21] E.g., *c. Gent.*, iii. 50. Cf. iii. 51: 'But since it is impossible for a natural desire (*naturale desiderium*) to be in vain (which would be the case if it were not possible to attain to understanding of the divine substance — a thing which all minds naturally desire), it is necessary to say that it is possible for God's substance to be seen by the intellect.'

[22] 'For it does not seem to be true that a created intellect naturally desires to see God: for nature does not bestow an inclination towards an object towards which the whole force of nature cannot lead' (*In Summam*, I.12.1). Cajetan goes on to admit that man experiences a natural curiosity which makes him wish to understand the 'effects of grace'; but he seems to envisage this as a natural desire for natural understanding.

[23] This possibility of a miraculous transformation is called an 'obediential potency'; Cajetan defines it as 'the aptitude of a being such that whatever God has ordained may be be brought about in it' (*In Summam*, I.1.1). He agrees that man possesses such a potentiality for a supernatural end, which consists in man's power of understanding; but, as the quotation given in the previous note shows, he does not accept that there can be in man any natural *tendency* towards the supernatural end. On the distinction between natural desire and obediential potency, see de Lubac, *Mystery*, p. 78, note 17.

of God; but in theory he could (and before baptism did) exist without this tendency in what came to be called a state of pure nature. By nature, man is equipped for a natural happiness; by grace he is supernaturally equipped for a supernatural happiness. From this it is but a short jump to saying that in the state of pure nature man is capable of a natural union with God. Cajetan's successors accordingly began to elaborate a system of natural counterparts to the gifts of grace, of the same order as the intellectual contemplation which Aristotle regarded as the greatest happiness in life. De Lubac produces a chilling list, documented from the works of Cajetan and his followers, of natural endowments of this kind that are attributed to man without grace. They speak of natural faith and prayer, natural love of God above all things, natural grace, friendship with God without grace, a certain most excellent natural love of God, a natural revelation, natural contrition, a natural possession of God, a natural direct vision of God. 'What remains peculiar to the supernatural order?', de Lubac asks in despair, 'except the word?' [24]

There are several criticisms that can be made of this distorted account of man's relations with God. It cannot be condemned precisely as Pelagian, for at least verbally the natural is sharply distinguished from the supernatural, to obtain which man has an absolute need for the help of God's grace. One thing, however, that should awaken our suspicions is the postulate of a complete natural spirituality which reproduces at a different level all the characteristics of a grace-given spirituality. A hypothesis that requires entities to be multiplied in this way will be hard put to it to establish its necessity. The most serious objection, however, to which this theory is vulnerable is that it makes the supernatural irrelevant.

No account of grace can claim to be faithful to the teaching of the New Testament and the Fathers unless it shows grace to be the renewing power of God's love. Even if a distinction between justification and sanctification is insisted upon, it still

[24] *Mystery*, pp. 51-2.

D

remains true that grace sanctifies man, and does not remain simply as the external approval of God. By grace man is born again, and becomes a new creation. And even though the new creation is not completed until we are united with God in heaven, the process begins on earth. We already have been granted the first fruits of the Holy Spirit, which we experience as a palpable guarantee of what is to come; we are already children of God, although 'it does not yet appear what we shall be'. Even in this life, therefore, the second gift becomes part of ourselves. An analogy could be drawn from the Greek legend of Pygmalion, who fell in love with a statue, which was brought to life in answer to his prayer. Grace makes us, like the statue, a new being throughout the whole of our personalities. The hypothesis, however, that we are considering makes it impossible for the second gift to become truly part of ourselves, because there is nothing in our natures which is attracted by it. The theory, in other words, falls into the error which the French call *extrinsicisme*.

On this theory it is also impossible to give a satisfactory account of heaven. The New Testament suggests, as we saw in Chapter One, both a continuity and a discontinuity between life in this world and life in the next. Heaven is not to be conceived simply as a reward for a good life; by the grace of God we grow in this world into the sort of person who can be gloriously transformed in heaven. We are caterpillars, whose humble growth is a stage in a continuous development which suddenly bursts into the splendour of the butterfly. The theory we are criticizing, on the other hand, suggests that heaven is an arbitrary reward, which is conditional upon man's progress in this life, but is not a growth from it. Indeed, the reward would be not only arbitrary but useless: as it would have no point of contact with our natures, it would be like a banquet, de Lubac suggests, set before a man who is not hungry. [25] In other words, this theory of heaven would be open to the same objections which are decisive against belief in the transmigra-

[25] *Ibid.*, p. 78, note 16.

tion of souls: such transformation would destroy the identity of the person in the successive states.

If Cajetan's attempt to account for the relation between the first and the second gifts is rejected, what other possibilities remain? Some possibilities can be briefly dismissed. It will not do, for example, to suggest that the natural is man's own preparation to receive the supernatural, for that would be a form of semi-Pelagianism. Peter Abelard's theory that man's unaided reason achieves inchoate faith as a preparation for the supernatural is subject to this criticism. [26] There are also pseudo-solutions, which appear to solve the problem verbally, but do so only by destroying either the supernatural or the natural. Thus, Baius in the sixteenth century regarded the share in the divine life as something which man needed so radically that God could not without injustice deny it to him: in other words, the supernatural is now relevant, but is no longer a second gift. [27] Some religions go further along this road and make the divine part of human nature; this belief, shared by Hinduism and some forms of gnosticism, denies the reality of the first gift.

The key to the true understanding of the supernatural is provided by Aquinas' theory which Cajetan misunderstood so catastrophically: man has a natural desire for the supernatural. There remained throughout the centuries a remnant of interpreters who were faithful to the mind of St Thomas, such as Soto and Toletus, and in our own century, Blondel and Rousselot: but Cajetan's theory gained general acceptance among Roman Catholic theologians, both as the authentic exposition of Thomistic thought, and as a satisfactory theory in its own right. It was not until the middle of the present century that, thanks largely to the work of Henri de Lubac, the arguments against Cajetan's position were clearly set out. His first full statement of his case appeared in 1946 under the title

[26] Cf. A. Dulles, *A History of Apologetics* (Hutchinson, London & Corpus, New York, 1971), p. 83.
[27] Cf. de Lubac, *Augustinianism*, pp. 1-33.

Surnaturel. It was inevitably misunderstood; as a result it was
attacked, though not by name, in the encyclical *Humani Generis*
in 1950, [28] and he and a number of like-thinking colleagues
were temporarily suspended from teaching. Fortunately the
wind rapidly changed, and what in 1950 was regarded as neo-
modernism has now an assured place, not only in academic
theology, but even in the popular paper-backs.

De Lubac shows that Cajetan's theory is unsound both as
exegesis of St Thomas and as a theory in its own right. What
Aquinas meant by the natural desire for the vision of God was
a natural appetite for the supernatural, not for some natural
Aristotelian contemplation. The first gift is a seed-bed for the
second, but does not contain the seeds of it. We are made for
God. 'Fecisti nos ad te', said St Augustine, 'et inquietum est
cor nostrum donec requiescat in te. You have made us for
yourself, and our heart knows no rest until it rests in you'. [29]
Browning's much-quoted saying bears precisely on this point:

> Ah, but a man's reach should exceed his grasp,
>   Or what's a heaven for?
>
> *(Andrea del Sarto)*

The supernatural is not irrelevant and exterior to man's nature,
but is on the contrary its fulfilment.

But it remains to explain in what sense the supernatural,
conceived in this way, really is *super*natural, a *second* gift. To
do this it is not necessary to maintain that at any time in his
history man has ever been left in a state of pure nature, without the possibility of receiving the second gift; still less does
it follow that individually we have experienced for ourselves
what it is like to be totally without the second gift. We can
cut ourselves off from the true Vine by our sins; but even then

---

[28] 'Some undermine the true *"character of freedom"* (*"gratuitatem"*)
of the supernatural order when they maintain that God could not
create beings endowed with understanding without destining and
calling them to the beatific vision' (DS 3891). De Lubac had never
maintained this.

[29] Conf. i.1.

we still belong to the race which Christ redeemed; and there still remain in us the habits formed under the influence of grace, as well as the constant prompting of grace towards repentance. No one leads a purely natural or a purely wicked or even a totally selfish life; even a Hitler can remain faithful to his Eva Braun.

Although by his first gift, of creation, God equips man to receive the second, of grace, the second gift is still above man's nature, and, when it comes, is the result of pure generosity on God's part — and not only in the sense in which each night's sleep and each sunrise and every breath we draw come to us from God's bounty. All these particular gifts are the result of God's original creation of us; but God *could* have left us a state of pure nature. Although he made us for himself so that instinctively we reach for him, and although he made us in this way because he intended to give the second gift, still he *need* not have given himself to us; he might have left us reaching for what we could not grasp.

An analogy may help to clarify the point. We were considering the original legend of Pygmalion; Bernard Shaw's adaptation of it may provide a better illustration. Professor Higgins did more than train Eliza Doolittle to take a place in high society; he transformed her so that it was possible for her to fall in love with him, and him with her. Let us suppose that he behaved honourably, and did nothing to encourage hopes that he had no intention of fulfilling; he could have trained her and then turned her out. That he should wish to give himself to her in marriage (if so brutally selfish a man was capable of giving himself to anyone) would be a further gift totally distinct from his education of her, though impossible without it. The first gift prepares for the second, though the second remains a *second* gift.

We can take the analogy further. Let us suppose that Higgins possessed some of the sensitivity of his friend Pickering, so that in educating Eliza he was aware that he was making her capable of loving him; let us suppose that all the time he was hoping that she would love him so that they could be married, though without ever presuming to trespass upon her freedom — even then his proposal of marriage would be a further gift of himself, even though it was planned and prepared for from the start. So too our natural endowment is a preparation for the supernatural, though grace remains a second gift.

The two gifts are not unconnected, as if one were to promise a favourite niece £5000 upon her coming of age, and another £5000 when she got married: rather, the first gift makes the second possible, and the second fulfils the possibilities inherent in the first. But the gifts are not connected in the same way as an engagement- and a wedding-ring. For the first ring is meaningless without reference to the second, of which it is the promise; but the gift of nature does not oblige God to give us grace. Of course, the Gospel is full of God's promises, and he is committed to them; but it is not the gift of our being that commits him, but his promise. Creation is not an engagement-ring; the second gift, though promised, is still a gift.

The consideration of different possible meanings of the word 'nature' may be an aid to clarity. First, the word could refer to a hypothetical nature without any aptitude for the supernatural. A being of this nature, however, would not be human; for this aptitude is as much a part of man as any of his other characteristics. Secondly, the word can denote what might be called 'pure' nature, in the sense of human nature with its aptitude for the supernatural present but unfulfilled. Such a human nature is not a contradiction in terms, but has never in fact existed. It would not have been incompatible with God's justice to leave a man without this second gift, but in his love he has not done so. Babies and great sinners may not at the moment possess grace as an actuality; but God destines them and is preparing them to receive it; and a sinner is a human being on whom the supernatural has left a mark. Thirdly, one can speak of 'historic' nature, the nature of man as he in fact exists, with his supernatural endowment. The term 'supernatural', therefore, is used in contrast, not with historic nature (which includes the supernatural), but with hypothetical pure nature. There is also a fourth sense of the term, which refers to man's lower instincts. It is in this sense that some spiritual writers, such as Thomas à Kempis, have spoken of a conflict between nature and grace — i.e. between man's irrational self and his rational self, which is under the influence of grace. The existence of such a conflict is undeniable, and St Paul describes it eloquently in the seventh chapter of the Epistle to the Romans; but in these pages I am not using the word 'nature' in this pejorative sense to denote the tendency in man to resist grace.

In the end, as de Lubac sees,[30] we are left with a paradox, indeed a double paradox. On the one hand, God has made us for himself, with a yearning for himself; on the other hand, he does not owe us the fulfilment of that yearning. On the one hand, the transforming power of his gift of himself reaches right down into the deepest levels of our personality; on the other, it is totally out of our range, and surpasses the innate capacities of any possible created being.

The New Testament compels us to grasp both horns of the paradoxes. The model of the supernatural has the advantage of emphasizing the second proposition of each paradox: the second gift is infinitely beyond our capabilities, rights and deserts; the infinite liberality and the otherness of God are safeguarded. The model does not however emphasize so well the first propositions: that grace is not alien to our natures, but fulfils them. Another defect of the terminology of the supernatural is that, by using it, we can slip into thinking of grace as a *thing* given us by God, rather than his own loving and transforming presence. I shall return to this point in the next chapter.

(b) *The Covenant*

I have spoken at such length about the supernatural because it is a harder model to interpret than the other two models which we must now discuss more briefly.

[30] *Mystery*, p. 217.

The image of the covenant has in recent times been frequently used to illustrate the distinction between the first and the second gifts. It appears repeatedly in the *Church Dogmatics* of Karl Barth. The Covenant, he reminds us, containing the promise, 'I will be your God', marks the emergence of God, not from a state of neutrality, but from what is already

> a gracious being and working as Creator and Lord in relation to man. That is more than the creation, more than the preservation, accompaniment and overruling of His creatures. That is the covenant of God with man, from which He has bound and pledged Himself always to begin, and in virtue of which He has constituted Himself his [man's] God. [31]

Here Barth is distinguishing the two gracious operations of God. In an earlier passage of the same book he had distinguished between the effects in man of these two facets of God's grace:

> According to the Christian message 'God with us' means God with the man for whom salvation is intended and ordained as such, as the one who is created, preserved and ruled over by God as man. It is not as though the expectation belonged to his created being. It is not as though he had any kind of claim to it. God cannot be forced to give us a part in His divine being. The matter might have ended quite well with that general grace of being — which even in itself is great enough. But where God is not bound and man has no claim, even more compelling is the will and plan and promise of God. It goes beyond, or rather it precedes His will and work as Creator. Therefore it has to be distinguished from it, as something prior which precedes it. [32]

However, the distinction between the effects in man of creation and the covenant does not mean that man has ever lived untouched by the covenant.

What God created when he created the world and man

[31] *Church Dogmatics,* ET IV/1.38.
[32] *Ibid.,* IV/1.9 (translation slightly modified).

was not just any place, but that which was foreordained for the establishment and the history of the covenant, nor just any subject, but that which was to become God's partner in this history, i.e. the nature which God in His grace willed to address and accept and the man predestined for His service. The fact that the covenant is the goal of creation is not something which is added later to the reality of the creature... It already characterises creation itself and as such, and therefore the being and existence of the creature. [33]

But the gap bridged by grace is not simply that between creator and creature; always, and above all, it is the gap between creator and sinful creature. The 'heart of the subject-matter of Christian faith' is that the covenant is 'fulfilled in the work of reconciliation'. [34]

It is characteristic of Roman Catholic theology to think of grace primarily as God's gift to the creature as such, so putting less emphasis on its redemptive aspect. For example, Piet Schoonenberg has put forward a theology of grace in terms of covenant which up to a point sounds very like Barth's. [35] But the Roman Catholic theologian feels much more than the Reformed the need to make covenant something more fundamental than forgiveness:

It is a question, however, of whether the unmeritedness of grace only holds in relation to the sinful element of our existence or with relation to our manhood as such... Insofar as grace is given to man as sinful, it presupposes sin; if it is given exclusively to sinful man, then grace presupposes sin without, conversely, sin presupposing grace. But this is precisely the case. Scripture always depicts sin as a break in the covenant, and this even holds for the 'first' sin in Genesis 3... Here too it is a matter of grace, of a giving — and demanding — encounter of

[33] *Ibid.*, III/1.231.
[34] *Ibid.*, IV/1.3; cf. IV/1.10ff.
[35] Cf. *Covenant and Creation* (ET Sheed and Ward, London, 1968), chap. 3; and *The Christ* (ET Sheed and Ward, London, 1972), pp. 32-8.

God, of unmerited gifts. For that reason the classical concept that grace precedes sin still seems the best, although it seems to us now that we do not know anything of the historical way in which it preceded and that it might possibly be conceived as merely a logical presupposition — as '*natura sed non tempore prius*'. Thus although the grace-nature relation appears to be accessible for us, merely in the grace-sin relation, it nevertheless lies at the foundation of the latter, and not vice versa. One can for that matter ask oneself why sin is made good by a merciful act of covenant of God, if it does not take place within a covenant-relation with him. Then it could also be rectified by such an act of creation that man, by his own powers, rectifies what he has spoiled by his own action. [36]

The covenant-analogy, as expounded by Barth and Schoonenberg, brings out clearly both sides of the paradoxes which emerged from our discussion of the supernatural: on the one hand the covenant-gift is a further exercise of God's liberality over and above creation, by which God receives man into a relationship which transcends his status as a creature; on the other hand, God has created man to receive the covenant. The model of the supernatural makes more immediately evident the infinite gap between the first and second gifts; the covenant-model makes it more evident that grace is not a thing, but a personal relationship with God.

(c) *Evolution*

Neither of the models so far considered makes clear the fact that the second gift is the goal of the first, and determines the nature of the first even before the second is given. Of course, theologians like de Lubac and Barth are well aware of this, and add comments to their analogies in order to make the point clear; but the analogies themselves do not convey it. Accordingly, precisely to emphasize this point, some theologians recently have turned to a third model, the model of evolution.

[36] *The Christ*, pp. 34-5 note.

The advantage of this model is that it represents God's action among his creatures as a unity. Evolution is not something that happens after or in addition to God's creative work; on the contrary, it is part of the process by which God creates. In this world-view, the second gift is not something added to creation, but is part of God's single creative activity. The creative action of Christ the Word, through whom all things were made by the process of evolution, is not distinct from the saving action of Christ, who is the source of all grace according to the same evolutionary process. Grace is not something foreign to man, but enters history according to the single evolutionary pattern in which God creates all things in Christ. This world-picture, which received such an impetus from the posthumous publication of the writings of Pierre Teilhard de Chardin, does full justice to one side of our paradoxes, for it sets out clearly the fact that we are endowed with a capacity to receive God. The evolutionary model is not, however, so well equipped to clarify the other wing of the paradoxes: that the gift is a second gift, because it raises man above the level of any creature, and is due, not necessarily to a separate *act* of giving, but to a higher level of giving on God's part.

In Teilhard's most straightforward exposition of his thought, the process of evolution in Christ towards Omega point is not interrupted by the Incarnation; rather, the Incarnation makes the whole process possible from the beginning.

> The unique business of the world is the physical incorporation of the faithful in Christ, who is of God. The major task is pursued with *the rigour and harmony of a natural process of evolution...*
>
> At its inception an operation of a transcendent order was required, grafting — in accordance with mysterious but physically regulated conditions — the Person of the Deity on to the Human Cosmos...
>
> *Et Verbum Caro factum est.* [37]

[37] From 'La Vie Cosmique', written in 1916, and reproduced in *The Future of Man* (ET Collins, London, 1964), p. 304.

The result of the Incarnation is that

> a new life was born, an unexpected enlargement and
> 'obediential' prolongation of our natural capacities:
> Grace. . . Christ is the Fulfilment even of the natural evolu-
> tion of beings. [38]

Grace, then, is a second gift, because it is the result, not of
creation, but of the Incarnation. Grace raises man above his
natural powers, but not in such a way that 'the rigour . . . of a
natural process of evolution' is destroyed.

Even in this early statement of his position, it is apparent
that Teilhard's thought starts from both ends, to achieve a
slightly uneasy synthesis in the middle. From the point of view
of man as we know him, Teilhard holds the development of
the history of man in grace takes place with the rigour of
natural evolution; but in the light of revelation he can affirm
that there is 'an unexpected enlargement and "obediential"
prolongation of our natural capacities'. The concept of the
supernatural has thus to be introduced to supplement the
evolutionary model.

Again and again in his writings Teilhard adopts this
expedient, partly no doubt to satisfy the misgivings of people
who doubted his orthodoxy. Thus in 1924 he wrote:

> In any hypothesis the world has to be centred in order
> to be thinkable. Consequently the presence of an Omega
> at its head has nothing to do with its 'supernatural eleva-
> tion'. What gives the character of 'gratuity' to the world
> is precisely the fact that the function of universal Centre
> has not been given to some supreme intermediary between
> God and the universe, but has been assumed by God
> himself, who in this way has introduced us into the depths
> of his immanent Trinitarian action. I say this to clarify
> my theological position. [39]

So too in 1940, after writing of confirming 'the presence at the

---

[38] *Ibid.*, pp. 304-5.
[39] From 'Mon Univers', quoted in C.F. Mooney, *Teilhard de Chardin
and the Mystery of Christ* (Collins, London, 1966), pp. 74-5.

summit of the world of what we have called the Omega Point',
he felt obliged to clarify his position in a footnote:

> To be more exact, 'to confirm the presence at the summit
> of the world of something in line with, but still more
> elevated than, the Omega point'. This is in deference to
> the theological concept of the 'supernatural' according to
> which the binding contact between God and the world,
> *hic et nunc* inchoate, attains to a super-intimacy (which
> is thus outside all logic) of which man can have no inkling
> and to which he can lay no claim by virtue of his 'nature'
> alone. [40]

In 1934, however, he had shown more confidence in dove-
tailing the concept of the supernatural into his evolutionary
framework:

> Whatever may be the precise positive content of the term
> 'supernatural', it cannot mean anything except 'supremely
> real', in other words 'supremely in conformity' with the
> conditions of reality which nature imposes on beings. If,
> then, Christ is to be *able* to be the saviour and the life of
> souls in their supernatural developments, he must first
> satisfy certain conditions in relation to the world, appre-
> hended in its experiential and natural reality. [41]

A. Hulsbosch's evolutionary picture of grace is more radical,
and sets out to dispense with the idea of a second gift altogether:

> There is still only one gratuitousness, namely, that of the
> creation in Christ. The creature has no single claim, except
> on the basis of the fundamental gratuitousness of the

[40] Postcript to *The Phenomenon of Man* (ET Collins, London, 1959),
p. 298 and note.

[41] 'How I believe', in *Christianity and Evolution* (Collins, London,
1971), p. 127 note. Throughout this discussion it needs to be borne
in mind that the word 'nature' can be used in two different senses:
(1) pure nature, i.e., nature without the vocation to grace; this is
a hypothesis which has never been fulfilled; (2) historic nature, i.e.,
nature as it exists with its vocation to grace. The term 'supernatural'
is used in contrast with nature in the first sense; it is nature in the
second sense which undergoes the process of evolution. I have
discussed some of the ambiguities of the term 'nature' more fully
on pp. 40-41.

creation itself, as this has been brought about by God in Christ. Completely in accord with traditional teaching, the supernatural gift of grace to man in Christ is treated purely as a gift. But this gift is now seen as the final phase of God's creative action, to which the preceding phases are directed... Looked at from this side the question about the gratuitousness of the supernatural becomes entirely superfluous, because we all see that the creation of man after the image of God was something in no way due. [42]

This passage may make the reader wonder whether Hulsbosch is distinguishing as clearly as he ought between man's natural capacity for grace and the grace itself. These suspicions are confirmed when in a later passage Hulsbosch reintroduces the idea of a second gift. We should not, he tells us, conceive evolution 'as if God in the beginning had given his creation the power to unfold itself in ever higher forms'. On the contrary, the regular process of evolution is simply the visible history of 'the progressively creative action of God'. 'Creation has not the built-in power to evolve independently to higher forms.' The same is true of the evolution of grace from nature, as it is of the evolution of one nature from another:

> Here we see with full clarity that there is in man a dis-
> position to receive a completion, but at the same time it
> is apparent that this disposition does not have the charac-
> ter of an inbuilt dynamic power which has merely to
> unfold itself in order to bring man to the sight of God.
> If we ascribe to man the possibility of reaching his end
> by his own powers, we should go contrary to the core of
> the Christian faith.

However, Hulsbosch does not show how the inability of man to attain the sight of God differs from the inability of any created thing to reach the next stage of its evolution. He tells us merely that the same can be said of each 'analogically and by extrapolation.' [43]

[42] *God's Creation* (ET Sheed & Ward, London, 1965), pp. 31-2.
[43] *Ibid.*, pp. 75-7.

Consequently, the evolutionary model, as employed by Teilhard and Hulsbosch, has a defect to balance the clarity with which it can represent the unity of God's creative and salvific action. Piet Schoonenberg sees this more clearly than either of them. For him it is only the disposition for grace (the 'natural desire') that fits into the evolutionary pattern; evolution can only prepare us for God's self-giving. [44] Only this self-giving of God, begun in life, makes heaven the full reality of grace.

> [Grace] is not the giving of God's constant creation in general, not even that of the constant creating of man in general, not even that of the perpetuation of the human person after death; it is precisely the encounter in which God gives himself to man as he already exists that constitutes grace. [45]

*   *   *

To sum up, each of the three models we have been considering contributes in a different way to the understanding of the way in which grace is a 'second gift'. Yet so far, though I have had much to say about the relation between grace and creation, I have made no attempt to say what grace is. I have used the word like an unknown x in an equation, in which the known quantities are God and ourselves: or like a foreign word with which we can stimulate a reaction in our hearers, though we do not know what it means. There has also been an unknown y: the aptitude for God, the natural desire for the vision of God. In the remaining chapters I shall try to go some of the way towards solving the equation and establishing a meaning for x and y.

---

[44] *The Christ*, p. 38.
[45] *Ibid.*, p. 37. For a rather different Christian interpretation of evolution the reader is referred to A.R. Peacocke, *Science and the Christian Experiment* (OUP, London, 1971), pp. 164-9.

CHAPTER 3

PARTAKERS OF THE DIVINE NATURE

So far all our attention has been directed to one point: that grace is a second gift of God. We have seen that this second gift is a theme which constantly recurs in scripture and in the Fathers, and we have considered various categories which theologians have adopted in order to express it. But we have not yet considered what this second gift consists of. Up to now we have been, as it were, feeling the parcel from the outside; it is time to take off the wrapping and see what it contains.

The first thing to be said is that the word 'grace' is used in many different, though related, meanings. For the sake of clarity three distinctions need to be drawn.

Healing and Elevating Grace

The first is the distinction between healing and elevating grace. On the one hand, grace can be considered as God's work of restoring us from a state of sin to a state of righteousness, of delivering us 'from the dominion of darkness' and transferring us 'to the kingdom of his beloved Son' (Col 1.13); this aspect of grace, which affects man in so far as he is a sinner, is called 'healing grace'. On the other hand, without direct reference to sin, grace can be considered as the work of the Holy Spirit as he makes us adopted children of God, members of Christ's Body, and partakers of the divine nature. Under this aspect, grace affects man in so far as he is a human being, and is called 'elevating grace'.

Healing and elevating grace are not two different kinds of grace, but rather two aspects under which grace is considered. The grace of God's forgiveness is always the grace by which God adopts us as his children; and conversely the grace of adoption always comes as forgiveness. But although all schools of theology agree that in practice healing and elevating grace, justice and sanctification, are connected, the Catholic and Protestant traditions place the emphasis differently. For Luther, for example, grace meant simply God's mercy by which he refrains from imputing to man his sin, and instead imputes to man externally through faith the righteousness of Christ; justification was the *articulus stantis et cadentis ecclesiae,* the article by which the Church stands or falls. Nevertheless,

> Luther never thought of a faith that is not already in itself regeneration (*regeneratio*), quickening (*vivicatio*) and there-fore good work (*bonum opus*). [1]

Similarly in Reformed theology, external, imputed justification is the fundamental grace of Christian life; but Calvin insisted that

> You cannot receive this [justification] without receiving sanctification at the same time. . . We may distinguish them, but Christ contains both inseparably in Himself. Do you wish then to obtain righteousness in Christ? You must first possess Christ: but you cannot possess him without being made a partner of his sanctification, seeing that he cannot be torn in pieces. [2]

Catholic theology, on the other hand, while well aware that

---

[1] A. Harnack, *History of Dogma* (ET William & Norgate, London, 1894-9), vol. vii, p. 209.
[2] *Inst. Christ.,* III.xvi.1. I have slightly modified the translation given in C. Moeller and G. Philips, *The Theology of Grace and the Ecumenical Movement* (ET Mowbray, London, 1961; reprinted by St Anthony Guild Press, Paterson, N.J., 1969), p. 38.

E

grace is always salvation from sin, teaches that it is far more than forgiveness, the healing and *restoration* of corrupted humanity; it is the *elevation* of corrupted humanity to a loving relationship with God; it is the communication of new life; it is adoption by the Father, membership of the Son's Body, the gift of God's own Spirit, a share in God's own nature. I shall have more to say about the connection between these two aspects of grace when we come to consider redemption in the fifth chapter.

Created and Uncreated Grace

The second distinction that has to be drawn is that between created and uncreated grace. One of the expressions used in the New Testament to describe God's self-communication is the image of the temple: 'Do you not know that you are God's temple and that God's Spirit dwells in you?' (1 Cor 3.16) Now this presence of God is dynamic, not static; the Spirit gives life; he cannot be present within us and leave us unaffected. Accordingly when grace is considered as God himself dwelling within us, it is called uncreated grace; but when it is considered as the transformation produced in us by God's loving presence, it is called created grace — created, because it is the work of God, God's achievement in our personalities, and not God himself.

Actual and Habitual Grace

There is much more that needs to be said about created grace, but it will be necessary first to introduce the third distinction, that between actual and habitual (sometimes called sanctifying) grace. All Christian traditions agree that God's self-giving is not ineffectual: 'my word ... shall not return to me empty, but it shall accomplish that which I purpose, and prosper in the thing for which I sent it' (Is 55.11). God's love empowers us to perform acts for love of him. The particular help God gives to empower us to perform a particular act is called actual grace.

However, actual graces are not to be considered as so many separate points at which God acts in us. Just as most of our actions are largely the result of our habits, so too God's particular, momentary helps that we call actual graces spring from a permanent disposition of ours which is the work of the Holy Spirit dwelling within us, and which is called habitual grace.

Actual and habitual grace are both aspects of created grace, the transforming effect upon us of the presence of God himself. The existence of created grace (in addition to uncreated grace), and in particular of habitual created grace, has for centuries been a fundamental hypothesis of Roman Catholic theology; it did not, however, receive explicit attention from the theologians until the thirteenth century. The term 'created grace' itself is certainly not found before then; and even though St Augustine could speak of a hidden grace not yet manifested in works, [3] the early scholastics thought of actual rather than habitual grace. Thus for St Anselm a baptized baby, in whom original sin has been forgiven, is still not in a state of justice, because 'justice is uprightness of will kept for its own sake'; [4] that is to say, if the psychological capacity to perform acts under the influence of grace has not yet developed, one cannot say that grace is present in the child. Peter Lombard reached the same conclusion from different premises. While acts of faith and hope, he thought, arise out of permanent habits or dispositions of faith and hope, there is no such permanent habit of charity in the soul: acts of charity are produced immediately by the Holy Spirit, who *is* himself charity. The reasons Lombard gave for holding this view, which is tantamount to a denial of created grace, are simply over-literal interpretations of St John's words, 'God is love' (1 Jn 4.8, 16), and of St Augustine's reflections on this text. [5]

---

[3] Augustine, *de Pecc. Mer. et Rem.*, I.ix.10 (PL 44.115). Cf. Moeller and Philips, *op. cit.*, p. 19.

[4] Anselm, *de Conc. Virg.*, 29. Here again, and indeed in all this section, I am indebted to the work of Moeller and Philips.

[5] P. Lombard, *Sent.*, lib. I, dist. xvii, c. 1.

In the thirteenth century, however, Alexander of Hales, St Albert the Great, St Bonaventure and St Thomas Aquinas all speak of created (i.e. habitual) grace. [6] The reasons that led them to this new insight were various. St Bonaventure sometimes speaks of man's helplessness and his need to be given by God a disposition to receive justification; in this way grace is seen as a preparation for the indwelling of the Holy Spirit. But Bonaventure and Aquinas, to name but two, also saw created grace as the transformation that is wrought in man by the indwelling of the Holy Spirit. For Bonaventure, to possess God (uncreated grace) is to be possessed by God, to love him and to be loved by him as a bride by the bridegroom, to be adopted as his child: which can only come about through 'a gift freely infused by God'. [7] Aquinas argues more metaphysically: 'Upon any expression of God's love there follows a goodness in the creature.' [8] Created grace is therefore not prior to uncreated; they are simultaneous and exercise a mutual causality. The presence of the Holy Spirit transforms a man so that he may receive the presence of the Holy Spirit.

It is well-known that Greek Orthodox theology soon came to follow the teaching of St Gregory Palamas, the fourteenth-century archbishop of Thessalonika, in rejecting the doctrine of created grace. In fact, however, Gregory's own position was much more nuanced. He accepts the fact that God's grace brings about a change in the individual, such as the 'new heart' and the 'new spirit' that Ezekiel speaks of, [9] and in the sense in which St Paul says that man becomes a new creature.

'There is a created grace and another grace uncreated',

he states; but he goes on to interpret created grace quite differently from the scholastics:

But since the gift which the saints receive and by which

[6] See the references in Moeller and Philips, *op. cit.*, pp. 24-28.
[7] *Breviloquium,* part V, c. 1.
[8] ST Ia IIae. 110.1 (trans. C. Ernst).
[9] Ezek 36.26.

they are deified, is none other than God himself, how canst
thou say that that too is a created grace? [10]

In the words of his most authoritative interpreter, John
Meyendorff:

> Palamas therefore accepts the idea of a 'created grace',
> but that by no means signifies that he is open to the
> conception of a 'created supernatural' in the Thomist sense
> of that term: the 'supernatural' can only designate the
> reality essentially distinct from the creature, the divine life
> itself. [11]

> The divine life — which is deifying grace when it is granted
> to man — therefore belongs to the divine nature even
> when men benefit from it. . . It is therefore just the oppo-
> site to an 'intermediary' between God and man; that
> would be the case with a created grace, for then it would
> be an intermediate nature, neither divine nor human. [12]

Palamas, therefore, like the scholastics, believed that grace was
the indwelling of the Holy Spirit, the self-giving of God; like
them he believed that this presence of God transformed the
human personality. But he differed from them in insisting that
this transformation was not itself supernatural; if it were supernatural, it would come between God and the soul, preventing
God's direct action.

In their wonderfully perceptive essay in ecumenical theology,
Charles Moeller and Gerard Philips have argued that the two
viewpoints are not, as was traditionally thought, incompatible:
as so often, the difference is rather one of emphasis, compounded
by the fact that the two sides were not using terms in the same
sense. [13] When Palamas rejected the notion of supernatural

---

[10] *Letter to Athanasius,* Coisl. 98, fol. 12-12v; *Against Akindynos,*
III.8, Coisl. 98, fol.76v. Both quotations from unpublished MSS,
are given in J. Meyendorff, *A Study of Gregory Palamas* (ET The
Faith Press, London, 1964), p. 164.

[11] Meyendorff, *op. cit.,* p. 163.

[12] *Ibid.,* p. 217.

[13] 'The East is concerned ... with what it is in God that makes it
possible for Him to give Himself; while the West is also concerned

created grace, he was rejecting a view which the best Western theology did not hold: namely, that grace is only a *thing* given by God to man and not the presence of God himself. In insisting that only God can be described as supernatural, and that man's co-operation with grace is natural, [14] Palamas was defining his terms differently from the West, in order to emphasise the primacy and immediacy of God's action on the soul. Western theology, on the other hand, while holding equally to this point, has been shaped by the need to face the issues raised by Pelagius, and therefore chose terms which stressed also man's inability without grace to take to himself the divine life. In any event, Palamas' battle was not against the West, but against the monk Barlaam and his supporters, who had ridiculed the traditional spiritual practices of the monks.

Martin Luther also rejected the doctrine of created grace, partly for the same reasons as Palamas, though the version of the doctrine with which he was familiar was the rationalistic travesty put forward by the nominalists, who separated created from uncreated grace, and made it no more than a quality in man. As Luther saw, created grace so conceived is simply a human possession, a thing, which is postulated as a means to unite man with God, but in fact only succeeds in keeping them apart. He also saw that such a doctrine comes close to Pelagianism, as it suggests that man, once equipped with this God-given disposition, is now capable on his own of gaining or meriting his salvation. [15]

The Council of Trent incorporated the idea of created grace in its teaching, though the term is not used. Instead the Council prefers to speak of God's charity *inhering* in man:

by the merit of his most holy passion, through the Holy

— though not to the exclusion of all else — with what it is in man that makes it possible for him to receive and take to himself God and His divine life... The East has never attempted a philosophical explanation of deification.' (Moeller and Philips, *op. cit.*, p. 16).

[14] Cf. Meyendorff, *op. cit.*, p. 165.

[15] Cf. Moeller and Philips, *op. cit.*, p. 29.

Spirit, the charity of God is poured out in the hearts of those who are justified and inheres in them. [16]

God's own justice (i.e. uncreated grace) is described in Aristotelian terms as 'the sole formal cause' of our justification; by this gift

we are renewed in the spirit of our mind, and are not only considered just, but truly are called and are just, so that each one *receives his own justice in himself*. [17]

These passages express the doctrine of created grace by insisting that God's charity and justice are not merely present to the individual, but become part of his being; we 'receive' God's justice in ourselves; God's charity 'inheres' in us.

The Council proposed this doctrine as a rebuttal of the Lutheran teaching that man himself is never just, but justice is imputed to him by God's grace. Although Luther was right to point to Pelagian tendencies in much late scholastic theology, [18] the Tridentine doctrine is quite the opposite of Pelagian. For according to it grace is not an independent faculty with which God endows man as he endows him with intelligence and will: it is God's own love which is poured out in our hearts and 'inheres' in them. As St Bonaventure saw, to possess grace is to be possessed by God.

This question of created grace is right at the heart of the theology of grace, and it is important to focus it as sharply as we can. The problem is this: granted that God's gift of himself by grace transforms the personality of the receiver, can this transformation itself be regarded as part of God's second gift, and that not only because it comes freely from God, but also in the sense that the gift itself raises man to a position above the natural powers of any possible created being?

---

[16] '...ipsis inhaeret' (Decree on Justification, ch. 7; DS 1530).

[17] '... iustitiam in nobis recipientes unusquisque suam' (DS 1529).

[18] 'For it is certain that the so-called Moderns agree with the Scotists and the Thomists in this matter (i.e. of free will and grace), with the sole exception of Gregory of Rimini, whom they all condemn. He himself rightly and convincingly showed that they were worse than Pelagians.' (WA II.394).

A negative answer to this question would imply that God came to man in his condition of a being with a natural desire for God, but did not raise man's personality or capacities above those of a creature. Actual grace would be whatever transient supernatural help was needed at any moment. By co-operating with grace, man would grow morally and spiritually, but his state would always be proper to a creature. The state of glory in heaven would not therefore be a further maturing of the growth God's grace has nurtured in a man on earth; it would simply be a reward for, or sequel to, the growth man's natural capacities had achieved by the help of grace.

Reasons for Believing in Created Grace

There are, however, several considerations which justify an affirmative answer to the question about the existence of created habitual grace.

(1) The language of the New Testament suggests unambiguously that God's presence in the soul is a transforming presence. There is no need to repeat the rapid glance which we took over some of the relevant texts in the first chapter. It will suffice, I hope, if we recall the various metaphors expressing the sharing of life, as in a human body or a plant; St Paul's doctrine that man participates in Christ's death and resurrection, and becomes a new creation; the Johannine doctrine of regeneration; the belief that God adopts Christians, not only in name but in fact. To say that such a transformation in man leaves him still within the limits of his human powers would be to divest these bold scriptural images of most of their meaning.

(2) Uncreated grace, the presence of the Holy Spirit, is not best conceived as a *local* presence (his presence *within* me), nor simply as a dynamic presence (his power *affecting* me), though this conception is much closer to the truth. His presence is a personal presence: he is present *to* me; with infinite generosity he initiates a personal relationship *with* me. To form

such a personal relationship with God is beyond the reach of a creature; it is only because God's transforming love makes him into a new creature that man is able to enter into such a relationship with God, so that he can call the Almighty and the All-holy one his Father.

(3) The glory of man is that he can serve God freely. The acts I perform by virtue of God's grace are still *my* acts. They are my acts, but not in the sense that a puppet's movements are the *puppet's* movements only because it is the puppet's limbs that jerk when the puppeteer pulls the strings. In so far as my acts are fully human, they are not a reflex reaction to stimuli coming from the outside, or even from God dwelling within me. A human being's free acts are his own in a unique way. If my acts performed under grace were simply a free but still natural co-operation with God's impulse of grace, they would cease to be mine precisely at the point at which they come under the influence of grace. God and I would be two co-operating agents; I acting by virtue of the first gift, my natural powers, he co-operating from outside my natural capacities. The doctrine of created grace, on the other hand, makes the actions totally mine while they are totally the work of grace, because they proceed from a grace-filled personality.

I would like to propose two analogies as illustrations rather than as proofs of this point.

(a) In a cricket match, a batsman plays a cover-drive which is a poem of footwork and timing. We are not, however, surprised, because we have often watched him bat, and have come to regard this stroke almost as his signature. In a reflective moment we may take pleasure in the thought of each occasion on which we have seen his bat swing with such easy elegance; and we know that this skill, though precariously held, no doubt, like most delicate arts, is his possession; it is something which is all his own. We do not simply enjoy a series of perfectly executed movements; we admire *him* for *his* skill. Now just as we recognize an abiding skill which underlies the individual strokes, so too, it seems that underlying actual graces there is

habitual created grace, an abiding disposition which is the fruit
of the presence of the Holy Spirit; because of it the actions I
perform under the influence of actual grace are *mine*.

(b) When a couple are happily married, each matures in
character as a result of the support that is given and received
by each. They will find that they can fulfil responsibilities to
an extent which would be beyond their capabilities alone. It
is true that in some cases the husband, say, is weak and needs
to be propped up by the wife every time a difficulty comes
along. But more often the new capabilities are due to a true
growth in character: each has a greater personal strength
because they are united. The strength comes from the continuing union, but is now part of the character of each. So too
God's presence (uncreated grace) supports us, not from outside
our personalities, but by transforming them.

(4) In the second chapter I put forward the view that
heaven is not an arbitrary reward, but is the maturing of our
growth in this life. We receive in this life the first fruits of the
gift of the Spirit God has promised us in the next. This can
only be so if God's presence transforms us, so that our growth
in this life is growth in the Spirit. For the same reason, the
doctrine of created grace shows hell to be not so much a
punishment devised by God, as the consequence of sin which
quenches the Spirit within us. [19] Without the Spirit, we slip
back to the limitations of a creature, and so become once more
incapable of enjoying the vision of God in heaven. Just as we
possess in this life the first fruits of heaven, so too in this life
we make our own hell. Hell is not a place but a state, as
Marlowe's Mephistopheles knew: 'Why, this is hell, nor am I
out of it'. In other words, the medieval representation of St
Michael at the Last Judgment, weighing the good works of the
dead man in the scales against his sins, misses the point: our
future life depends not on the balance of our good and bad
deeds, but on the sort of person we have allowed God's grace
to make of us on earth.

[19] Cf. 1 Thess 5.19.

(5) The existence of habitual grace helps to explain what we hope for when we pray for the grace to meet a particular need, that is to say, when we pray for actual grace. It is surely mistaken to regard such grace as a quasi-miraculous help which somehow makes easier what we naturally find hard; this model of the spiritual shot in the arm makes grace too external an influence. Now it is true that the help God sends may be totally external, like a word from a friend, or a passage read in a book; but this is not supernatural grace. It is only the natural psychological stimulus in response to which we can *grow* in grace, since the grace which transforms us is a developing, vital principle which is part of ourselves. An actual grace is a particular moment in the permanent capacity of our personalities, filled with the continuous personal presence of the Holy Spirit, to respond to a particular situation in which God's providence places us.

These are the reasons — and they seem to me strong — in favour of the theory of created grace. Yet it is certainly true that at the heart of the doctrine lies an enormous paradox. For if grace is to enter fully into our lives, it must become part of ourselves; yet it is always God's self-communication, his gift of himself. How can God's gift of himself become a part of ourselves without making us lose our identity in God? Gregory Palamas was well aware of the paradox, although he sought a solution to it in different terms from ours:

> You see that the teaching of the most venerable theologians [Maximus, Athanasius, Basil and John Chrysostom] contains two elements? On the one hand they tell us that the divine essence is incommunicable, on the other hand they tell us it is in some way communicable; on the one hand they tell us that we participate in the divine nature, on the other hand they tell us that we do not participate in it at all. We must therefore hold to both sides of their teaching, and make them the test of our spirituality. [20]

Let us remind ourselves once more how deeply rooted this

[20] *Theophanes* (PG 150.932D).

paradox is in the New Testament. On the one hand, the divine essence is incommunicable. He 'alone has immortality and dwells in unapproachable light, whom no man has ever seen or can see' (1 Tim 6.16). By no stretch of the imagination can the New Testament be made to yield a doctrine of pantheism: God alone is adorable, his will is supreme, his power is unassailable, and by his judgments all creation will be judged. He is totally self-sufficient and totally other.

On the other hand, the divine essence is communicable. We *receive* the Spirit, who dwells within us, as do also the Father and the Son; to reverse the imagery, we are in the Spirit, we live in Christ, as branches in the vine or organs in the body; we put on Christ; 'God's love has been poured into our hearts through the Holy Spirit who has been given to us' (Rom 5.5); we are baptized into Christ's death and raised together with him. This is a true communication of life, a sharing, not a manipulation: we become a new creation; we are born again; we become the scent of Christ rising up to the Father. We find ourselves most truly and attain to our fullest freedom and humanity, the more we receive the divine life. 'It is no longer I who live, but Christ who lives in me' (Gal 2.20).

This paradox cannot be resolved, for it is at the heart of the mystery of Christianity. We can however hope to penetrate a little more deeply into its meaning by the use of various analogies.

When jelly is poured into a mould, the mould imparts its shape to the jelly; and if the jelly sets properly, it retains the shape when the mould is taken off. Although the mould gives the jelly its shape, the mould itself never becomes part of the jelly, even while the jelly is still in the mould. Now no analogy of this kind can adequately represent God's union with his children. The mould gives its shape to the jelly, and God communicates to us his image; but to make God a cause who shapes us while remaining apart from us as the mould is apart from the jelly, would be to lose sight of the second wing of the paradox, namely that the divine essence is communicable.

Let us seek a second analogy in the work of an artist. It is not only his hand that applies the paint to the canvas or chips away at the marble until the beauty of the human form emerges from it; the form exists in his imagination even before it is realized in paint or stone. This remains true even if his conception to begin with is vague, and achieves precision only as he works, so that the eventual form seems to have grown out of the material he uses. So too God not only creates us, but imprints upon us his grace, which is his own form, the form of his Word, having already prepared our natures to receive that form. The divine artist is like a painter in the Ditchling tradition painting a self-portrait: he first weaves his own canvas and blends his own paints, and then creates from them his own image. But this analogy does not go far enough either. For when he has finished painting his work is over, though the picture continues to hang on the wall portraying his features; but the soul possesses God's grace only because of God's continuing self-giving.

Let us try to express this point in Aristotelian categories. The work of the artist exemplifies several different types of causality. There is the action of the artist in wielding his mallet and chisel or his paint-brush; in Aristotelian terms, he is an efficient cause. There is also the form that the material assumes under the artist's creative touch; this is called the formal cause. The efficient cause remains outside the effect; the formal cause is always part of the effect. In so far as the form exists in the artist's mind before being realized in the material, it is not a formal cause but a particular kind of efficient cause called an exemplar cause. Now God in conferring grace certainly acts as an efficient cause, even an exemplar cause, as he shapes us by grace after his own likeness. But any analogy which leaves God only as an efficient cause will fail to do justice to the intimacy involved in God's second gift, for it is the gift of himself. On the other hand it seems that we cannot very well say that God is the formal cause of the grace he bestows on

us, for that would imply a pantheistic type of divinisation. [21]
We seem therefore bound to conclude that God exercises upon
us a peculiar kind of causality which is more intimate than
efficient causality but less intimate than formal causality. Karl
Rahner invented for this the name of 'quasi-formal causality'. [22]

The theory was first clearly stated, though in different
terms, by Maurice de la Taille in 1928. [23] He pointed out
three instances in which God exercises on his creation a
causality which is more intimate than efficient causality, but
less so than formal causality. The first instance is God's action
in glorifying the saints in heaven so that they become able to
see him face to face; this transformation has been known since
the thirteenth century as the 'light of glory', in reference to
the words of the psalm: 'In thy light do we see light' (Ps 36.9).
The second instance is the one we are considering: God's
communication of himself to a person in grace. The third
instance is the union of the divine Word with the humanity
of Jesus. To this third instance we shall shortly return.

De la Taille's point is that in each case God fulfils the
potentiality of a created being, not simply as an efficient cause
operating from outside, as he does when he creates the world,
but by sharing himself with the other being. This sharing he
calls 'actuation', because it fulfils or makes actual the possibilities of the creature; further, he calls it 'created actuation',
since it is in its own being that the creature receives the new
form. In ordinary cases of actuation, it is the form in the
material that fulfils or actuates the potentiality of the material;
the new shape of the carved marble, for example, fulfils or
actuates the potentiality of the marble. In such cases (to retain
his French terminology) *actuation* implies *information*. But

---

[21] To speak in the terms of the Council of Trent, God's justice is
'the sole formal cause of our justification' (see above, p. 57).

[22] K. Rahner, 'Some Implications of the Scholastic Concept of Uncreated Grace', *Theological Investigations* i (ET Darton, Longman
& Todd, London and Helicon Press, Baltimore, 1961), pp. 329-331.

[23] 'Actuation Créée par Acte Incréé', *Recherches de Science Religieuse*,
18 (1928), pp. 253-268.

when God actuates human potentialities in the three ways just mentioned, his is the *actuation* but not the *information;* he shares his being without himself becoming a human form or perfection. What takes place de la Taille calls the created actuation of the creature by uncreated act.

Incidentally, this distinction between efficient and quasi-formal causality opens the way to the solution of a famous *crux theologorum*. Theologians had long been puzzled about the way to explain the relation between the Christian and each of the three Persons of the Trinity. On the one hand the New Testament and the creeds describe the actions of each of the three Persons towards the Christian in different terms: the Father, for example, is the Creator; the Son is the one *through* whom all things were made and who was made flesh to save us; it is the Holy Spirit who leads the Church into the fullness of revelation. On the other hand, since the three Persons are not three Gods but one, they act towards man with a single activity; the 'Athanasian' creed declares that there are not in God three almighty powers, but only one; [24] and it was the faith of the Council of Florence that in the Trinity everything is one, except the relationships of the Persons one to another. [25] Until recently the generally accepted position in Roman Catholic theology at least was that, while men have a special relationship with the manhood of the *incarnate* Christ, in other respects they are created and redeemed equally by all three divine Persons; the attribution of a particular role to each of the three Persons is simply a convention adopted to illustrate the relationships of the Persons among themselves. This convention was called appropriation. For example, because the Father is the source of the Son's being, it was a suitable convention to speak of the First Person only as the creator, even though the Son and the Holy Spirit are equally creators of the world, as

[24] 'Similiter omnipotens Pater, omnipotens Filius, omnipotens Spiritus Sanctus; et tamen non tres omnipotentes, sed unus omnipotens.' (DS 75).
[25] 'Omniaque sunt unum, ubi non obviat relationis oppositio.' (Decree for Jacobites; DS 1330).

all things in God are one, apart from the relationships of the
Persons one to another. On the other hand the New Testament
appears to give such a clear and consistent account of the
Christian's different relationship with each Person of the
Trinity that it seems unjustifiable to dismiss such meaningful
language as mere conventional appropriation. The distinctions
drawn by Rahner and de la Taille point the way to a solution.
Even if one feels bound to admit that God's work of creation,
including the constant sustaining and providential guidance
of his creatures, is a work of efficient causality proceeding from
God as such, [26] and therefore equally from each of the three
persons, nevertheless with grace it is quite different. Grace is
not God's external activity performed by efficient causality; it
is God's gift of himself, his actuation of the creature with his
own form. This self-communication by God takes man up into
the internal life of the Trinity, into what one might call God's
own family life, where all is not one but three. The Holy Spirit,
the Spirit of adoption, is given to us, so that we become one
with the Son made man, and therefore ourselves become sons
and daughters of the Father.

The theory of de la Taille which we have just been considering suggests a third analogy which may shed some light on
the paradox that God's essence is both communicable and
incommunicable: the analogy between the union of the
Christian with God by grace and the union of the humanity
and the divinity in the person of Jesus Christ. It is only to
be expected that there would be points in common, as we live
in Christ and Christ in us. According to the definition of
Chalcedon, in the incarnate Christ the divinity and humanity
are united in one *hypostasis*. Some modern theologians profess
to find in this definition no help towards understanding the
mystery of Christ; but in fact it contains an essential truth.

---

[26] 'The activity which is common to all three persons and appropriated
only to one is (as with the divine essence) possessed by each of the
three persons in his own proper way.' (K. Rahner, *The Trinity*,
Burns & Oates, London and Herder & Herder, New York, 1970,
p. 77).

The word 'hypostasis' does not denote a person in the modern psychological sense, but an existing being. [27] What the definition implies then is that, in so far as God the Son in his love for men chose to enter human history, he *was* and *is* the man Jesus. In Jesus there is no hypostasis, no existing being, apart from that of God the Son. The words and acts and experiences of that man are not simply the instruments of the eternal saving power of God the Son; they *are* that saving power projected into human history. Jesus, in his full humanity, *is* God the Son made man to save us.

De la Taille, as we saw, observed that the divinity of the Son is more than an external, efficient cause of the humanity. It will not do, however, to speak of the divinity as a form communicated to the humanity; that would be either a logical contradiction, or a monophysite confusion of the natures, or both. Although the man Jesus *is* God the Son, his divinity is not his humanity. In de la Taille's terminology, the divinity is the *actuation* of the humanity but not the *information* of it.

The analogy however between grace and the hypostatic union of the two natures in Christ is not exact. Although the humanity is not the divinity, Jesus is God the Son; but the Christian, though sharing in the divine life, is not God the Son, nor the Father, nor the Holy Spirit. What then is the effect of this actuation by God's own form, if it does not make us identical with him? The Christian does not *become* a Person of the Trinity, but receives a capacity to *relate* to the Persons of the Trinity in knowledge and love. 'This is eternal life, that they *know* thee, the only true God, and Jesus Christ whom thou hast sent' (Jn 17.3). 'God's *love* has been poured into our hearts through the Holy Spirit who has been given to us' (Rom 5.5).

The analogy, then, drawn from the creative work of an artist does shed some light on the way in which the Christian

---

[27] Cf. A. Grillmeier, *Christ in Christian Tradition* (Mowbrays, London, 1965), pp. 410-412.

F

shares in the divine life by grace, but not without the danger
of making us lose our way in the entanglements of abstract
terminology. We might accordingly make a fresh start by turning
to a biological model; there are obvious precedents for this in
the New Testament. A shoot grafted on to a stock, or an organ
grafted on to a body, becomes part of the main organism and
draws its nourishment from it, and in turn contributes to the
life of the whole, but the identity of the grafted shoot or organ
is not totally merged into that of the fostering plant or body.
So too, when we are grafted on to Christ, and so share in the
divine life, we draw this life from him without losing our
personal identity. In other words, the analogy brings out the
intimacy with which God gives himself to the Christian in
grace. But it fails to represent the transforming power of grace:
a grafted kidney remains a kidney, and a grafted rose remains
a rose, whatever St Paul may have thought happened when
a wild olive shoot is grafted on to a cultivated olive; [28] but when
we are grafted on to Christ we become a new creation.

So let us try a fifth analogy, an analogy drawn from human
relationships, especially the analogy of love, which recurs so
frequently in St Augustine's writings, and which the Christian
mystics of all ages have found an indispensable mode of
expression. 'God is love, and he who abides in love abides in
God, and God abides in him' (1 Jn 4.16). The analogy is
derived from the deepest form of union that we know, the love
of one person for another. For a person whom I know and
love, while remaining distinct from myself, becomes a second
centre of reference for my values, my emotions and my choices.
The image is especially apt, because love is transforming. We
grow by loving and by being loved; while retaining our own
personality we mature through the experience of love, and as
we learn to respond to and complement the other we draw
strength from him. So too in grace God's love unites us with
him and transforms us, so that we are able to know him (not
in the abstract but as a person) and to love him. To paraphrase

[28] Cf. Rom 11.17, 24.

a saying of St Augustine's: because you loved me, you made me lovable and capable of loving. [29] This effect of God's love as it breathes over us and makes us lovable and loving is created grace.

The Experience of Grace

Here we have reached the central point of our investigation. Grace, the share in Christ's life, the indwelling of the Holy Spirit, adoption by the Father, is, I have maintained, not something merely extrinsic to man, but something that transforms him. We have received from Christ's fullness; we reflect his Father's glory. [30] This share we receive in the divine life takes the form of a capacity to relate to the Persons of the Trinity in knowledge and love. Now in St Paul's thought this capacity or disposition falls within our experience: the Spirit enables *us* to cry 'Abba! Father!'; [31] though 'too deep for words', it is a recognizable cry which affords evidence that we are God's children. How then do we experience this cry to the Father in our hearts? How do we experience grace?

It may be helpful to return here to a conclusion that was reached in the second chapter: there must be in our natures a point of contact with grace, a capacity for the supernatural, a natural desire for God. If we can succeed in identifying in our experience this natural aptitude for grace, we will have gone a long way towards identifying the experience of grace itself. To put the question in another way, what is there about man which marks him off from the rest of creation (leaving angels out of the account) so that he alone can become a partaker of the divine nature? Or again, if our hearts know no rest until they find their rest in God, how do we experience this restlessness?

[29] This analogy of love is developed perceptively by P. Fransen, *The New Life of Grace* (ET G. Chapman, London, 1969), pp. 7-23. Fransen makes great use of the Augustinian text: 'Quia me amasti, fecisti me amabilem.'

[30] Cf. Jn 1.16; 2 Cor 3.18.

[31] Rom 8.15; cf. Gal 4.6; Rom 8.26.

St Augustine identified the image of God in man's rational
soul as his 'power to use reason and intellect for the understanding and the beholding of God'.[32] Philosophers, before
empiricism robbed them of their innocence, used to wax lyrical
about the infinite range of the human intellect. *Mens est
quoddammodo omnia*: the human mind, like Proteus, can
assume any shape. 'The whole universe', said Longinus,

> is not wide enough to contain the drive of man's contem-
> plation and thought; often his ideas reach even beyond
> the boundaries of space.[33]

We have not only an open-ended ability to learn, but also an
instinct to learn, an intellectual curiosity. Even the spiritual
cabbage who has taken root in front of the television set wants
to learn — even if it is only to know what comes next in the
story or who will win the wrestling-match. We are not cameras
impersonally recording information: we direct our lens at
what interests us; or to change the metaphor, we are blood-
hounds who sniff information out.

Thinkers in the Augustinian tradition can proceed a stage
further still: knowledge of any object includes knowledge of
God. This is not to say that when I look at any group of
people surrounding me my mind is immediately filled with the
thought of God. The point is rather that God is the light in
which we know whatever we know. When the mind, says St
Augustine,

> is directed to intelligible things in the natural order,
> according to the disposition of the Creator, it sees them
> in a certain incorporeal light which is *sui generis*, just as
> the corporeal eye sees the objects that lie before it in this
> corporeal light.[34]

Aquinas followed St Augustine on this point:

> Every being that knows, knows God implicitly in every-

[32] *De Trin.*, xiv.4 (CC 50A.428; PL 42.1040).
[33] *On the Sublime*, 35. I owe this reference to H. de Lubac, *The
Mystery of the Supernatural*, p. 138.
[34] *De Trin.*, xii.15 (CC 50.378; PL 42.1012).

thing that it knows. For just as nothing is desirable except in so far as it resembles fundamental goodness, so too nothing is knowable except in so far as it resembles fundamental truth. [35]

This argument may seem to depend on too intellectual a picture of man; the blank spaces in the picture need to be filled in by a similar argument derived from man's free will and his capacity to love. God's grace is able to transform these powers too into the free and conscious love of himself. The Augustinian will again venture further, and maintain that every act of freedom and every movement of love is implicitly a movement of the will towards God himself, the supreme good.

It will be seen that these arguments can be stated at three levels:

(1) Man has limitless powers of knowing and loving. God is able to transform these capacities by his grace so that he himself becomes their object, not as the object of abstract speculation, but as the partner in a personal relationship.

(2) Man not only has limitless powers of knowing and loving, but his longings never find satisfaction; his heart knows no rest until it finds its rest in God. In Tertullian's fine phrase, the soul is a natural Christian; [36] man's longings are a witness to the fact that he was made to receive the second gift of grace. This form of the argument appeals to the existentialist tendencies of modern continental theologians. De Lubac speaks of 'that mysterious lameness, due not merely to sin, but primarily and more fundamentally to being a creature made out of nothing, which, astoundingly, touches God'. [37] And Karl Rahner, in one of his characteristic outbursts of lyricism, writes of man's longings in which grace is experienced together with the natural being of man:

The beginnings of this fulfilment already exist — the

[35] *De Veritate*, 22.2 ad 1.
[36] *Apologeticum*, xvii.
[37] *Op. cit., pp.* 147-148.

experience of infinite longing, radical optimism, discontent which cannot find rest, anguish at the insufficiency of material things, protest against death, the experience of being the object of a love whose absoluteness and whose silence our mortality cannot bear, the experience of fundamental guilt with hope nevertheless remaining etc. [38]

(3) The third form of the argument has already been indicated: every act of knowing and loving contains a recognizable movement of the intellect and the will towards God, and is possible only because it does contain this movement. Grace is God's free fulfilment of this basic tendency in man. This form of the argument I have called 'Augustinian', but its twentieth-century revival owes most to the Louvain philosopher Joseph Maréchal. The aim of Maréchal's monumental work *Le Point de Départ de la Métaphysique*,[39] which began to appear soon after the first World War, was to establish the validity of objective knowledge in the face of the Kantian criticism. To accomplish this purpose he followed and extended Kant's own methods, and tried to establish not only logical but also psychological demonstrations that any act of knowing involves a movement of the mind towards infinite Being and absolute Good, and the simultaneous implicit affirmation of the objective existence of that Being and that Good. Unlike Kant, however, Maréchal maintained that the absolute is not only a postulate of knowledge, but is actually apprehended in all knowledge, although it is not itself an object of explicit awareness.

It is easy to find another example of such implicit awareness: my self-awareness. We are aware of ourselves explicitly

---

[38] *Nature and Grace* (ET Sheed & Ward, London, 1963), p. 36. There is a different translation of the same passage in *Theological Investigations* iv (Darton, Longman & Todd, London and Helicon Press, Baltimore, 1966), pp. 183-184.

[39] The first edition of the first of the five volumes was published in 1922 (Museum Lessianum, Louvain and Libraire Félix Alcan, Paris). The later editions were published by L'Edition Universelle, Brussels and Desclée de Brouwer, Paris.

when we practise introspection and think about ourselves, especially when we ask ourselves questions: Am I making a success of this job? Am I warm enough in bed without another blanket? We are aware of ourselves implicitly or indirectly as the subject of every experience; for I am implicitly aware that it is *my* experience and not somebody else's, although of course I do not normally tell myself this in so many words. Besides this, in all my conscious activity there is an attachment towards my own good; it is *my* hunger that craves to be appeased; it is *my* sense of beauty that seeks satisfaction when I move my eye over a landscape. In some such way, Maréchal argued, underlying all my knowledge is an implicit awareness of absolute truth and an implicit movement of the will towards absolute goodness; and that truth and goodness is God.

Maréchal's attempt to demonstrate that every act of knowledge has God as its implicit object has been called the Transcendental Method — transcendental, because it is based on knowledge of God, not as an explicit object, but as an object of a higher order, which is implicit in all knowledge and postulated by it. This method is followed by such leading figures in Roman Catholic theology today as Karl Rahner and Bernard Lonergan. [40]

The third, namely the transcendental, form of the argument we are considering makes this implicit knowledge of God and this implicit movement of the will towards him the point at which man's nature is open to grace. I myself do not find this third form convincing, and I have reservations about the second. But the first form of the argument I am prepared to accept: namely that it is man's unlimited powers of knowing

[40] E.L. Mascall discusses various expositions of this theory, called Transcendental Thomism, in chapters 4 and 5 of *The Openness of Being, Natural Theology Today,* the Gifford Lectures of 1970-1 (Darton, Longman & Todd, London, 1971). Cf. E. Coreth, *Metaphysics* (Herder & Herder, New York, 1968), p. 35: 'I call every knowledge transcendental which occupies itself not so much with objects, but rather with our way of knowing objects, in so far as this is to be possible *a priori*.'

and loving that make him capable of receiving God's second gift.

Piet Schoonenberg has pointed to another characteristic in man which makes him capable of receiving grace: his nature, which is both free and social. Alone among living creatures human beings depend upon one another for help freely sought and freely given.

> The instincts of mother and child are oriented towards a dialogue of love. . . One of the most eloquent expressions of it is to be found in the fact that the human child must still learn all the patterns of movement with which the young animal is equipped from birth. Thus man shows himself as a nature most profoundly defined by its openness... — for the gift of others. The dialectics of a natural longing for an unmerited gift, of a desire for what can only be gift and be desired as gift, is proper to man; it almost forms his definition. [41]

So far in this chapter I have tried to show that grace is not just God's presence within me, but his creative presence transforming me, enabling me to relate with him in knowledge and love, as one person relates with another. Then I suggested that the aspect of my nature which makes God able to transform me in this way is the openness of my powers of knowing and loving, together with the peculiar character of my social instincts. At last we can attempt an answer to the question, How do we experience grace?

We experience grace in three ways. First, although I am not able to accept fully the results that Maréchal claimed for his transcendental analysis of consciousness, his method can help us. I suggest that we do experience God's grace implicitly, as a transcendental, within and beneath all our actions and thoughts, in so far as in them we seek the truth and respond to the needs of others. I do not, like Maréchal, claim that there are logical and psychological demonstrations; the only demonstration is by faith. We know by faith that these actions and

[41] *The Christ* (ET Sheed & Ward, London, 1972), pp. 37-38.

thoughts are the fruit of grace; therefore we know that in experiencing them we are experiencing grace. *Ubi caritas et amor, Deus ibi est.* 'He who abides in love abides in God, and God abides in him.' This is the experience of actual grace.

Secondly, I have tried to show that created grace is not only a transitory burst of power enabling us to act, but is (in the Aristotelian sense) a habit, a disposition, an abiding vital principle, an enduring personal relationship. 'As the branch cannot bear fruit by itself, unless it abides in the vine, neither can you, unless you abide in me' (Jn 15.4). Now by definition a habit possesses a certain permanence; I do not cease to know French at a moment when I am giving all my attention to the struggle to speak German; when we speak of a 'good' person, we do not mean only that he performs separate good acts. [42] My individual acts, then, which I perform by the power of grace, are the fruit of a permanent principle or habit, which is the transforming effect in me of God's gift of himself, and which is called habitual grace. Like any habit, habitual grace is experienced only in the acts that flow from it, that is to say in the experience of actual grace.

Thirdly, although the experience of grace is clothed in the experience of acts proceeding from the habit of grace, we cannot rule out the possibility of what I shall call extraordinary graces, through which a person comes to act in a way which is discontinuous with his previous development. The most spectacular examples are sometimes called miracles of grace. Thus Gerard Manley Hopkins, in a prayer that God's grace will have its way in man, contrasts the patient, gradual working of grace in St Augustine with the abrupt conversion of St Paul:

[42] 'We act rightly "when the time comes" not out of strength of will but out of the quality of our usual attachments and with the kind of energy and discernment which we have available.' Iris Murdoch, *The Sovereignty of Good over Other Concepts,* the Leslie Stephen Lecture for 1967 (CUP, Cambridge, 1967), p. 21; reprinted in *The Sovereignty of Good* (Routledge & Kegan Paul, London, 1970), pp. 91-92.

With an anvil-ding
And with fire in him forge thy will
Or rather, rather then, stealing as Spring
Through him, melt him but master him still:
Whether at once, as once at a crash Paul,
Or as Austin, a lingering-out sweet skill,
Make mercy in all of us, out of us all
Mastery, but be adored, but be adored King.

(The Wreck of the Deutschland)

CHAPTER 4

THE GRACE OF OUR LORD JESUS CHRIST

St Luke tells us, in two somewhat conventional phrases, that the grace of God was on the child Jesus, and that 'Jesus increased in wisdom and in stature, and in grace with God and man'. [1] It would clearly be an anachronism to interpret the word 'grace' in these two passages as if it meant exactly what later theologians have meant by the word. The word here probably means 'favour', the same kind of favour as that expressed by the Father's voice at the Jordan: 'Thou art my beloved Son, with thee I am well pleased.' [2] The reference is to God's love; but since God's love is creative and transforming, it would be equally mistaken to interpret these Lucan texts as if they excluded any allusion to the personal qualities of Jesus. Similarly, Luke's reference to Jesus' increase in grace *with men* would have no significance unless he had in mind the holy child's own moral and spiritual growth. However, most people, I think, would feel more at ease in speaking of the 'grace of our Lord Jesus Christ' in the sense that St Paul gives the phrase in the benediction at the end of 2 Corinthians [3] —

---

[1] Lk 2.40,52. (The RSV Common Bible has 'favour' in preference to 'grace'.) A similar phrase is used in the OT of Samuel (1 Sam 2.26); cf. Jdg 13.24 in connection with Samson.

[2] Lk 3.22.

[3] 2 Cor 13.14.

namely, the love of Christ for us and the grace that he confers on us.

The subject of this chapter is the grace of Jesus in both senses, and it is my contention that the two senses are very closely connected: it is because Jesus in his human nature is himself full of grace that we are able to receive from that fullness.

Jesus the Source of Grace

St Thomas Aquinas distinguished three senses in which one could speak of the grace of Christ. First, there is what he calls the grace of union, through which the human nature was assumed by the divine Person; this can be described as a grace because it is a free gift of God to human nature which no man has done anything to deserve. [4] Secondly, Jesus possessed habitual grace; his humanity was not only united with the divinity by the grace of union, but was itself transformed by the presence of the Holy Spirit. [5] Thirdly, Jesus possesses the grace of headship of the Church, not only in so far as he rules over the Church, but also in so far as the members of his body derive their grace from the created, habitual grace of Christ the head. 'The personal grace by which the soul of Christ was justified is in essence the same as the grace by which, as head of the Church, he justifies others, though it is considered from a different point of view.' [6]

Cornelius Ernst points out how frequently in the Third Part of the *Summa* St Thomas refers to a particular passage in the *de Praedestinatione Sanctorum* of St Augustine. [7] The passage runs:

[4] ST III.2.10.
[5] III.7.13. Cf. III.7.9; III.8.5.
[6] 'eadem est secundum essentiam...; differt tamen secundum rationem.' (III.8.5).
[7] C. Ernst, *Summa Theologiae*, vol. 30, *The Gospel of Grace* (Eyre & Spottiswood, London and McGraw-Hill Book Company, New York, 1972), pp. xxi-xxii. The passage quoted is taken from Augustine, *de Praed. Sanct.*, xv.31 (PL 44.982). I have ventured to make small changes in Ernst's translation.

> Let there become manifest to us, then, in our Head, the very source and spring of grace, from which grace flows out to all his members according to the measure of each. From the beginning of his faith each man becomes a Christian by the same grace by which that man from his first beginning became Christ.

Aquinas employs a variety of images to illustrate the operation of this grace of headship. Grace is 'transferred', [8] 'channelled off' [9] or 'communicated' [10] to us from the humanity or soul of Christ. Christ's grace is 'prior' to ours, not necessarily in time, but because 'other men have received grace with respect to his grace'. [11] The human body is so constructed that the head exercises not only an external control over the rest of the body by means of the senses, but also an interior influence in that the power of sensation and of moving are derived from the head; so too 'the interior effusion of grace (*interior effluxus*) comes . . . from Christ alone, whose humanity has the power of justifying because it is united with the divinity'. [12]

St Thomas's contention, then, is that the humanity of Jesus is not only the means by which God grants us grace or the model after which we receive and grow in grace; it is also the source from which we receive grace. The Platonism of this conception is unmistakable. In the last chapter I discussed the theory which makes God the quasi-formal cause of our grace; here Aquinas seems to be attributing a similar function to Jesus' humanity. Because it is united with the divinity, his humanity is the source of our grace.

This use of material rather than personal analogies to describe the working of grace may leave us uneasy today. It is not, however, far removed from the language of the New Testament. 'From his fullness have we all received, grace upon

[8] 'transfunderetur', III.7.9.
[9] 'profluens in nos deducatur', Ia IIae.108.1; 'derivatur', III.8.5 ad 1.
[10] 'communicatur', III.7.10.
[11] III.8.1.
[12] III.8.6.

grace' (Jn 1.16). St Paul speaks of 'the Head, from whom the whole body, nourished and knit together through its joints and ligaments, grows with a growth that is from God' (Col 2.19). The word 'knit together' (*sunbibazomenon*) is only one of a large number of words beginning with the prefix *sun-*(with) which St Paul uses, and sometimes apparently coins, in order to express the Christian's unity with Christ in his Paschal actions. We are 'formed in the likeness of his death' (*summorphizomenos*); [13] we suffer (*sunpaschomen*), [14] died (*sunapethanomen*) [15] and were buried (*sunetaphēmen*) [16] with him; our old self was crucified (*sunestaurōthē*) [17] with him. God has brought us to life (*sunezōopoieisen*) [18] with Christ, raised us up with him (*sunēgeiren*), [19] and made us sit with him in heaven (*sunekathisen*), [20] where, as his fellow-heirs (*sunklēronomoi*), [21] we shall be glorified with him (*sundoxasthōmen*) [22] and shall reign with him (*sunbasileusomen*), [23] St Paul's favourite expression 'in Christ' sums up the intimacy of man's dependence on Jesus. 'It is no longer I who live, but Christ who lives in me' (Gal 2.20).

This emphasis on the sanctifying role of Jesus' humanity is expressed in other ways. 'There is one mediator between God and men, the *man* Christ Jesus' (1 Tim 2.5). Systematically St Paul allows the image of the Body and its members, which refers directly to the manhood, to slip into the image of the eucharistic Body, which is equally associated with the man-

[13] Phil 3.10.
[14] Rom 8.17.
[15] 2 Tim 2.11.
[16] Rom 6.4; cf. Col 2.12.
[17] Rom 6.6; cf. Gal 2.19.
[18] Eph 2.5. So too 'we shall live' (*sunzēsomen*) with Christ. (Rom 6.8; 2 Tim 2.11).
[19] Eph 2.6. Cf. Col 2.12; 3.1.
[20] Eph 2.6.
[21] Rom 8.17.
[22] Rom 8.17.
[23] 2 Tim 2.12.

hood. 'The Bread which we break, is it not a participation in the body of Christ? Because there is one bread, we who are many are one body' (1 Cor 10.16-17). Jesus' saying 'I am the way, and the truth, and the life; no one comes to the Father, but by me' (Jn 14.6), also seems to refer to his humanity.

Now what meaning can be attached to this doctrine which St Thomas states so clearly and repeatedly, and which is so deeply rooted in the New Testament — that the humanity of Jesus is not only the cause and the model of our sanctification, but is the source from which our sanctification is derived? We can say that our grace and Christ's are one and the same, in that sense that, in Cornelius Ernst's phrase, they result from 'a single divine initiative of grace'. [24] We can also seek an explanation in terms of human solidarity: because of the unity of the race in Christ, the last Adam, Jesus' human moral achievement can be shared by the rest. This is the message of the Epistle to the Hebrews: Jesus has to experience the moral struggle himself so as to be the 'pioneer' (*archēgos*) of our salvation, the 'forerunner' (*prodromos*); he leads the way so that we may 'have confidence to enter the sanctuary by the blood of Jesus, by the new and living way which he opened for us through the curtain, that is, through his flesh'. [25] But are not St Paul and St Thomas saying more than this?

It would of course be perverse to insist on the literal truth of the statement that created grace in us is identical, i.e. numerically identical, with that of Jesus. For this would be altogether to do away with the distinction between Christian and Christ. Besides, literally to share grace with another is a contradiction in terms. The grace in question, habitual created grace, is a permanent personal relationship with God, the ability to know and love him which is the result of the abiding presence of the Holy Spirit. It would make sense to say that God the Father

---

[24] Ernst, *op. cit.*, p. xxii. However, this is an explanation only in terms of *uncreated* grace.
[25] Heb. 2.10; 6.20; 10.19-20.

loves us with the same love with which he loves his Son; the phrase 'love me, love my dog' supposes that even on the human level the same movement of love can embrace two objects. What does not make sense is to suggest that two persons can know and love a third with numerically the same love.

Perhaps some light can be shed on this point by Dom Odo Casel's use of the term 'mystery'. [26] In the pagan mysteries the initiation-rites re-enacted certain crucial events of the god's life; by taking part in the rites, the votaries entered mystically into the god's own experience. So too one can speak of the mystery of Christ, not only in the sense that he is the revelation of the Father's love, but also in so far as the Christian can enter into his saving actions, especially his death and resurrection. This is done above all in the Church's worship, particularly in the initiation-rites of baptism, confirmation and Eucharist; [27] for they are the 'sacred rites which imitate and pass on the mystery of Christ', 'the sacred actions by which we are taken up and engrafted into this one mystery' of Christ, the images 'filled with the reality of the new life which is communicated to us through Christ'. 'What is necessary is a living, active sharing in the redeeming deed of Christ; passive, because the Lord makes it act upon us, active, because we share in it by a deed of our own', namely the liturgical celebration. [28]

It seems, then, to be the Christian tradition that Christ's humanity plays a role in our sanctification which goes beyond

[26] O. Casel, *The Mystery of Christian Worship* (ET Newman Press, Westminster, Maryland and Darton, Longman & Todd, London, 1962). See also E.J. Yarnold, 'Baptism and the Pagan Mysteries in the Fourth Century', *Heythrop Journal*, 13 (1972), pp. 247-267. The link between mystery (in this sense) and the doctrine of grace is made by C. Davis, *Liturgy and Doctrine* (Sheed & Ward, London, 1960), ch. 5.

[27] The Anglican/Roman Catholic Statement on the Eucharist of 1971 (the 'Windsor Statement') speaks in a similar sense of the Eucharist as the 'memorial' (*anamnesis*) of Christ's atoning work (para. 5; cf. paras. 3-4).

[28] Casel, *op. cit.*, pp. 16, 17, 14.

the notions of a cause or model of our grace. In explanation of
this doctrine we can say that the Father's gift of grace to Jesus
and to ourselves is due to one and the same gracious action
that is based on the unity of Christians in Christ. We can say
that the Father initiates and deepens the life of grace within
us by allowing us to share through the Church's liturgy in
the saving achievement that Jesus accomplished in his own
person. Beyond this point for the present I cannot go. I shall
return to the subject in the next chapter, where redemption
will be discussed. For the moment I must content myself with
adding two corollaries.

(1) Professor E.J. Tinsley has shown that the ideal of
imitating Christ has much stronger warrants in the New
Testament than many theologians have allowed.[29] Nevertheless
there are serious difficulties involved. First, the Gospels do
not provide the kind of biographical information which would
allow us to imitate Christ systematically and with certainty.
Secondly, there is the danger that the Christ we imitate is not
Christ at all, but the projection of our own preferences. Harnack,
for example, if George Tyrell was right, looked 'back through
nineteen centuries of Catholic darkness' and saw 'only the
reflection of a Liberal Protestant face ... at the bottom of a
deep well'. [30] Thirdly, the circumstances of our lives are so
different from Christ's that imitation of him can rarely be a
practical criterion of choice. These difficulties would be decisive
if what the New Testament enjoined on us were the literal
copying of Jesus' actions. But what discipleship involves is
not the copying, but the *following* of Christ; what the German
writers call *Nachfolge* rather than *Imitatio*. [31] We have to take
up the cross after Christ, put on his self-sacrificial mind; we

[29] Cf. E.J. Tinsley, *The Imitation of God in Christ* (SCM, London,
1960).
[30] G. Tyrrell, *Christianity at the Cross-roads* (Longman, Green & Co.,
London, 1909), p. 44, quoted by J. Ashton, 'The Imitation of Christ',
The Way, Suppl. 16 (1972), p. 30. The whole article is worth
reading for its critical examination of the concept of imitating
Christ.
[31] Cf. Tinsley, *op. cit.*, p. 23.

have to make our lives, like his, conform to the pattern of the grain of wheat which must die in order to bear fruit; [32] we have to make his *values* ours.

But there is another sense in which we imitate Christ, or rather grow in his likeness. God's second gift of grace means that Christ lives in us. In the words of John Robinson, interpreting the mind of St Paul: 'The Christian, because he is in the Church and united with Him in the sacraments, is part of Christ's body so literally that all that happened in and through that body in the flesh can be repeated in and through him [the Christian] now.' [33] Therefore to suffer, for example, with Christ does not mean 'external concomitance, like the P.T. instructor who says, "Now do this with me" ', but a 'common organic functioning'. [34]

> The Christian life . . . does not consist of an external imitation of the character and actions of Jesus of Nazareth or of an external obedience to his commands; those are its fruits, not its roots. In its essence, it is the reproduction of Christ in us, or, viewing it from the opposite aspect, it is our continual and progressive fashioning into him. The Christian virtues are nothing less than the manifestation of Christ in his members. [35]

It follows then that we could imitate Christ even if we knew nothing about his life, provided we put no obstacle in the way of his growth within us.

The transmission of human life provides an analogy. A child grows to be like his parents, partly because he copies their mannerisms and assimilates some of their attitudes, but more basically because many of the child's characteristics are fixed by his genetic structure, which in its turn was determined by the genetic structure of the parents, which itself determined

---

[32] Mk 8.34; Gal 3.27; Phil 2.5ff.; Jn 12.24-26.

[33] J.A.T. Robinson, *The Body* (SCM, London, 1952), p. 47.

[34] *Ibid.*, p. 63.

[35] E.L. Mascall, *Christ, the Christian and the Church* (Longmans, Green, London, 1946), pp. 204-5, quoted in Tinsley, *op. cit.*, p. 179.

many of their characteristics. Now habitual grace, which is the gift of the abiding Spirit within us, leads us to grow in the likeness of Christ, because it, so to speak, communicates to us his genetic code. It is a share in, an expression of, the divine life of the Trinity, and in particular of the life of God the Son; consequently it also assimilates us to the human life of Jesus, for his manhood is the human expression of his divine life. Jesus is therefore not so much a model to be consciously imitated, as the supreme example of the same power of God that works in us. His human life is the highest achievement of grace, the same grace which can flower in all the other members of the human race. Moreover, if the argument of the first part of this chapter is accepted, the Christian's life of grace is even more closely related to Christ's human life. He participates first in the grace-filled humanity of Jesus, and only as a consequence of this fact does he share in the divine life of the Trinity.

(2) The second corollary concerns devotion to the sacred humanity of Jesus, and in particular devotion to his sacred Heart. If this does not seem a sufficiently academic subject for theological lectures like these, I would only say that in one of the most influential sets of Bampton Lectures to be delivered since the beginning of the Second World War, G.L. Prestige devoted his last lecture to these precise themes. [36] My approach, however, is different from Prestige's: he concentrated specifically on devotion paid to the humanity; I am interested rather in the way in which the humanity of Jesus is seen in popular devotion as the source of grace.

Such is the belief expressed in Toplady's elemental hymn:

Rock of ages, cleft for me,
Let me hide myself in thee.

Hugo Rahner suggests that:

the sublime picture which the early Christians had of the Sacred Heart, as the fountain which dispenses Spirit from

---

[36] *Fathers and Heretics,* the Bampton Lectures for 1940 (SPCK, London, 1940).

the wounded side, was formed by connecting John 7.37 ['If any one thirst, let him come to me, and let him who believes in me drink. As the scripture has said, Out of his heart shall flow rivers of living water'.] with John 19.34 ['One of the soldiers pierced his side with a spear, and at once there came out blood and water.']. Gospel, Church, Grace, Baptism: these are the gifts of the transfixed heart of the glorified Lord, and the symbol which crystallizes them is the water of the Spirit. Even the early Christians at their simple prayer knew and loved this thought. On the wall of the Baptisterium in the Catacomb of Priscilla, some anonymous Roman scratched the words from John 7.37: *Whoever thirsts, let him come.* Another hand wrote: 'Redeemed through the wound of Christ'. We know from the Church regulations made by Hippolytus at the beginning of the third century, that at the ninth hour of the day Christians meditated with special intensity on the piercing of Christ's side... Ambrose gathered all these ideas into a prayer which has the mystical ardour and beauty of a genuine canticle to the Sacred Heart. He is exhorting the faithful to drink at the fount of living water, which is Christ himself:

> Drink of Christ, for he is the rock,
>   from which the water springs.
> Drink of Christ, for he is the fountain of life.
> Drink of Christ, for he is the stream whose
>   torrent brought joy to the city of God.
> Drink of Christ, for he is Peace.
> Drink of Christ, for streams of living water
>   flow from his body. [37]

Another biblical image that has been used to illustrate the origin of salvation from the body of Christ is the birth of Eve from the side of Adam. Thus Tertullian writes:

[37] H. Rahner, 'The Beginnings of the Devotion in Patristic Times', in *Heart of the Saviour,* ed. J. Stierli (ET Nelson, Edinburgh and London, and Herder & Herder, New York, 1958), pp. 48-49. The Ambrosian hymn comes from *Expl. Ps.,* i.33 (CSEL 64, p. 29). In Jn 7.38 the Greek word for the source of living water is *koilia* (literally, 'belly'), rather than *kardia* ('heart'). For this verse I have adopted the punctuation which represents the living water flowing from the heart of Christ, rather than from the heart of the believer.

> If Adam was a prefiguration of Christ, the sleep of Adam
> was the death of Christ, who was to sleep in death, so
> that the wound in Adam's side could also be the pre-
> figuration of the Church, the true mother of the living. [38]

From the time of St Augustine, alongside the devotional
expressions concerning Christ's side, references to the heart
(*cor*) begin to occur. Augustine himself writes of the Evangelist
John:

> At the Supper he lay in his [Christ's] bosom, signifying
> that he drank in deeper mysteries from the centre of his
> [Christ's] heart. [39]

In the middle ages references to the Heart of Jesus became
more common. One historian of the devotion, Josef Stierli,
distinguishes two aspects of it: first, the heart of Jesus is seen
as the centre and symbol of Jesus' own inner life; second, —
and it is with this aspect that I am more concerned — the
'pierced Heart of our Lord, pouring out blood and water on
Golgotha, is seen objectively in its redemptive role, as the
source of all the messianic treasures of salvation.' [40]

This devotional writing assumes a close connection between
Jesus' own grace and the grace which he communicates to his
followers. The comparison of two prayers, one of the fourteenth
century and one of the seventeenth, illustrates the development
of this idea. The *Anima Christi*, which is known from fourteenth-
century manuscripts, and received a new popularity from its
inclusion in the *Spiritual Exercises* by St Ignatius Loyola, [41]
is content in terms that recall St Ambrose's prayer, to regard
Christ's humanity, and in particular his body, as the source
of grace:

[38] Tertullian, *de Anima*, 43, quoted in H. Rahner, *op. cit.*, p. 54.
[39] *Tr. in Jo.*, xviii.1 (CC 36.179; PL 35.1536).
[40] J. Stierli, 'Devotion to the Sacred Heart from the End of Patristic
times down to St Margaret Mary', in *The Heart of the Saviour*,
pp. 59-60.
[41] Cf. H. Thurston, 'Anima Christi', in *Dictionnaire de Spiritualité*
(Beauchesne et Fils, Paris, 1937), vol. i, 670-672.

> Soul of Christ, sanctify me;
> Body of Christ, save me;
> Blood of Christ, inebriate me;
> Water from the side of Christ, wash me;
> Passion of Christ, strengthen me;
> O Good Jesus, hear me;
> Within thy wounds hide me. . .

In the seventeenth century the founder of the seminary of
Saint-Sulpice, Jean-Jacques Olier, taught his seminarians to
say twice daily a prayer which links the Christian's grace
specifically with that of Christ; each particular virtue of the
Christian is now seen to be vitally connected with the corresponding virtue in Christ, which he already possessed even in
the womb:

> O Jesus, living in Mary, come and live in your servants,
> in the Spirit of your Sanctity, in the fullness of your
> strength, in the perfection of your ways, in the truth of
> your virtues, in the communion of your mysteries. Be
> Lord of every opposing power, in your Spirit, for the glory
> of the Father. [42]

Two centuries later Gerard Manley Hopkins linked this
idea with Mary's motherhood of all Christians:

> If I have understood,
> She holds high motherhood
> Towards all our ghostly good
> And plays in grace her part
> About man's beating heart,
> Laying, like air's fine flood,
> The deathdance in his blood;
> Yet no part but what will
> Be Christ our Saviour still.
> Of her flesh he took flesh:
> He does take fresh and fresh,
> Though much the mystery how,
> Not flesh but spirit now
> And makes, O marvellous!

[42] Cf. H. du Manoir, *Maria*, vol. iii (Beauchesne et Fils, Paris, 1954), p. 159.

New Nazareths in us,
Where she shall yet conceive
Him, morning, noon, and eve;
New Bethlems, and he born
There, evening, noon, and morn —
Bethlem or Nazareth,
Men here may draw like breath
More Christ and baffle death;
Who, born so, comes to be
New self and nobler me
In each one and each one
More makes, when all is done,
Both God's and Mary's Son. [43]

A moving expression of this belief in the connection between the experiences of the Christian and those of Christ was given by the martyr St Felicity. In prison awaiting martyrdom she gave birth to a daughter. When she cried out with the pain of labour, one of the soldiers guarding her taunted her in these words: 'If you feel so much pain now, what will it be like when you are thrown to the beasts?' She replied: 'Now the suffering is mine. But when that happens, there will be someone else inside me suffering in my place, because I will be suffering for him.' [44]

Jesus' Experience of Grace

Because of the decisive importance for us of the grace of the man Jesus, I wish to devote the rest of this chapter to a discussion of his experience of grace. It is of course true that the position of Jesus is unique, because, to borrow St Athanasius' terms, he is the Son by nature, and not, like us, by adoption or decree; [45] the man Jesus *is* God the Son incarnate. Yet he is as human as we are. His humanity is not only

---

[43] *The Blessed Virgin Compared to the Air We Breathe, The Poems of G.M. Hopkins,* ed. W.H. Gardner & N.H. McKenzie (OUP, London, 4th ed. 1967).

[44] *Martyrdom of SS. Perpetua and Felicity,* 15, in H. Musurillo, *The Acts of the Christian Martyrs* (Oxford Early Christian Texts, Clarendon Press, Oxford, 1972), pp. 122-4.

[45] *Or. adv. Arian.,* ii.59 (PG 26.273). See above, p. 21.

united to the godhead of the Son as one hypostasis; the man Jesus, as man, is caught up into the life of the Trinity, is elevated and divinised by habitual created grace. It is created grace, because it transforms his created humanity; and it is because his humanity is transformed in this way that we can be caught up into the life of the Trinity too. It is this created grace of Jesus that I wish to examine.

The theme of this book is the threefold pattern of the impact of grace on our lives: first, as habitual grace, it is a permanent ontological fact, an enduring and transforming personal relationship with the three-personal God, an abiding vital power to know and love God; secondly, as actual grace, it is experienced in the particular acts of knowledge and love which flow from habitual grace, and is experienced indirectly as a transcendental within and beneath all our moral delibera-tions and choices; thirdly, and more problematically, it is experienced in God's particular interventions in our conscious lives, as it were from outside. I wish to consider how Jesus experienced grace in these second and third ways.

This consideration inevitably leads to the discussion of the psychology of Jesus. Some may think that this mine has already been fully worked. But it appears to me that there are certain seams that have still to be explored, and I would like to offer my own contribution towards the surveying of them.

Eric Mascall believes that nothing useful can be said on this topic. He protests against the way in which by many theologians 'the problem of the Incarnation is taken as simply the problem of describing the mental life and consciousness of the Incarnate Lord', [46] and in this protest I agree with him. But I cannot altogether agree with the way he develops his argument:

> For this problem [concerning the consciousness of Jesus] seems to me to be strictly insoluble... If I am asked to say what I believe it feels like to be God incarnate I can

[46] E.L. Mascall, *Via Media* (Longmans Green, London, 1956), p. 117.

only reply that I have not the slightest idea and I should not expect to have it. [47]

I feel considerable sympathy with Professor Mascall's reverent silence. Indeed, besides reverence, there is another reason for silence, namely common-sense humility: it is hard enough to imagine what it feels like to be a saint, let alone one who could say with total truth: 'My food is to do the will of him who sent me' (Jn 4.34). Nevertheless there are reasons why we must take off our shoes and walk as far as we can on this holy ground. For the doctrine of Chalcedon, that Christ is 'not only one in substance with the Father in godhead, but also one in substance with us in manhood', [48] must be capable of some degree of elucidation in terms of human experience. Granted Mascall's point that a description of Jesus' mental states cannot be a full theological account of the Incarnation, the declaration of Chalcedon remains a mere algebraic formula unless we are able to state some of its practical implications. What, for example, is the difference in psychological terms between the phantom man of the docetists or the divinely-souled body of the Apollinarians and the complete man of Chalcedon? It is not enough to say that full humanity is necessary to explain the redemption, if we cannot say what full humanity means.

It is not in fact a straightforward concept. I am inclined to think it is no easier, perhaps even harder, to explain the implications of 'full manhood' than it is to explain those of 'full godhead'. Full manhood implies being 'born of woman', as St Paul saw; [49] but traditional theology did not think that the virgin birth made Jesus less of a man. The criterion, as the Fathers constantly repeated, is functional: Jesus has all the properties of manhood that are necessary for the redemption of man. Among these a normal human psychology must be included. For, first of all, the suffering and death of Christ

[47] *Ibid.*
[48] DS 301.
[49] Gal 4.4.

loses its power to inspire love in us if we cannot understand
from our own experience something of the generosity and self-
sacrifice that was involved. Secondly, his life loses its validity
as a standard for our own if the choices Jesus had to make did
not involve a psychological cost. How can we 'put on Christ', [50]
if he was merely going through the motions of doing what costs
us so much effort and pain? Thirdly, and most importantly,
since our grace is a participation in his, the life of grace that
Jesus lived must have involved the same sort of experience
that a similar life would involve for us. For grace is not a
static possession, but a principle of life that bears fruit in
particular experiences; if our experiences of grace bear no
comparison with his, neither will the habitual grace itself.
To put the argument in a different way, Jesus is able to redeem
us only because he is able to 'sympathize with our weaknesses',
because in every respect he 'has been tempted as we are, yet
without sin', because he was 'made like his brethren in every
respect'. [51]

Theologians who followed Aquinas have distinguished three
kinds of knowledge which Jesus possessed with his human
mind: the beatific vision, infused knowledge and acquired
knowledge.[52] The beatific vision is the vision of God face to
face which the saints enjoy in heaven and which will replace
the glimpses of God, as if in a clouded mirror, which is all we
have in this life. [53] Jesus, it was said, being himself divine,
must have enjoyed the direct vision of God in this life, but by
accepting human limitations he renounced the beatitude that
it brings in heaven. [54] Acquired knowledge is the normal sort

[50] Gal 3.27.
[51] Heb 4.15; 2.17.
[52] ST III.9.2-4.
[53] Cf. 1 Cor 13.12.
[54] Pius XII, in his encyclical *Mystici Corporis,* insisted that Christ
possessed the beatific vision on earth (DS 3812); but K. Rahner has
indicated that it is more accurate to speak of this vision of Christ's
as 'immediate' rather than 'beatific'. See 'Dogmatic Reflections on
the Knowledge and Self-Consciousness of Christ', in *Theological
Investigations* (ET Darton, Longman & Todd, London and Helicon
Press, Baltimore, 1966), vol. v, pp. 202-3.

of knowledge that human beings gain by experience. Infused knowledge is in content like acquired, but is different in origin: it is not, it was said, learnt by experience, but miraculously communicated by God. Various reasons were alleged to prove that Jesus needed infused knowledge: that, since ignorance is an imperfection, he must have possessed from the cradle all possible knowledge, though he abstained from using it; that God must have communicated at least all that he needed to know in order to fulfil his saving mission.[55] Some theologians added a fourth kind of knowledge: because of his direct awareness of God, Jesus simultaneously perceived all truth.[56] Although this is a totally different kind of knowledge, what I have to say about infused knowledge will also apply to this fourth kind.

Now this account of Jesus' knowledge is totally inconsistent with the considerations I was putting forward a few moments ago. There is no hint here of a life of grace, or even an ordinary natural human life, with which we can feel the slightest affinity. Moreover, this account of Jesus' psychology is quite incompatible with the many references the Gospels, especially the synoptic Gospels, make to ignorance and even error on Jesus' part. There are, in fact, two very different pictures of Jesus in the Gospels. On the one hand, Jesus is the Son who is in the bosom of the Father from all eternity, who receives all knowledge from the Father, who sees events at a distance and in the future, who reads hearts; such is the impression left above all by the Fourth Gospel.[57] But there is a second portrait, found mainly in the synoptics, and especially in Mark, of a Jesus whose knowledge is limited: the boy Jesus grows in wisdom; he does not know the time of the last day; he thinks that it will come within a generation; he chooses a disciple

[55] ST III.9.3 contains an argument from Jesus' perfection. It is of course true that Jesus knew all he needed to know in order to redeem the world; but it does not follow that he needed infused knowledge.
[56] ST III.10.2.
[57] For example, cf. Jn 1.18, 48; 2.25; 5.19; 8.58. See also the notoriously 'Johannine' passage in Mt 11.25-30.

who lets him down; he prays for things that are not granted
— that the cup may be removed from him, that his followers
may all be one. [58] If one of these mutually inconsistent portraits
was an invention of the early Church, it is more likely to have
been the portrait of the omniscient Christ. This Johannine
portrait adds a new dimension to the historical portrait by
references to the divine powers of the Son or to the powers
of the risen and glorified Christ.

It is not only Roman Catholic theologians who have felt
obliged to give an account of Jesus' psychology which would
put him in practice outside the human race. Canon H.P.
Liddon, for example, in the Bampton Lectures of 1866, judged
that 'the Gospel history implies that the knowledge infused
into the Human Soul of Jesus was ordinarily and practically
equivalent to omniscience'. Liddon is compelled by the words
of Mark 13.32 to admit that Christ did 'deny to His Human
Soul at one particular date the knowledge of one fact',
namely the knowledge of the date of the day of judgment.
But he continues:

> that He was ever completely ignorant of aught else, or
> that He was ignorant on this point at any other time, are
> inferences for which we have no warrant, and which we
> make at our peril. [59]

But from the time of Charles Gore many Anglican theologians
came to accept the view that Jesus' knowledge was subject to
normal human limitations. It became customary to expound
this theory in a form called kenotic, with reference to the
self-emptying of Christ which St Paul speaks of in Philippians
2.7.

The former Archbishop of Canterbury, Dr A.M. Ramsey, has
provided a useful account of the development of this theory
in his study of Anglican theology entitled *From Gore to
Temple*. Dr Ramsey distinguishes between two versions of the

---

[58] For example, cf. Lk 2.52; Mk 13.32, 30; 14.36; Jn 17.21-23.
[59] *The Divinity of Our Lord and Saviour Jesus Christ* (Longmans
Green, London, 14th ed., 1890), pp. 474-5.

kenotic doctrine: the 'classic', 'extreme', 'full-blooded' version of continental Lutherans on the one hand, and the 'restrained and imprecise Anglican form' on the other. According to the continental interpretation of kenosis, during his earthly life the Word renounced the divine attributes so completely that God the Son simply ceased during this time to be omniscient and omnipotent. [60] Gore was aware that this view was unacceptable philosophically and incompatible with scripture and the councils of the Church. His theory implied that, while there was no diminution in the powers of the unchanging and eternal Son of God, 'He emptied Himself of divine prerogatives so far as was involved in really becoming man, and growing, feeling, thinking and suffering as man'. [61] Christ's limited human knowledge therefore coexisted with his infinite divine knowledge; but, as Gore well says, we must not

> so juxta-posit the omniscient Godhead with the limited manhood as to destroy the impression that He, the Christ, the Son of God, was *personally* living, praying, thinking, speaking, and acting — even working miracles — under the limitations of manhood. [62]

Gore's theory, so expressed, seems to me in general to be convincing. There are however some details of it which are open to objection. (1) He refuses to decide whether the kenosis was a once-for-all act of renunciation, or whether it involved a continual refusal to accept the divine knowledge. 'We have not the knowledge of the inner life of Jesus which would make an answer possible.' [63] However, the theory of the continually-repeated renunciation cannot be right. For either the continual repetition took place in the divine mind, which seems to put God *as God* within time; or else the repeated

---

[60] A.M. Ramsey, *From Gore to Temple* (Longmans, London, 1960), pp. 32, 42.

[61] C. Gore, *Belief in Christ* (John Murray, London, 1922), p. 226.

[62] C. Gore, 'The Consciousness of Our Lord in His Mortal Life', in *Dissertations on Subjects Connected with the Incarnation* (John Murray, London, 2nd edit., 1896), p. 203.

[63] C. Gore, *Belief in Christ*, p. 226.

renunciation took place within Jesus' human consciousness, which already implies that his human consciousness operated beyond human limitations in order to make the renunciation. The once-for-all renunciation seems the only tenable theory. (2) Gore sometimes speaks as if the renunciation of divine knowledge was an extra self-emptying in addition to that involved in becoming man. 'The self-sacrifice of the Incarnation appears to have lain in great measure, *so far as human words can express it,* in His refraining from the divine mode of consciousness within the sphere of His human life, that He might really enter into human experience.' [64] At other times Gore suggests that the renunciation of omniscience is implied by the Incarnation, and is *not* an additional sacrifice. This second view seems preferable: the purpose of the Incarnation, as I have tried to show, could not have been fulfilled if Jesus had retained divine omniscience in his human mind. Besides, it is a truism that if God the Son is to become man, it must be a man with human limitations, so that it is *in* these human limitations and not *in spite of* them that God and the properties of God, his omniscience and omnipotence, as well as his goodness and wisdom are revealed. I shall return to this point later.

(3) Some of Gore's conclusions now seem surprisingly timid. Although holding that Jesus was 'living, praying, thinking, speaking, and acting . . . under the limitations of manhood', Gore rejected 'the *a priori,* humanitarian and also unhistorical view that the Son in becoming man ceased to be conscious of His own eternal sonship, and became, not merely a human, but a fallible and peccable teacher'. [65] In this compendious sentence Gore lumps together three totally different things: consciousness of divine sonship, infallibility as a teacher and sinlessness. His insistence on impeccability seems well-founded: a sinful Jesus could not be God the Son in human terms. But it is not on *a priori,* humanitarian and unhistorical

[64] C. Gore, *Dissertations,* p. 97; cf. p. 94.
[65] C. Gore, *Dissertations,* pp. 95-96.

grounds that Jesus' infallibility and self-knowledge can be questioned; theological considerations have great relevance. The infallibility of Jesus' teaching I shall consider when I come to discuss revelation in Chapter Six. The question of Jesus' knowledge of his divine sonship cannot be answered without drawing distinctions, and I shall return to the point shortly.

Despite these reservations, it seems to me that there are overwhelming reasons for accepting Gore's general thesis, and rejecting the picture of a Christ in habitual or continual receipt of infused knowledge. We have already considered how the theology of the redemption leads us to this conclusion, and how the evidence of the Gospels points in the same direction. The first of these arguments can well be pursued a little further.

(1) For Jesus to be the source of our grace, and the standard and inspiration of our lives, his mental processes must have been comparable with ours — sin alone excepted. Now our minds are not like data-banks which gradually increase their store of information; rather, our personality grows with our expanding knowledge, in the effort to appropriate experience and to assess it, and in the attitude we form to it. [66] If Jesus, therefore, had possessed this fund of infused knowledge, he would not only have had more facts at his disposal than we have, but the development of his personality would have been radically different from ours. In particular, he would not have undergone the process of learning in those keenly-impressionable first weeks after birth which do so much to determine the shape of our future personal development.

(2) The extent of the infused knowledge would have to be either much smaller or much greater than proponents of the theory normally envisage. For infused knowledge would be incomprehensible unless the recipient had the appropriate

[66] It is of course possible that a person can fail fully to assimilate the information he acquires; it then remains mere *learning,* a collection of facts which he can repeat, rather than *knowledge* which has become an enrichment of his personality.

experience with which to interpret it, just as a man born blind cannot understand descriptions of colours, and a child cannot understand erotic literature. Therefore, to be usable, infused knowledge would either have to be limited to the facts that Jesus' experience would enable him to assimilate, or else would have to include the direct implanting in Jesus' mind of all the background of knowledge and experience needed to interpret it.

(3) Since human beings learn and remember through the biochemical functioning of the brain, the amount of knowledge Jesus could assimilate would be limited to the capacities of the biochemical processes.

However, of more decisive importance than these considerations is the fact that there is no need to postulate infused knowledge in Jesus. Now I do not wish to rule out on *a priori* grounds the possibility that Jesus could have received any knowledge of this kind. I see no reason why God should not be able to give a human being miraculous knowledge of the future or extraordinary mystical experience (I shall speak of mysticism in the last chapter). It is possible that Jesus possessed the ability to read hearts and tell the future in particular cases because of a kind of infused knowledge; though perhaps one need seek nothing further than a natural power of empathy into other men's characters, and a spiritual insight into the meaning of the Old Testament. But though Jesus may have received special enlightenment from his Father in particular instances, the grounds alleged for his need of habitual enlightenment are insufficient.

On the one hand it is said that Jesus needed such infused knowledge because ignorance is an imperfection. Now imperfections are of several kinds. First, there are moral imperfections, which involve culpability; Jesus could not have been subject to such imperfections, but ignorance is not one of them. Secondly, there are limitations which follow by logical necessity from the fact of the Incarnation: for example, Jesus could not have been both male and female, both a Jew and a gentile. Now it follows from what has been said already that some degree of ignorance is a logically necessary condition of human existence; in this sense, therefore, the imperfect state of Jesus' knowledge presents no special problem. Thirdly, it might be said that someone possessed a quality imperfectly, in the sense that he possessed it to a less than ideal extent. However, this conception seems to rest on a fallacy, for there is no ideal degree of human size, strength, beauty, knowledge, etc. Fourthly, a quality possessed by Jesus might be said to be imperfect if other people possessed this quality to a higher degree. Now it seems to be possible, and even necessary, to admit such imperfection in Jesus, even with regard to his knowledge. It is clearly unnecessary to maintain that he had the best voice in Judea, and the greatest strength; that he was the fastest sprinter as well as the fastest three-miler. I see no reason why similar conclusions should not be maintained about Jesus' mental powers. There may have been people who knew more than he did, or who possessed a higher I.Q. He may not have been potentially both the best scientist and the best artist.

Besides the claim that Jesus was free from imperfections, there is also the more modest claim made that he needed infused knowledge of his saving mission in order to carry it out. This claim simply cannot be proved. Neither, of course, can the opposite be proved, namely that Jesus never experienced moments of divine illumination; all that one can say is that such moments must have been so limited that normal psychological development was not made impossible.

Jesus' Self-knowledge

There is one area of Jesus' knowledge which is so important and so unique that it needs to be considered separately: his awareness of his divinity and of his saving mission. A very plausible argument can be constructed in favour of the view that in his human mind Jesus was aware of these two facts: since God the Son became man, it was God the Son who was the subject of all the operations of the manhood, including the psychological; when Jesus thinks and feels it is the one divine

K

person of the Son thinking and feeling. Therefore the divine knowledge cannot be kept separate from the human knowledge; and in particular, the divine self-knowledge must have over-flowed into the human self-knowledge.

There are two ways of answering this line of reasoning. The first is to concede the point that the human knowledge is not insulated from the divine. However, the divine knowledge will be received in the human consciousness *in a human way*. For, first of all, only on this supposition can it be said that Jesus had the normal psychological development which was necessary for our salvation. And secondly, the Incarnation means that the human life of Jesus is the 'extrapolation' of the Son's life in the bosom of the Father *into the totally human sphere,* its revelation *in wholly human terms;* it is a totally human psychology that is the translation of the divine consciousness into the mode of the Incarnation. Human knowledge in his human mind according to human limitations is the incarnate equivalent of the infinite divine knowledge of the divine mind.

A second, bolder answer could be given to the argument that the unity of person demands that the divine knowledge overflowed into Jesus' human mind: a flat denial. Was it necessary for the human mind to receive any echoes from the divine mind at all? The Chalcedonian formula, it is true, speaks of a single Person, but the word 'person' was not chosen for its modern psychological connotations, which include a certain continuity of consciousness. By person (or hypostasis) Chalcedon meant a single ontological subject or existent being, such that all the properties, actions and achievement in each nature belonged to the same individual. [67] Now does unity of person in this sense necessarily imply the overspill of the divine consciousness into the human? Bernard Lonergan's answer is 'No', and he argues that his answer, so far from contradicting the Chalcedonian formula, is actually supported by it; he finds further support in the later definitions concerning the two wills and two operations in Christ.

[67] Cf. A. Grillmeier, *Christ in Christian Tradition,* pp. 410-412.

A parallelism is to be recognized between ontological and psychological statements about the incarnate Word. The main parallel statements are that, as there is one person with a divine and a human nature, so there is one subject with a divine and a human consciousness. As the person, so also the subject is without division or separation. As the two natures, so also the divine and the human consciousness are without confusion or interchange. . . As the two natures do not prove two persons, so the divine and the human consciousness do not prove two subjects. [68]

In other words, in his divine consciousness Christ is conscious of himself as God; but this consciousness does not spill over into his human consciousness, which is consciousness of himself as man, though the self is the same in both cases.

But let us take the less radical course, and assume that the divine self-consciousness was expressed in Jesus' mind, though only in a human way. This cannot have taken the form of explicit, verbalized knowledge of his divinity. For, first of all, it is difficult to conceive how and when this knowledge came into the mind of the growing Jesus. If it was there from the beginning, how could it be intelligible to a new-born baby? If it was not there from the beginning, why is it necessary to postulate it at all? Secondly, there was no terminology available to a first-century Jew which was capable of expressing to Jesus' mind the fact that he, a man, distinct from God his Father, was himself God.

There is however another possibility. Underlying every one of our experiences there is a non-verbal, non-conceptual self-awareness. Every experience I know as *my* experience: I think, I see, I taste, and therefore indirectly I know myself. On the other hand, if I turn my mental gaze in on myself, and watch myself thinking and seeing and tasting, I am moving from indirect to direct knowledge of myself, a knowledge which may take the form of verbal statements to myself about myself. Now

[68] B. Lonergan, *Collection* (Darton, Longman & Todd, London, 1967), p. 196.

Jesus, like any other human being, was continually indirectly aware of himself, but the self of which he was aware was the self of the second person of the Trinity. The overspill of the divine self-knowledge was certainly at least of this indirect kind. But should we also postulate a direct, verbalized or conceptualized overspill?

The Gospels do not provide a clear answer either way: the divergence between the Johannine and the synoptic views, which we noted earlier, is evident again here. The many references in the Fourth Gospel to Christ's life with the Father before the Incarnation suggest an explicit verbal knowledge of his divinity; but the synoptic portrait seems to suggest that Jesus grew in self-awareness. It is difficult to reconcile the temptations in the desert, the uncertainty and fear in the Garden, and the cry of dereliction on the cross with a direct, articulated knowledge of his divinity. Once again it seems justifiable to argue that if one of these two conceptions of Jesus' self-knowledge has allowed theological considerations to colour the presentation of historical facts, it is more likely to have been the conception contained in the Fourth Gospel.

The most reasonable conclusion therefore seems to be that Jesus' self-awareness in his divine mind affected his human consciousness only in the form of indirect, non-conceptual and unreflective awareness of his divine self. The conclusion is in fact very similar to Lonergan's theory of the two separate consciousnesses of the single self, without confusion or interchange. [69] Jesus' growth in self-awareness would then consist in the developing insight with which he reflected on this self-awareness, and so turned it into direct, verbalized self-knowledge. He had to find from his human experience forms of words to match this non-verbal self-consciousness. He would be helped by his reading of the scriptures, and by the knowledge he could gain from other people, especially his mother and St Joseph, who could teach the unique circumstances that surrounded his

---

[69] See p. 101. On the overspill of the divine self-knowledge into the human, see the article of K. Rahner referred to in note 54.

birth. It was necessary that Mary should keep 'all these things, pondering them in her heart', [70] for the recollections and reflections which she could pass on to her Son would help him to grow in understanding of his person and his mission.

Nowadays we are all aware that the Gospels are not intended to be detailed biographies of Jesus or to provide material for a study of his psychological development. Yet, if the theory I have put forward is correct, there must have been such a psychological development, and such incidents as the Gospels contain must have marked stages in this development. It seems certain that his self-awareness was linked with a sense of intimate connection with his heavenly Father. At some stage Mary and Joseph told him the facts of his birth. This information, communicated perhaps when at twelve he came of age, can hardly have failed to cause an upheaval in his self-understanding, and perhaps led him to stay behind in Jerusalem in his Father's house. The synoptic Gospels show the baptism as another moment of illumination: Mark and Matthew state that it was Jesus himself who saw the Spirit descending, and in Mark and Luke the words from heaven, 'Thou art my beloved Son', are addressed to him and not to the bystanders. [71] All three evangelists show him at once driven by the Spirit into the desert, where he is tempted; in Matthew and Luke this temptation takes the form of the attempt to discover his Father's will through the painful sifting of the Old Testament. He realizes by now that he is the subject of the scriptures in a unique way: the problem is to apply them correctly. Is he to be a miracle-working religious leader? A military conqueror? A prophet? The suffering servant of Isaiah? The humble king of Zechariah? Is he to call himself Messiah? The questions recur at various points in his life: for example, when he is faced with the need to work his first miracle; [72] perhaps at Caesarea Philippi, when he first prophesies his death and Peter

[70] Lk 2.19; cf. 2.51.
[71] Mt 3.16-17; Mk 1.10-11; Lk 3.22.
[72] At Cana, according to Jn 2.11.

plays the part of Satan; [73] above all at Gethsemane. The explanation he gives after the resurrection, that 'everything written about me in the law of Moses and the prophets and the psalms must be fulfilled' (Lk 24.44), is perhaps a clue to the process by which he himself learned his Father's will, to do which was his food, [74] so that only when on the cross he has received the drink and fulfilled the last prophecy can he say, 'It is finished'. [75]

Further light is thrown on his self-awareness by the unparalleled authority which is revealed in his actions and his teaching. For example, to forgive sins with such authority shows that he was aware of a unique relationship with his Father. On the subject of Jesus' teaching, I can do no better than to quote my colleague John Ashton:

> Most Christians would be surprised to learn just how much of Jesus' ethical teaching can be paralleled from contemporary rabbinical sources; but however small the amount of original teaching it is quite decisive: it was Jesus, not Paul, who rendered inevitable the rupture between christianity and judaism that followed years later. He was the only teacher of his time to reject the established belief that the law and the prophets included all God required of men and to insist instead that God's demands were absolute and irreconcilable with any written formula, however comprehensive. Such a break from established tradition, revolutionary in effect if not in intent, argues an immense confidence in his own position. No doubt it was this assurance of the divine origin of his message, an assurance unaccompanied by any self-centred call for deference to his own person, that gave his teaching that indefinable stamp of God-given authority which made it seem so unlike that of the scribes and pharisees and which, paradoxically enough, offered the kind of surface to which the glorious titles attested by the tradition would naturally adhere. Even John's sophisticated

[73] Mk 8.31-33.
[74] Jn 4.34.
[75] Jn 19.30.

and apparently alien theology of the word (anticipated anyway in some degree by Mark) finds a firm historical foothold in the tradition of a man who challenged the authority of the Torah, the Word of God *par excellence,* by declaring it insufficient: the young man whom Jesus loved, loyal to the law in its every detail, is still short of perfection: 'Come, follow me'. [76]

But despite the degree of self-knowledge his words and his actions imply, there could still come Gethsemane and the cry of desolation on the cross; it was not until the resurrection that the process of illumination was complete.

However, the objection might be made that Jesus' miracles imply that he possessed an explicit knowledge of his divinity, especially as he appeals to them as signs. 'Even though you do not believe me, believe the works, that you may know and understand that the Father is in me and I am in the Father' (Jn 10.38). In reply I would make four points. (1) Jesus' awareness of power to work miracles was not necessarily knowledge of divine power; it could be knowledge that God had chosen to work through him. Even though in the Fourth Gospel he claims to have power to lay down his life and take it up again, he goes on to say that he is not his own master in this: 'this charge I have received from my Father'. [77] In the same Gospel Jesus raises Lazarus not apparently by his own power, but by praying to the Father to raise him: 'Father, I thank thee that thou hast heard me. I knew that thou hearest me always' (Jn 11.41-2). (2) Even though Jesus regarded the miracles as *signs,* it does not follow that they were signs of his own divinity; he may have regarded them as signs of the *mission* given him by the Father. (3) Luke and John seem to have regarded the first miracle as an important stage in Jesus' developing self-awareness. Luke makes the turning-point Jesus'

[76] J. Ashton, 'Theological Trends: The Consciousness of Christ III', in *The Way,* 10 (1970) pp. 253-4. All three of the author's articles on the subject in this volume repay study (pp. 59-71; 147-157; 250-259).
[77] Jn 10.18.

sermon at Nazareth on the text: 'The Spirit of the Lord is
upon me, because he has anointed me to preach good news to
the poor. He has sent me to proclaim release to the captives
and recovering of sight to the blind. . .' (Lk 4.18-19, quoting
Is 61.1-2). Before that sermon he has toured Galilee preaching
and has gained a reputation; but it is only after this sermon
that Luke narrates the first miracle at Capernaum. [78] Similarly
in the Fourth Gospel Jesus' abrupt reaction to his mother's
suggestion at Cana indicates that the decision to perform the
first sign was not easy. [79] (4) So far are the Gospels from
regarding the miracles as conscious exercises of divine power that
from time to time they let us see him in moments of weakness:
for example, sitting travel-weary by Jacob's well, while the
apostles have the energy to go shopping; [80] lying asleep in the
boat while the apostles labour at the oars; [81] on one occasion
unable to do any 'mighty work . . . except that he laid his hands
upon a few sick people and healed them' (Mk 6.5); on another
occasion having no intention to work a miracle, but 'perceiving
in himself that power had gone forth from him' (Mk 5.30).

In this chapter I have been trying to make two points:
first, that the grace of the man Jesus is not only the cause and
the model but the source of the grace of his followers. Secondly,
Jesus' experience of grace must therefore have been comparable
with ours. As we are indirectly aware of grace as a transcendental
in our actions, so was he. Nevertheless, since he *is* the Son of
God by nature and not only by grace as we are, there was
perhaps a unique element in his experience which contributed
to his knowledge of a unique relationship to the Father and
of a unique mission. This knowledge, however, was not of such
a kind as to render his normal human psychology irrelevant.

[78] Lk 4.14-15, 31-35.
[79] Jn 2.4.
[80] Jn 4.6,8.
[81] Mk 4.38.

CHAPTER 5

SAVED BY GRACE

I wish to consider in this chapter the saving power of grace, the ways in which we experience it, and the need for it. The supply of material available for the study of the experience is rich and varied. Let us consider some examples:

John Pentland Mahaffy, Provost of Trinity College, Dublin, when asked by an evangelist whether he was saved, replied in his customary lisp: 'Yes, but it was such a vewwy nawwow squeak that I never boast about it.' [1]

'In my most clear-sighted moments not only do I not think myself a nice man, but I know that I am a very nasty one. I can look at some of the things I have done with horror and loathing.' These are the words of a most conscientious Christian, C.S. Lewis. [2]

John Wesley: 'In London alone I found 652 members of our Society who were exceeding clear in their experience, and whose testimony I could see no reason to doubt. And every one of these (without a single exception) has declared that his deli-

---

[1] W.B. Stanford and R.B. McDowell, *Mahaffy: A Biography of an Irishman* (Routledge & Kegan Paul, London, 1971), p. 128.
[2] C.S. Lewis, *Mere Christianity* (Fontana, Collins, London, 1955), p. 102.

verance from sin was instantaneous; that the change was wrought in a moment... I cannot but believe that sanctification is commonly, if not always, an instantaneous work.' [3]

Professor E.D. Starbuck quoting an American woman's testimony:

> I know not how I got back into the encampment, but found myself staggering up to Rev. ......'s Holiness tent — and it was full of seekers and a terrible noise inside, some groaning, some laughing, and some shouting, and by a large oak, ten feet from the tent, I fell on my face by a bench, and tried to pray, and every time I would call on God, something like a man's hand would strangle me by choking... I thought I should surely die if I did not get help, but just as often as I would pray, that unseen hand was felt on my throat and my breath squeezed off. Finally something said: 'Venture on the atonement, for you will die anyway if you don't.' So I made one final struggle to call on God for mercy..., if I did strangle and die, and the last I remember that time was falling back on the ground with the same unseen hand on my throat... When I came to myself, there were a crowd around me praising God. The very heavens seemed to open and pour down rays of light and glory. [4]

The Council of Trent, against the Lutheran doctrine of justification by faith:

> On the one hand no good Christian should have any doubts about God's mercy, Christ's merit or the power and efficacy of the sacraments: but on the other hand any man, when he considers himself and his own weakness and incapacity, can feel anxiety and fear about his grace, for no one can know with the infallible certainty of faith that he has received the grace of God. [5]

---

[3] Quoted in W. James, *The Varieties of Religious Experience* (Longmans Green, London, 1st ed. 1902), p. 227.

[4] Quoted in the same work, p. 250.

[5] Decree on Justification, c. 9 (DS 1534; cf. 1563).

Theories of the Atonement

Since Gustaf Aulén's work on the Christian idea of the atonement was published in Swedish in 1930 and in English (under the title *Christus Victor*) in 1931,[6] many theologians have felt obliged to write on the redemption according to the categories which he impressed upon the material with such a firm hand. It will be recalled that Aulén distinguished three types of atonement-theory: the classic, the Latin and the subjective types. The classic type — he calls it classic, because it recurs so persistently in both East and West — represents the atonement as a victory which God, through Christ, has won over the power of sin, often described in personal terms as the devil. The great exponent of this view, Aulén held, was St Irenaeus. The Latin model, put forward above all by St Anselm, explains redemption as the satisfaction which, by the merciful dispensation of God, the God-man Jesus is able to offer to his Father on behalf of sinners. The subjective view, of which Peter Abelard was a pioneering exponent, thought of the atonement above all in terms of the power of Christ's teaching and example to turn men away from sin.

Aulén's book was especially influential in three ways. First, he argued that the classic view was the most common one throughout the whole of Christian history, and showed that, despite the mythological form in which the Fathers clothed it, it provides a serious and illuminating account of the atonement. Secondly, he showed, against Harnack, that the Latin theory did not teach 'the propitiation of an angry God by a sacrificial death',[7] for it was God himself who initiated his Son's sacrifice'. Thirdly, he was a persuasive champion of the classical view at a time when it was commonly assumed, in Protestant circles at least, that there was a straight choice between the other two theories.

---

[6] (SPCK, London). References are given here according to the edition of 1965.

[7] A. Harnack, *History of Dogma*, vol. iii, p. 313.

Nevertheless Aulén is open to the charge of over-simplification. It is only with some degree of violence that the teaching of a biblical or later author can be confined within a single category. Moreover, Aulén's three categories are not enough. I suggest that there are four main models: the models of a transaction, of teaching, of conflict and of solidarity. However, these are not rival theories; although I consider one of them to be basic, the truth about the redemption will not be reached except by a combination of them all.

Atonement as a Transaction

The model of a transaction represents atonement in terms of a law-suit or negotiation. Support for this view seems to lie readily at hand in those passages in the New Testament which say that we were ransomed or bought, and that the price was Christ's death or his blood. [8] Several of the Fathers, beginning with Irenaeus, assumed that the price was paid to the devil; in a more subtle form of the theory, Jesus was the bait which the devil has to be tricked into swallowing and so forfeiting his powers over the human race. [9] These theories are all open to the objection that they presuppose the dualistic view that God and Satan are two comparable opposing powers who have to respect one another's rights. St Augustine was aware of this difficulty, and pointed out that man had put himself in the devil's power, so that it befits God's justice to respect the rights we have given the devil until he abuses them. [10] But this is no solution; there can be no obligation on God to respect male-volent power achieved by trickery.

Some historians of doctrine attempt to uncover the truth

[8] For example, Mk 10.45; 1 Cor 6.20; 7.23; Eph 1.7; 1 Pet 1.18; Heb 9.12.

[9] Christ's blood paid to the devil: Irenaeus, *Adv. Haer.*, V.i.1-2 (Harvey ii.315); Christ the fish-hook to catch the devil: Gregory of Nyssa, *Or. Cat.*, 24, 26; Christ the mouse-trap: Augustine, Serm. 263.1. Cf. J.N.D. Kelly, *Early Christian Doctrines* (A. & C. Black, London, 4th ed. 1968), ch. 7 and 14.

[10] Augustine, *de Trin.*, xiii.12-14 (CC 50A.402-7; PL 42.1026-8).

which is expressed in the mythological form of a transaction between Christ and the devil. For J.N.D. Kelly 'the essential truth' was 'the wholly Scriptural one (cf. Acts 26.18) that fallen man lies in the Devil's power and salvation necessarily includes rescue from it.' [11] I would myself rather say that God respects, not the devil, but our power to determine our own destiny; salvation consists in our rescue from the consequences of our own misuse of our free will and from the consequences of other people's similar misuse.

Some of the Fathers and later theologians, recognizing the difficulties involved in the theory of a transaction with the devil, consider that we are redeemed by a transaction between Christ and the Father. This transaction is often described as a sacrifice. The question then arises: in what way was the sacrifice that Christ offered on our behalf pleasing to his heavenly Father? Most theologians who put forward this theory took it for granted, in St Anselm's words, that 'there is no need to explain what a great gift the Son gave freely'. [12] However, that original but shadowy figure, the Ambrosiaster, had seen the need to explain the value of Christ's sacrifice, and indicated that it was the love and obedience involved in it that gave Christ's sacrifice its sweet savour to the Father. It was clearly unthinkable to him that the Father could take pleasure in his Son's pain. [13] After the reformation, however, the theory grew up that the transaction was one of vicarious punishment rather than vicarious satisfaction: Christ was restoring God's injured justice not so much by a pleasing offering as by bearing the punishment on our behalf. This doctrine was more common in Protestant circles, but it can hardly have been put forward in a more sick form than by the great Catholic preacher Bossuet:

[11] *Op. cit.*, p. 376.

[12] *Cur Deus Homo?*, II.xix; cf. xiv. Anselm in fact gives two subtly different versions of the transaction theory: (1) in terms of vicarious satisfaction; Christ paid what is owing for the sins of the world (II.xiv); (2) in terms of the recompense for his sacrifice, which he shared with mankind (II.xix). Aquinas also adopts this second line of reasoning (ST III.48.1).

[13] Ambrosiaster, on Eph 5.2 (CSEL 81.iii, p. 110).

The sweetest consolation of a man who is suffering is the thought of his innocence... Jesus, the innocent Jesus, did not enjoy this relief in his passion... God arms against him his avenging hand, and breaks a criminal soul under the intolerable weight of his vengeance... It had to be, my brethren, that he should proceed himself against his Son with all his lightnings; and since he had laid upon him our sins, he had to lay upon him also his just vengeance. That he did, Christians, we can be sure of that... God fixed on his Son that blazing eye; he looked at him, not with the gaze which brings peace, but with that terrible gaze which kindles fire where it falls... He rejected his Son, and opened his arms to us. [14]

This theory of vicarious punishment represents God the Father as if he fell short of elementary human standards of justice and love, and it must consequently be discarded. But underlying both this model and the model of vicarious satisfaction is an important truth which St Anselm saw with great clarity: sin does harm which needs to be repaired. As the theory has generally been put forward, the emphasis has been on the affront which sin inflicts upon God, and which God cannot forgive until the wrong is righted. This is however a conception which does not appeal readily to the modern mind: it seems it would be unworthy of God to insist on satisfaction. But it may be that if one had a fuller understanding of the holiness of God and the evil of sin, the need to make satisfaction to God would become evident. Failing that, we may prefer to think of the obligation to repair, not the wrong done to God, so much as the wrong done to the sinner himself and to his fellow men. There is certainly a connection between them: by repairing the damage done to men we do make satisfaction to God. This takes some account of St Anselm's insight that it is incompatible with God's justice (and, we may add, his holiness) to leave sin unatoned for, and that we are incapable of atoning, even granted a change of heart. Sin leaves something owing to God.

[14] Bossuet, *Oeuvres Oratoires,* ed. Lebarq, tome III (Hachette, Paris, 1916), pp. 367, 368, 369, 385, 387, 389.

However, the shortcoming of all these transaction theories is that they adopt an emphasis which is scarcely present in the New Testament. Despite the frequent occurrence of the language of ransom, it is never said that the ransom is paid to God the Father; on the contrary, he is regarded as the giver rather than the receiver, the reconciler rather than the reconciled. 'God so loved the world that he gave his only Son.' [15] 'He . . . did not spare his own Son but gave him up for us all' (Rom 8.32). 'God was in Christ reconciling the world to himself' (2 Cor 5.19). Of course, there are passages in which God is regarded as the receiver of an offering from the Son: 'Christ loved us and gave himself up for us, a fragrant offering and sacrifice to God' (Eph 5.2). But God already has mercy on man, and that is why the Word can become flesh and make the fragrant offering of himself to God.

It is in fact quite likely that the reason why the 'ransom' passages do not state to whom the ransom is paid, is that they are not about ransom at all. A plausible case can be made out for saying that in general they refer to the 'liberation' of those who are captives to sin and the 'acquisition' by God of a people; the idea of a price paid to another is not necessarily part of their meaning. [16]

Aulén finds fault with all attempts to explain the atonement in terms of satisfaction paid by Christ to God, on the grounds that 'the continuity of Divine operation is lost'; for although the initiative in bringing about the Incarnation is taken by God, 'the satisfaction is offered by Christ as man, as the sinless Man on behalf of the sinners'. [17] It appears, however, that a Protestant fear of anything that sounds remotely like salvation by man's works (even Christ's works!) has prevented Aulén from grasping the full implications of the Incarnation. According to the

---

[15] As Abraham gave up Isaac (Jn 3.16).
[16] Cf. S. Lyonnet and L. Sebourin, *Sin, Redemption and Sacrifice,* (Analecta Biblica 48, Biblical Institute Press, Rome, 1970), part ii, especially pp. 118-119.
[17] Aulén, *op. cit.,* p. 146.

view proposed in the last chapter, it is the *man* Jesus who is the mediator between God and man; but at the same time his mediatorial work is wholly God's. There is no discontinuity; the redeeming act is God's from first to last: 'God was in Christ reconciling'. But it must also be man's work; humanity as a whole must be redeemed by the second Adam in his own person before individuals can be redeemed.

This brings us to the hidden problem which lies at the heart of the transaction theory: how does Christ's offering make satisfaction for the sins of the rest of the human race? One possible answer is that God, out of love for his Son, freely chooses to regard his Son's offering as satisfaction for our sins. This was St Anselm's explanation; it entered into the nominalist tradition, [18] and from there made its way into the thinking of the Reformation. The shortcoming of this explanation is that it attributes to God a loving arbitrariness; *stat pro ratione voluntas*: God's love knows no reason. A less arbitrary explanation will be found shortly in the fourth model, the model of the solidarity of the human race in the person of Christ.

Atonement as a Conflict

A similar problem lies hidden beneath the second model we are considering, Aulén's classic model of a conflict between God and the forces of evil, [19] who are defeated at Christ's death, the very moment when they seem to have triumphed.

---

[18] The two key nominalistic doctrines in this regard are: (1) God's gratuitous acceptance (*acceptatio*) of Christ's merits on our behalf; and (2) the distinction between what God can do in theory (*potentia absoluta*) and what he has bound himself to do in the present order of things (*potentia ordinata*). On the debt that nominalist theology of the redemption owed to Scotus, cf. L. Richard, *The Mystery of the Redemption* (ET Helicon Press, Baltimore, 1965), pp. 198-200. On the soteriology of Gabriel Biel, the last great nominalist theologian, cf. H. Oberman, *The Harvest of Medieval Theology* (Harvard University Press, Cambridge, Mass., 1963), pp. 42-47.

[19] Cf. Col 2.15: 'He disarmed the principalities and powers and made a public example of them, triumphing over them in him.' Cf. Heb 2.14-15, quoted on p. 119.

This again is an incomplete model, because once the imagery of the tricking of the devil is eliminated, it offers no explanation of the way in which the forces of evil are defeated. If the victory was won through the power of Christ's teaching and example, we have come to depend on our third, the didactic model. If it was won through a sacrifice made to God, we are back with the transaction theory and its attendant problems. If it was through our solidarity with Christ, we are once more forced to rely on the fourth model. In other words, the defeat of evil is the result of Christ's saving work, rather than the process by which we are saved.

Atonement as Enlightenment

The third model I have called the didactic. It includes what are often called exemplarist or subjective theories, but has a wider range, for it not only takes in the example that Christ gave us by his life and self-sacrifice, and the guidance afforded by his teaching, but gains its full impact from the fact that the example and teaching are those of God who became man, suffered and rose again for us. In Reinhold Niebuhr's words: 'The Cross, which stands at the centre of the Christian world-view, reveals both the seriousness of human sin and the purpose and power of God to overcome it.' [20] Pelagius, though not consistent in his language, preferred the didactic model, and identified grace with the teaching and example of Christ; [21] Abelard plumped for the same model in preference to the transaction theory put forward by his elder contemporary Anselm; [22] and Schleiermacher won for it wide acceptance among continental Protestants. [23]

---

[20] Quoted in F.W. Dillistone, *The Christian Understanding of Atonement* (J. Nisbet, Welwyn, 1968), p. 111.

[21] Cf. R.F. Evans, *Pelagius: Inquiries and Reappraisals* (A. & C. Black, London, 1968), pp. 106-113.

[22] Abelard holds that we are redeemed by the 'manifestation' of God's grace through the cross, which binds us to him by love. (*Exp. in Rom.*, lib. ii, PL 178.836A).

[23] Cf. Aulén, *op. cit.*, pp. 135-138.

I

The theory can claim considerable support in the New Testament. In the prologue to the Fourth Gospel great emphasis is laid on the fact that the Son is the Word of God who makes the Father known; he is the true light that enlightens every man. [24] In the Pastoral Epistles we are reminded that we were saved 'when the goodness and loving kindness of God our Saviour appeared' (Tit 3.4). So too in later Greek thought the Incarnation is an epiphany, a revelation of God, and baptism is illumination.

Another form of the didactic theory envisages the redemption in terms of explanation. 'Thanks to the Incarnation, nature and man make sense, and the world has unity and meaning.' In this conception, explanation tends to replace atonement. Dr A.M. Ramsey confesses that this tendency to reduce atonement to the provision of an explanation of life has been a sad consequence of the interest shown by Anglican theologians in the Incarnation. [25]

No form of the didactic theory can provide a complete account of the redemption. In the New Testament there are other aspects of the doctrine which cannot be reduced to example or teaching. If atonement and redemption are identified with instruction and motivation, 'the idea of sin', as Aulén pointed out, 'has become altogether weakened'. [26] As we have already seen, it is the merit of the transaction model that it shows that because of sin, something is owing to God which is appropriately described as satisfaction. Besides, if it is maintained that Christ died simply to teach a lesson, that lesson is in consequence robbed of much of its power to instruct and move. And finally, if redemption is identical with the enlightenment brought by Christ, those millions of people who know nothing of Christ would be totally unredeemed.

[24] Cf. Jn 1.1,18,9.
[25] Ramsey, *op. cit.*, p. 27.
[26] Aulén, *op. cit.*, p. 148.

Atonement through Solidarity

The fourth model, which I have called the model of
solidarity, sometimes goes by the name of the physical or
mystical theory. It expresses the unity of the human race in
Christ, because of which all mankind is caught up in Christ's
passage from suffering and death to the resurrection, so that
what happened to Jesus happens to all men. It links up also
with two points which I was considering in the last chapter:
first, that man's grace is organically connected with the grace
of Jesus and is derived from it; secondly, that it is through
the Church's worship, especially baptism and the Eucharist,
that the Christian becomes associated with the death and
resurrection of Jesus.

The theory of redemption through solidarity with Christ
appears in the New Testament in many forms. It underlies the
Pauline *leitmotiv* expressed by the phrase 'in Christ'. It underlies also the doctrine of the last Adam: the obedience of Christ
repairs the universal ruin caused by the first Adam's disobedience, [27] and repairs it not so much because a transaction
is made with God, as because Christ is 'the first fruits of those
who have fallen asleep' and who are 'made alive' in him. [28]
In Hebrews Jesus' endurance is held out as an example and an
encouragement to Christians, but it is much more than this:
he is the path-finder who obtained remission for the sins of all
by himself leading the way into the presence of his Father,
and who opened 'a new and living way ... through the curtain,
that is, through his flesh'. [29] In Ephesians men are saved from
their evil desires and cease to be 'children of wrath' and to be
dead through their trespasses, because God has 'made us alive
together with Christ ... and raised us up with him' (Eph 2.3-6).

Many of the Fathers are even more explicit about man's
redemption through unity with Christ. This is the meaning of

[27] Cf. Rom 5.12-21.
[28] Cf. 1 Cor 15.20-22.
[29] Heb 10.20; cf. 2.10; 6.20.

St Irenaeus' doctrine of the recapitulation. All mankind was
involved in the sin of Adam; but Christ sums up all humanity
in his own person, re-enacts human history on the right lines
by his life of obedience and his death, and so repairs the
effects of Adam's sin for the whole race.[30] St Athanasius,
besides explaining the redemption in terms of sacrifice and
teaching, also uses the model of solidarity: since all were held
to die with Christ, the sentence against man was deemed to
be executed; moreover Christ abolished death for all mankind
by uniting human nature with the godhead, and also by involving the whole race in his resurrection. His flesh was the first
to be 'saved and liberated'.[31]

Some of the Fathers attempt to explain *how* the glorification
of Christ's own humanity affects other men; this is, as was
said earlier, the fundamental question. For St Irenaeus it is
because Christ is the Word that he can be the representative
man.[32] Sometimes a Platonic doctrine of universals seems to
underlie their thinking; once human nature, in the person of
Christ, has been repaired and divinised, all individuals who
share that nature are affected. St Paul's teaching that all mankind is united in Christ is also influential, which in turn owes
much to the rabbinical speculations concerning the unity of
mankind in Adam.[33]

In the first chapter we considered how the Fathers take
the divinisation of man as an agreed axiom from which they
can draw polemical conclusions.[34] The same is true of the

[30] Cf. Kelly, *op. cit.*, pp. 172-173, with references.
[31] *Or. adv. Arian.*, ii.61; cf. iii.33-34 (PG 26.277, 393-397). Cf. Kelly,
op. cit., pp. 377-380.
[32] 'For the maker of the universe is truly the Word of God..., because
he is the Word of God governing and disposing all things; and
for this reason he came invisibly to his own and was made flesh,
and hung upon the cross, to sum up all things in himself.' (*Adv.
Haer.*, v.18.3; Harvey ii.374-5).
[33] Cf. W.D. Davies, *Paul and Rabbinic Judaism* (SPCK, London,
2nd ed., 1955), ch. 3.
[34] pp. 22-24.

doctrine of human solidarity and the redemption of all human nature in the person of Jesus. To refute the view of Apollinarius that all sinful human flesh is healed because the human flesh is united, not with a human soul, but with the divine Word, St Gregory of Nazianzus argued that *because human nature is healed in the person of Jesus,* his humanity must have been complete, body and soul: 'what was not assumed was not healed.'[35] Theodore of Mopsuestia and Nestorius made use of the same line of reasoning in support of the distinctive formula of Antiochene Christology, that Christ was constituted by a union of the divine Word with a man: there must be full manhood in Christ *in order that humanity may be saved in him.*[26] Nestorius in fact explained the working of human solidarity in two ways: first, Christ, in his own human nature, restored the original image of human nature; secondly, in transactional terms, 'Christ assumed the person of the nature which owed the debt'.[37]

The theory of solidarity is accordingly not only a theory of atonement in its own right, but it can be used to explain the transaction theory. It also underlies the theory of the defeat of sin and death, because it is the solidarity of the race in Christ that makes his victory the victory of all. Thus, the Epistle to the Hebrews, which I have quoted as an exposition of the solidarity model, uses the model also to shed light on the model of conflict and victory: 'Since therefore the children share in flesh and blood, he himself likewise partook of the same nature, that through death he might destroy him who has the power of death, that is the devil, and deliver all those who through fear of death were subject to lifelong bondage' (Heb 2.14-15). There are, therefore, good reasons for concluding that it is the solidarity model which deserves the name 'classical' and which is truly fundamental, rather than the sacrificial form of the

---

[35] Ep. 101 (*Contra Apoll.,* 1) (PG 37.181C).
[36] Cf. R.A. Norris, *Manhood and Christ* (Clarendon Press, Oxford, 1963), pp. 191-7. Norris calls this the 'homo victor' theme (p. 194).
[37] *Lib. Her.* (Nau), p. 78; Serm. 1 (Loofs), p. 255. To this extent, at least, Nestorius' Christology was orthodox.

transactional model, [38] or the conflict theory, which is championed by Aulén. Although it is not possible to state with any confidence *why* Christ's achievements can be shared with the rest of the human race, and though the theory does not readily accord with twentieth-century individualism, it seems to me to be the indispensable basis of the doctrine of the redemption.

But, of course, all four models are needed for a balanced understanding of the redemption. The transactional model brings out the truths that sin needs to be atoned for, and that man would have been incapable of making that atonement unless Christ had made it on man's behalf. The model of conflict emphasises the truth that sin constitutes an evil force in the individual and in society which needs to be overcome. The didactic model highlights the fact that the teaching and example of Christ and his revelation of God's love have the power to correct the self-indulgent and aggressive tendencies in man. The model of solidarity stresses every man's need for new life derived from Christ himself, if he is to recover from the deadly effects of his own sin and the sins of the race.

Not only are all four models needed for a full understanding of the doctrine, but they are logically interconnected. If man is reconciled to God (transaction), the power of sin is broken (conquest). When the power of sin is broken (conquest), the risen life of Christ becomes ours (solidarity); and the logical order here can be reversed. Because we are one in Christ (solidarity), his sacrifice avails on our behalf (transaction). Christ's sacrifice (transaction) reveals the love and mercy of God (didactic).

There has, however, been a stream of theological thought which tried to separate some of these aspects of redemption.

[38] 'Running through almost all the patristic attempts to explain the redemption there is one grand theme which, we suggest, provides the clue to the fathers' understanding of the work of Christ. This is none other than the ancient idea of recapitulation which Irenaeus derived from St Paul, and which envisages Christ as the representative of the entire race.' (Kelly, *op. cit.*, pp. 376-377).

Scotus, for example, with his passion for distinctions, considered it a theoretical possibility (though not a real possibility in the present order of providence) that a man might be in a state of grace while in mortal sin, or free from sin but not in a state of grace. [39] In other words he thought it possible that a man could be one with Christ, without the conquest of evil or satisfaction being made for his sins. The same tradition is represented in a more extreme form by Ockham [40] and the nominalistis; and the same tendency was followed by those Lutherans who insisted that justification, being external, did not necessarily bring with it internal holiness. This was the theory that Bonhoeffer was to attack under the name of 'cheap grace': 'the justification of sin without the justification of the sinner.' [41] In Chapter Three we considered how Luther himself, and Calvin also, insisted that justification is accompanied by 'regeneration' or 'sanctification'. [42]

The Experience of Redemption

It is a characteristic of the present age that many people have lost the sense of sin, and consequently no longer feel the need of redemption. It is strange, incomprehensible even, that in an age when totalitarian regimes have revealed the potentialities of evil in a starker light than the world has ever seen before, when governments have at their disposal instruments of oppression and destruction which are unparallelled in their efficiency, when the hard selfishness of the rat-race marks so much of our industrial and commercial life, leaving us insensitive to family and neighbourly obligations, at such a time a great number of people have ceased to believe in the fact of sin.

These pages are not the place for an attempt to analyse the causes of this moral blind-spot. Nor must one exaggerate

[39] See note 18, on Scotus' theology of the redemption.
[40] On the Ockhamist theory of justification, see P. Vignaux, 'Nominalisme', DTC xi.769-776.
[41] *The Cost of Discipleship* (ET SCM, London, 1964), p. 35.
[42] p. 51.

its extent: evangelism is still successful, and people still come to confession, though perhaps less frequently than before. My concern is simply to indicate some of the ways in which we experience the grace of redemption. The Lamb of God takes away the sin of the world; if we say we have not sinned we make him a liar. How do these truths impinge upon our consciousness?

The reader will remember that grace is being considered at three levels: actual grace, extraordinary grace and habitual grace. Let us try to discover how the experience of redemption is verified on each of these levels.

A. *Actual Grace*

Dr F.W. Dillistone in his sensitive and comprehensive work *The Christian Understanding of Atonement* takes the essence of atonement to be reconciliation, the healing of man's alienation. He examines eight ways in which man is alienated from his surroundings and within his own personality, and shows how the saving work of Christ repairs these external and internal divisions.

First, for all man's mastery over nature, nature is not always his obedient servant; we are never wholly free from the threat of disease and natural disaster. Christ redeems us by sharing our condition and shouldering our burdens; and by finding them not an obstacle but a means to growth, he enables us to do the same.

Secondly, we live amid not only physical evil but moral evil, which infects us, so that we in turn add to the general infection. Christ redeemed us by sharing our insertion into the evil world but resisting the infection, and so enabling us to overcome it too.

Thirdly, we are often at odds with our fellow men; we quarrel, we torment, and sometimes ruin one another. Christ heals us by enduring the enmity of society, like a tragic hero who by his own death brings healing to his people.

Fourthly, though man's social nature demands a system of moral and civil law, we each fail to fulfil our obligations, and so need some way of absolving our guilt. Christ 'in some mysterious way . . . has borne the stripes and the chastisement which should, by strict desert, have fallen upon' us. [43]

Fifthly, by our self-assertion we poison human relationships. Christ's perfect love of his Father heals our relations with the Father and with one another.

Sixthly, we each suffer wrongs for which we need to forgive others without condoning the fault, and ourselves need to be forgiven in the same way. Christ is the supreme model of forgiveness without moral compromise, and so mediates God's forgiveness to us.

Seventhly, few if any of us are fully integrated in our personalities. We can make St Paul's words our own: 'I do not do the good I want, but the evil I do not want is what I do' (Rom 7.19). We need a symbol, an ideal, round which to unify our lives. We find this symbol in the lifelong self-sacrifice of Christ, and especially in his passion and death.

Finally, from time to time men experience a greater or lesser degree of despair, when no past assurances seem capable of indicating a way forward. Sometimes this darkness can take the form of a crisis of faith. Christ rescued us from our despair when in his own darkness and fear he accepted the cup in Gethsemane.

We need to look more closely at what Dr Dillistone is doing in his book. He is not attempting to provide eight explanations of the *means by which* what Christ has done is communicated to us. Rather in each of his eight treatments of the theme, he begins at both ends, our end and Christ's, without being very concerned to bridge the gap in the middle. He indicates eight ways in which we need redemption, and eight corresponding ways in which Christ achieves wholeness in his own person,

[43] Dillistone, *op. cit.*, p. 214.

without always showing the connection between Christ's wholeness and our need. He considers himself to be providing eight
analogies — he calls them 'ranges of comparison' — to 'expand'
and 'make ... meaningful' the text, 'God was reconciling the
world to himself in Christ.' [44]

But in fact Dr Dillistone is doing more than provide analogies. He is not just listing eight experiences which are *like* the
experience of redemption; he is indicating eight of the ways in
which we actually experience redemption. To be reconciled in
these eight ways is to be redeemed, and to be redeemed by
Christ. All true reconciliation is the saving work of Christ; at
whatever level we experience it, in every apology genuinely
meant and sincerely accepted, in the forgiveness of others and
of ourselves without compromising our ideals, we are experiencing Christ's redeeming power.

These experiences of redemption are not distinguishable
from ordinary psychological experiences, because it is precisely
in our ordinary psychological experience that redemption affects
our daily lives. The grace of redemption is experienced as a
transcendental; it can be experienced only in the form it takes
in natural experience, as a piano can be heard only through
the music that is played on it. Nevertheless there are purer,
intenser moments of grace, when the experience of redemption
in the natural situation can be more clearly identified, even
though the experience can never be distinguished into two
elements, namely of natural psychology and of grace.

Karl Rahner tries to identify them in a short essay entitled
'Reflections on the Experience of Grace'. He begins by asking
a series of questions:

> Have we ever kept quiet, even though we wanted to defend
> ourselves when we had been unfairly treated? Have we
> ever forgiven someone even though we got no thanks for
> it and our silent forgiveness was taken for granted? ...
> Have we ever sacrificed something without receiving any

[44] *Ibid.*, p. 405, quoting 2 Cor 5.19.

thanks or recognition for it, and even without a feeling of inner satisfaction? ... Have we ever decided on some course of action purely by the innermost judgment of our conscience, deep down where one can no longer tell or explain it to anyone, where one is quite alone and knows that one is taking a decision which no one else can take in one's place and for which one will have to answer for all eternity? Have we ever tried to love God when we are no longer being borne on the crest of the wave of enthusiastic feeling, when it is no longer possible to mistake our self, and its vital urges, for God? ... Have we ever tried to love God when we seemed to be calling out into emptiness and our cry seemed to fall on deaf ears, when it looked as if we were taking a terrifying jump into the bottomless abyss, when everything seemed to become incomprehensible and apparently senseless? Have we ever fulfilled a duty when it seemed that it could be done only with a consuming sense of really betraying and obliterating oneself, when it could apparently be done only by doing something terribly stupid for which no one would thank us?

Rahner then comments:

... we know — when we let ourselves go in this experience of the spirit, when the tangible and assignable, the relishable element disappears, when everything takes on the taste of death and destruction, or when everything disappears as if in an inexpressible, as it were white, colourless and intangible beatitude — then in fact it is not merely the spirit but the Holy Spirit who is at work in us. [45]

Rahner does not however fail to keep his feet firmly on the ground: he reminds us that 'grace can also sanctify everyday and reasonable activities and can transform them into a step towards God'. [46]

Our experience therefore of the redemption as an actual grace is clothed in the experience of taking moral decisions. Most of

[45] *Theological Investigations,* iii, pp. 87-89,
[46] *Ibid.,* p. 88.

these decisions are inextricably interwoven with our characteristic human values; but occasionally our habitual values become so irrelevant to our choices that Rahner can speak of 'the taste of the pure wine of the spirit'. [47] But even in these choices which Rahner describes, grace is not experienced directly, but only as a transcendental underlying the experience of rising above our habitual values.

B. *Extraordinary Grace*

Apart from these experiences of actual grace, there seems also to be the possibility of the experience of extraordinary graces, miracles, so to speak, of the grace of redemption. By these extraordinary graces I mean something similar to Rahner's 'taste of the pure wine of the spirit', the difference being that with extraordinary graces the discontinuity between the new decision and the habitual values is so dramatic that it is easy to conclude that one is witnessing the action of grace. The most obvious example of an extraordinary experience of the grace of redemption is spectacularly sudden conversion, like the conversion of St Paul. I am not speaking here of spectacular psychological accompaniments to conversion, like the experience of the lady outside the holiness tent; for it seems that such experiences can accompany what is only the final eruption of a process that has been building up for some time. I am thinking rather of conversions for which there seems to have been very little psychological preparation. Nevertheless it seems that a conversion can never be totally discontinuous with a person's previous development, because it cannot come totally from outside. A miracle of grace is not like a miracle of healing or the miraculous change of water into wine: a conversion is the free response to the prompting of God's grace. A conversion represents a personal decision, and must therefore be an expression of the convert's personality, even though the expression is totally unpredictable, even though it needed a violent stimulus from outside to trigger it off, and even though the new decision marks a decisive

[47] *Ibid.*, p. 89.

development of personality. Even St Paul's conversion was not wholly, in Hopkins's phrase, 'at once . . . at a crash'; [48] for the goad had presumably been there for some time if he had been kicking against it.

C. *Habitual Grace*

The third way in which God gives men his grace is by effecting in them that abiding transformation which comes from the presence of his Spirit, and which is called habitual grace. By it a person is changed inwardly and endowed with a new vital principle, a new enduring relationship with God, from which there grow his particular graced actions, the particular experiences of actual, and even extraordinary grace. In the light of what has already been said about redemption through solidarity with the human Jesus, the last Adam, it appears that man's share in the redeeming triumph of Jesus' humanity is to be identified with this new life of grace, this share in the divine nature which is the source of each individual action performed under the influence of grace. That is to say, men receive redemption, not as something imputed to them externally, as when a person unqualified to sit for a university examination is 'deemed' to be qualified; nor as a help which God gives them moment by moment from outside their personalities, to reconcile them with himself, with themselves and with other people. Redemption is a permanent transformation in the human being by which he becomes 'dead to sin and alive to God in Christ Jesus' (Rom 6.11); by which God makes him a new creature, transferring him from the kingdom of darkness into Christ's kingdom of light. [49]

The relevance of the sacraments, and infant baptism in particular, to the grace of redemption I shall discuss in Chapter Seven. Those to whom God's grace first comes when they are of maturer age, can receive his redemption only freely and by faith. No one, however, could perform this first movement

[48] *The Wreck of the Deutschland.*
[49] Cf. Col 1.12-13.

towards God in faith so as to accept God's redeeming grace, i.e. habitual grace, unless he had already received the help of grace. This initial grace, without which one could not perform the first movement towards God in faith, does not proceed from a life already transformed by habitual grace; it is totally God's gift from outside, and is sometimes called prevenient (i.e. preparing) grace. But once one has responded by faith to God's call, one is redeemed, reborn, a new creature filled and transformed by that abiding presence of the Holy Spirit which is habitual grace. It is possible, however — and I incline to this view — that the distinction between prevenient and habitual grace, i.e. between grace before and after faith, is a logical distinction only, and not one of time: that is to say, the act of accepting prevenient grace is faith, and faith at once results in habitual grace and redemption.

The first acceptance of grace is always a conversion. It may be a conversion from personal sins. In every case, however, this first grace comes to one who is a member of a sinful race which is united in alienation from God; the fact that mankind is created to enjoy solidarity with Christ makes it possible for the human race to be at one in separation from God. Every human being is created and equipped to receive God's second gift, but comes into the world without it; this absence of grace is the most important aspect of original sin. [50] It is not personal guilt, but it is a deficiency, an emptiness, which God designed to be filled by himself. It is called sin because it has the same effect as sin, [51] namely separation from God, and because it is due to the personal sins of the race; without personal sin there would be no original sin, no congenital absence of God. When a man first receives the gift of the Spirit and so first enters a state of habitual grace, his alienation from God is brought to an end; the habitual state of grace is accordingly the state of redemption. The words of St Paul can be applied to original as well as to personal sin:

[50] For an explanation of this view of original sin, cf. E.J. Yarnold, *The Theology of Original Sin* (Mercier, Cork, 1971), Part II, ch. 4.
[51] Cf. Council of Trent, Decree on Original Sin (DS 1515).

... since all have sinned and fall short of the glory of God, they are justified by his grace as a gift, through the redemption which is in Christ Jesus (Rom 3.23-4).

By serious (mortal) sin man can re-erect the barrier between himself and God, driving the Holy Spirit out of his temple, and blotting out in his own being that reflection of God's glory which we call grace. He can be justified again by contrition and the sacraments, so that habitual grace is restored to him, once more as the grace of redemption, only this time it is redemption from his personal sins alone.

However, not all man's acts of meanness and selfishness have the disastrous and lethal power of destroying in himself the image of God. His many daily sins, traditionally called venial sins, weaken the habitual life of grace in him without killing it, blot the image of God in him without utterly obscuring it, strain his relationship of a son to his heavenly Father without completely rupturing it. When St Paul told the Thessalonians not to quench the Spirit,[52] he seems to have been referring to the gift of prophecy; but to quench the Spirit in a more general sense is in fact the effect of venial sins. Yet they do not quench him altogether: he remains within men as in his temple, transforming them, so that through his persisting action they retain the power to repent, and then he can cleanse their tarnished image of God. It is one aspect of habitual grace, therefore, that it is God's gift of the power to be converted from daily sins. Redemption from them does not come from outside, but from the Christian's abiding, most intimate union with the wounded Surgeon whose bleeding hands bring healing.

[52] 1 Thess 5.19.

CHAPTER 6

GRACE AND REVELATION

Ink and paper can never make us Christians, can never beget a new nature, a living principle in us; can never form Christ, or any true notions of spiritual things, in our hearts. The gospel, that new law which Christ delivered to the world, it is not merely a letter without us, but a quickening spirit within us. Cold theorems and maxims, dry and jejune disputes, lean syllogistical reasonings, could never yet of themselves beget the least glimpse of true heavenly light, the least sap of saving knowledge in any heart... The secret mysteries of a Divine Life, of a New Nature, of Christ formed in our hearts, they cannot be written or spoken, language and expressions cannot reach them; neither can they ever be truly understood, except the soul itself be kindled from within, and awakened into the life of them. [1]

In this sermon delivered before Cromwell's Parliament in 1647 Ralph Cudworth was concerned with the connection between knowledge of the truth and holiness of life. My subject in this chapter is very close to his: the connection between revelation and grace. That there is a connection is evident. Both are means by which God communicates himself to us;

---

[1] *A Sermon Preached before the Honourable the House of Commons on March 31st 1647* (Rivingtons, London, 1812), p. 5.

revelation as well as grace can be called a second gift. Both are concerned with the knowledge of God; for habitual grace is a power to relate with God in knowledge and love.

Are Grace and Revelation Identical?

So close is the connection between grace and revelation that a recent Roman Catholic theologian, J.P. Mackey, has identified them altogether.

Mackey points out that most theologians of his own Church take great pains to discuss the relationship between grace and nature, but make almost no attempt to say what grace is. In his search for the missing definition, he adopts what he claims to be a neo-Protestant position derived from Barth and Brunner; though, as we saw in the last chapter, the theory in fact includes Pelagius and Abelard in its ancestry. Grace, Mackey maintains,

> is God's self-revelation to man in words specially addressed to man and in action on the human scene... Grace, from man's side, is first and foremost the knowledge that man now has of God as a result of God's self-revelation to man in word and action . . . , the love that this knowledge inspires in man for God . . . , the hope that maintains itself on this knowledge and love. [2]

Now it is of course possible to adopt so wide a definition of revelation that it is made to embrace all that I have been including under the second gift. I would have no quarrel with such a treatment of the subject apart from its choice of terms. Mackey's exposition, however, seems to limit the sense of grace so as to make it mean nothing more than knowledge and the motivation that springs from knowledge. This theory seems to me inadequate for three reasons:

(1) The images used in the New Testament and the Fathers to describe grace suggest something far beyond the provision of knowledge and motivation. Organic metaphors are used: Christians live in Christ, like the branches of a vine or the

[2] J.P. Mackey, *Life and Grace* (Gill, Dublin, 1966), pp. 61, 50.

J

organs of a body; they die and rise with him by the Father's mighty power; they are born again, and become a new creation. St Paul's statement that Christians are adopted as sons through the Spirit combines the images of biology and family relationships. Since even this language is not strong enough, other images are used: men reflect God's glory, even share his nature; God is present in them as in a temple. The Fathers develop this idea in their theologies of the Logos, the image of God in man and divinisation. In other words this second gift of God is described, not as man's reaction to God's self-revelation, but as a direct transformation in man consisting in God's gift of himself.

(2) This leads to the second weakness of the theory under examination: it implies an attenuated view of faith. Faith is not simply man's acceptance of God's revelation; it is man's God-given power to accept the revelation. Both the revelation and the power to accept it are a second gift. It is true that 'the words that I have spoken to you are spirit and life' (Jn 6.63). But this does not mean that a man, by virtue of his natural, God-given intelligence, can understand Christ's words and derive spirit and life from them. To be able to understand them is itself a special gift, for Jesus continues in the same passage: 'But there are some of you that do not believe... This is why I told you that no one can come to me unless it is granted him by the Father' (Jn 6.64-5). God's word is life-giving only if God gives the grace of understanding. Ralph Cudworth's words with which I began this chapter apply here, even though he was speaking with a slightly different purpose: 'the soul itself' must be 'kindled from within and awakened into the life' of the Gospel, if the Gospel is not to remain 'a dead letter without us'.

(3) All Christian traditions which practise infant baptism agree that if a baptized baby dies he is saved. There seems in addition to be a growing consensus — and it has the support of the Second Vatican Council [3] — that good pagans are saved.

---

[3] *Lumen Gentium* (Decree on the Church), 16.

Karl Rahner, for example, speaks of them as anonymous Christians, [4] though perhaps 'implicit Christians' would be a better term. Such terminology, though admittedly in certain circumstances less than diplomatic, can readily be justified. A good Buddhist is an implicit Christian not only in the sense in which a good Christian is an implicit Buddhist, namely in so far as the two religions, despite differences of expression and practice, hold many truths in common; a good Buddhist is an implicit Christian because he was created through Christ and saved by Christ, the one mediator, whereas the good Christian has no such dependence on the Buddha. Now the baptized baby and the good unbeliever receive salvation neither as a reward for natural efforts in this life, nor as a gift in the next life which has no preparation in this. What they receive in heaven is the full flowering of a life lived in this world in the Spirit, who is the 'first-fruits' and the 'guarantee'. They are saved because they have received God's grace, but they have not received his revelation.

Of course, one could use the term revelation in the sense of man's natural knowledge of God from created things that St Paul speaks about in the Epistle to the Romans (1.19-21); in this sense it is true that the good pagan may receive God's revelation. But those who equate grace with revelation have in mind God's revelation in Christ contained in the New Testament, and this revelation *ex hypothesi* the good pagan and the baptized baby have not accepted. They have the gift of grace without the gift of revelation.

There is, however, a difficulty concerning the hypothesis of implicit Christians: the New Testament seems to teach that faith in Christ is necessary for salvation. 'He who believes in him is not condemned; he who does not believe is condemned already, because he has not believed in the name of the only Son of God' (Jn 3.18). Thus the Fourth Gospel seems to insist upon the need for belief in Christ. Similarly the Epistle to the

[4] 'Christianity and the Non-Christian Religions', *Theological Investigations,* v. ch. 6.

Hebrews teaches the necessity of faith in two propositions about
God: 'And without faith it is impossible to please him. For
whoever would draw near to God must believe that he exists
and that he rewards those who seek him' (11.6). The Epistle
to the Romans points to the connection between faith and the
proclamation of the Gospel; [5] it was for this reason that the
Council of Trent included 'fides ex auditu' as part of the
process of preparation for justification. [6]

But how can the pagan, the agnostic and even the atheist
be said to have faith? It would be too easy a solution to say
that the salvation of the unbeliver raises problems that the
New Testament writers had not envisaged, and that therefore
what they have to say about the necessity of faith is not relevant
to the question we are asking. For the passages from Hebrews
and Romans ask quite explicitly what one needs to believe in
order to be saved. Besides, the case for the need of faith does
not rest upon the literal interpretation of a few New Testament
texts. Since heaven is not an arbitrary reward for a good life, the
vision of God in the next world is the fullness of the gift of the
Spirit in this; that is to say, the vision in the next world seems
to grow from faith in this. 'When the perfect comes, the imperfect will pass away... For now we see in a mirror dimly,
but then face to face' (1 Cor 13.9, 12). The new state grows
from the old, as the man's thoughts grow from the child's.
Moreover, the New Testament writers speak of salvation as a
'call' to be freely accepted; it is an invitation to be welcomed in
freedom and knowledge, and therefore in faith.

But what *is* the faith by which the unbeliever is saved?
On the one hand it can hardly be an explicit faith in Christ,
or only professing Christians could be saved; on the other hand,
to reduce it to knowledge of God based on natural reason would
be ultra-Pelagian, and would provide an explanation only for
the salvation of the good pagan theist, not the good agnostic or

---

[5] 'So faith comes from what is heard, and what is heard comes by
the preaching of Christ.' (Rom 10.17).
[6] Decree on Justification, ch. 6 (DS 1526).

atheist. It seems necessary therefore to postulate the existence of a third kind of faith, which might be called implicit faith. Such faith has not yet been articulated into propositions about God or Christ; indeed many people with implicit faith would presumably doubt or deny propositions asserting the existence of God. Nevertheless, if they are saved, it is not only by grace but also through faith. For good actions are unselfish actions; they are in accordance with the second great commandment. To put others before oneself is to accept Christ, to submit to the claims of others is to submit to Christ, even though he is not explicitly recognized. [7] 'When did we see thee hungry and feed thee? ... As you did it to one of the least of these my brethren, you did it to me' (Mt 25.37, 40). The argument is not that such a person is unwittingly doing what Christ requested; the argument is rather from the personal relationship involved. By relating to another in love, one is relating to Christ, and this relationship it is reasonable to call implicit faith. Indeed, the object even of explicit faith is the person of Christ; faith is essentially knowledge *of* him, not *about* him; the propositions in which we believe, the things we know *about* him, are simply the means by which we know *him*. [8]

So too one can speak of an implicit revelation [9] which is neither the revelation spelt out in articles of the creed and definitions nor merely the natural evidences in the world for the existence of God. Implicit revelation is the experience, contained in every moral choice, of God's self-communication in grace; for if every choice of the good involves faith in Christ, it is made under the influence of grace. This implicit revelation

[7] St Thomas Aquinas came to believe that to make a good moral choice is to accept God. Speaking of the grace of the unbaptized, he says that when a man experiences his first moral awareness, 'if he directs himself to his due end, he will obtain the remission of original sin by grace' (ST Ia.IIae.89.6).

[8] Cf. Aquinas, ST IIa.IIae.1.1: the fundamental object of faith is not propositions, but God himself. Cf. *de Ver.*, 14.8.

[9] Cf. K. Rahner, 'Revelation: B. Theological Interpretation', *Sacramentum Mundi*, v (ET Burns Oates, London and Herder & Herder, New York, 1970), pp. 348-353.

and the offer of grace can never be separated, as the revelation is simply the experience of the offer of grace. To this extent Mackey is right in identifying grace with revelation. But his concern seems to be to identify grace with explicit revelation, and the case of the implicit Christian, who possesses grace and implicit revelation but not explicit revelation, proves that the identification is false.

The case of the baptized baby is similar to that of the implicit Christian to the extent that neither possesses the Christian revelation in explicit form. They differ in that the implicit Christian receives the revelation in implicit form when he makes moral decisions; the baptized baby, on the other hand, is presumably incapable of receiving any form of revelation. Whether he receives implicit revelation before explicit revelation must remain uncertain, though a child psychologist might make an informed guess. If the child could understand right and wrong before he could understand Christian teaching, it would seem that implicit revelation came first; if he was first capable of a rudimentary understanding of Christian teaching, it would seem that explicit revelation came first.

The consideration of explicit revelation leads to the central theme of this chapter, the experience of revelation. Throughout this investigation we have had before our eyes a triple division of grace: first, habitual grace, which is not itself experienced, but which is the vital and personal principle of the second aspect of grace, actual grace, which is experienced only transcendentally, i.e., as a dimension of all moral experience; the third aspect is extraordinary grace, which is less consistent with normal experience than actual grace, and therefore reveals an extraordinary activity of God in comparison with the rest of what is already a second gift. The question before us now is whether the same triple scheme applies to revelation. The second, transcendental level has already been considered; at this level there is the implicit revelation contained in the experience of actual grace within every moral decision. At the first level, the permanent, vital level, there is that principle in man which makes the acceptance of revelation possible, namely the gift of faith. As habitual grace is a disposition to relate to the Trinity in knowledge and love, faith is a consequence of habitual grace. [10] What then of the third level, the extraordinary manifestation? Is there an experience of revelation at this level, as perhaps there is of grace?

From one point of view the answer Yes can readily be given. For all explicit revelation by definition comes from outside; I accept it, not as the fruit of my own experience, but as the word of God; 'faith comes from what is heard'. God's extraordinary entry from outside into human history is the subject of all statements of Christian faith. When in faith I read the scriptures, or hear them read in church, or listen to the Church's appointed minister explaining them, God is continuing to make his revelation to me from outside.

The Nature of Inspiration

But let us consider revelation at an earlier stage, namely the process by which God inspired the biblical author to write his book. Here again there seems to be a clear case for the existence of extraordinary revelation, for it seems that light comes to him from outside by the direct action of God in the form of an experience which is discontinuous from the normal. For scripture is the word of God, and the Holy Spirit is its author.

However, biblical inspiration does not provide so straight-

---

[10] Experience seems at first sight to indicate that faith and habitual grace are separable. For, on the one hand, a person by serious sin can apparently forfeit his state of grace while still retaining some religious beliefs; and on the other hand, an apparently good person can 'lose his faith'. But the separation is perhaps not real. For in the first case the man in question retains, not faith in the person of Christ, but the intellectual habit of believing certain propositions. In the second case, if the man remains good, he becomes an implicit Christian; what is lost is not faith in the person of Christ, but the ability to express that implicit faith in propositions, and to recognise Christ in his visible Church.

forward an example of extraordinary revelation as the foregoing argument suggests. For it does not follow that the human author can separate in his own mind the prompting of the Holy Spirit from his own efforts at composition. In the words of a recent study of biblical inspiration:

> The writer(s) of a biblical book is not like the Egyptian scribe Ra-messe-naki of the nineteenth Dynasty . . . whose statue we see in the Cairo museum. He is seated cross-legged with the papyrus on his knee and a baboon, the emblem of Thoth, the god of learning, on his head. The god whispers wisdom into the scribe's ear. The biblical writer receives no dictation. He uses every faculty that a man normally uses in writing and the Spirit respects his person entirely. [11]

The apologies at the end of Ecclesiastes and 2 Maccabees and the introduction to St Luke's gospel [12] make it clear that inspiration does not take away from the writer the labour of composition. When then are the respective functions of the human and the divine authors?

John Baptist Franzelin, [13] whose thinking had such a great influence on the decree on revelation of the first Vatican Council, maintained that the Holy Spirit put the ideas into the head of the human authors, even the ideas which they could form by natural means, but left them with the task of expressing the ideas in their own words. Critics have sometimes maintained that Franzelin's theory is philosophically intenable, because ideas cannot be possessed, still less communicated, without words. [14] Such criticism is, however, too sweeping: Michael

---

[11] J. Scullion, *The Theology of Inspiration* (Mercier Press, Cork, 1971), p. 91. For a fuller survey of Roman Catholic understanding of inspiration see J.T. Burtchaell, *Catholic Theories of Biblical Inspiration since 1810* (CUP, Cambridge, 1969).

[12] Eccles 12.9-10; 2 Macc 15.37b-38; Lk 1.3.

[13] Franzelin, *De Divina Traditione et Scriptura* (Typographia Polyglotta, S.C. de Prop. Fide, Rome, 3rd ed. 1882). Cf. Scullion, *op. cit.*, pp. 25-27; Burtchaell, *op. cit.*, pp. 98-101.

[14] E.g., Scullion, *op. cit.*, p. 27.

Argyle [15] has reminded us of the importance of communication by non-verbal means like touches and gestures, while investigations into telepathy and extrasensory perception should make us hesitant to assert that ideas can never be communicated without any signs at all. It would be more to the point to object that Franzelin's theory would reduce the role of God's inspiration to too small a compass: a non-verbal idea is of its nature vague; the crystallization of the inarticulate inspiration into words, which would be the human author's share in the process, would be too large a matter to be outside the range of inspiration (to say nothing of inerrancy).

But a more fundamental fallacy in Franzelin's theory is the attempt to assign to God and man different stages of the work of composition. He dispenses with the distinction at one end, when he allows that God can inspire a person with ideas that are already his through his own experience; but at the other end he insists on separating the functions, and maintains that the work of verbalization is all man's. An analogous, but far more harmful error was made at the end of the sixteenth and the beginning of the seventeenth centuries by the theologians of grace. Both Molinists and Banesians were seeking a solution to a false problem: what part of an act performed under the influence of grace is man's and what part is God's? [16] The solution to both problems is the same: just as a free human act is all man's and all God's, so too the whole process of the composition of the scriptures belongs both to God and to man.

There is another fundamental misconception in Franzelin's theory: he considers only one moment in the process of composition, the point at which the works are being written down for the first time. As Lagrange pointed out long before anyone

---

[15] *The Psychology of Interpersonal Behaviour* (Penguin Books, Harmondsworth, 1967), ch. 2, 5, 6.

[16] Banesians emphasised God's sovereignty at the expense of man's freedom; Molinists emphasised man's freedom at the expense of God's sovereignty. Cf. H. Rondet, *The Grace of Christ* (ET Newman Press, Westminster, Maryland, 1967), pp. 322-339; P. Schoonenberg, *The Christ*, pp. 13-15.

else, [17] this is a vast over-simplification. Even the writing of
what has come down to us as a single book of the Bible is in
many cases a very complicated process. Many of the books
(or groups of books) are compilations of earlier written or un-
written sources; some underwent subsequent modification, such
as the Gospel of Mark with the several versions of its ending.
But, more fundamentally, the genesis of any biblical book began
long before any author put pen to papyrus. Apart from the
sources that a writer expressly draws upon, his thought is
necessarily formed by the whole width and depth of the culture
of his society. If he is a writer of originality he will transform
the tradition handed on to him; but even the writer who transforms it has already been moulded by it. Therefore, just as it
places too narrow a limit on inspiration if the process of verbal
composition is considered immune from it, so too it seems
necessary to extend the range of inspiration backwards so that
it can include all the factors which formed the mind of the
writer. [18]

John L. McKenzie makes an even higher estimate of the
debt which the biblical author owes to his society. Pointing to
the spirit of anonymity in which the authors composed, he
writes:

[17] Especially in his lectures given in the Institut Catholique of Toulouse
in 1902 (ET *Historical Criticism and the Old Testament,* Catholic
Truth Society, London, 1905). Lagrange maintained that 'inspiration
has as its primary object not to teach, but to record the memory of
revealed truths..., although the aim of the sacred writer himself be
to teach' (p. 100). God 'does not teach... imperfect ideas to us in the
form in which they are expressed.'

[18] Lagrange (*op. cit.,* p. 97) asks of books like Proverbs, which were
apparently the work of a commission: 'Who was inspired? The
sages, or the compiler? The first writer, or the commission? It is
enough for us to know that the work we read is canonical, and is
therefore inspired.' God uses the formative elements to shape the
mind of the author; God's direction of them forms part of the
process by which he inspires the author; but this does not mean
that we need say that the sources themselves are inspired. For
example, if the two-document hypothesis is true, God inspired St
Matthew partly by means of the source Q; but it would not accord
with traditional theological language to conclude that the author
of Q was himself inspired.

I suggest that the ancient author was anonymous because he did not think of himself as an individual speaker, as the modern author does. He was anonymous because in writing he fulfilled a social function; through him the society of which he was a member wrote its thoughts. He was its spokesman, and the society was the real author of the literature. What he wrote were the traditions of his people, or the record of the deeds of his people, or the beliefs and cult of his people. [19]

However, McKenzie overstates his case, as more than one subsequent critic has pointed out. The writer is not always the self-effacing mouthpiece of his people. Sometimes he criticises and modifies the traditions he has inherited, as the author of the Book of Job questions the traditional view of God's justice; sometimes he is forced to choose between traditions, as the author of Samuel-Kings does when he attacks the people for infidelity to their authentic spirit.

With this criticism of McKenzie's position in mind, it should still be possible to outline what might be called a *social* theory of inspiration, according to which inspiration would be seen as part of God's general providential action, in this case exercised for the sake of the Church, of which, as Rahner maintains, [20] the scriptures are the foundation-documents. According to the social theory it would follow that God in his providence arranged that in the fullness of time there would emerge men of genius, or at least of some originality, whose religious development would inevitably be shaped by the traditions of their society, but who might rebel against these traditions or seek to modify them, and who would be impelled to commit their insights to writing. Throughout the whole development of the tradition God's grace, as well as his providence, will be at work, for we are concerned with the moral

[19] *Myths and Realities: Studies in Biblical Theology* (G. Chapman, London and Bruce, Milwaukee, 1963), p. 64. For criticisms of McKenzie, see Scullion, *op. cit.*, p. 48; D.J. McCarthy, 'Personality, Society, and Inspiration', *Theological Studies*, 24 (1963) pp. 553-576.

[20] *Inspiration in the Bible* (ET Herder, Freiburg and Nelson, Edinburgh and London, 1961).

and religious values of a society, and there are no such values in man which are not achieved under the influence of grace. In other words, throughout the whole of the process God has been making his *implicit* revelation, prompting countless anonymous individuals to hand on and develop the tradition, prompting the religious genius to wrench it into a new shape.

This brings us back to our original question: Is there then any need to postulate the existence of explicit, direct, extraordinary illumination of the human mind by God? Are God's providence and his normal communication of himself in habitual grace sufficient explanation of the genesis of scripture? Of course, the New Testament writers proclaim God's decisive entry into the world from outside by the incarnation of his Son; but does God also need to intervene in the normal thought-processes of the biblical author?

At first sight there are perhaps three reasons why we should give to this question the answer Yes, but on examination none of them will be found convincing.

First, to seek to identify inspiration with the influence of a culture on the mind of the author is simply to push the problem back a stage. An explanation of inspiration must be in terms of divine activity: how then does God shape the culture that influences the author's mind? If we suggest that God does it by implanting ideas in the minds of certain individuals at decisive moments in the development of the tradition, we have denied that God acts upon the mind of the biblical author in this way, only to postulate similar action by God in the mind of the people who influence the author. Does God then shape the culture by material means: climate, topography, fertility of the soil, etc.? This would be to offer a Marxist explanation of inspiration, which would be an oddity, and, more important, would seem to remove the process too much from the sphere of human freedom. Did God then exert his influence by altering the genetic structure of certain members of the Hebrew nation so as to ensure that individuals of a certain natural talent would emerge at decisive moments to direct the development of posterity in a particular direction? If one grants that God can work miracles, one should not deny this possibility; all one can say is that it does not seem to be God's way to intervene habitually, so that a miracle becomes ordinary. God is not a separate cause sharing an effect with human agents. [21] Did God then shape the tradition by giving individuals such grace that they developed the spiritual and moral qualities needed to form the Hebrew tradition? This will be a helpful suggestion only if it is easier to explain God's direction of history by grace rather than by his manipulation of material causes or his implanting of ideas in people's minds. And perhaps it is easier; for the whole of God's action in conferring grace is a continual intervention in human history, for it is a second gift, the communication of himself. Each gift of grace is an individual gift — the white stone bearing the name which no one else knows, the name by which the Good Shepherd calls each sheep. [22] By contrast, God's direct action in implanting ideas or manipulating physical causes would be an intervention at the level of the first gift, and therefore not typical of God's action in the world. It seems therefore that grace can provide a sufficient explanation of God's influence on the mind of the biblical author, both directly and through his cultural tradition: there is no need to postulate that God implants ideas in the author's mind.

The second reason which seems to suggest that God implants ideas directly in the minds of the biblical authors is connected with the scriptures of other religions. If inspiration is God's grace which shapes the religious consciousness of a people, and prepares individual prophets and writers to express and react to this evolving consciousness, the Christian scriptures seem to be no longer unique; for, once it is admitted that non-Christians are not outside the economy of grace, the same process of grace must have been present among pagan peoples also, forming their traditions and preparing the minds of

[21] Cf. Schoonenberg, *The Christ*, part I, 'God or Man: a False Dilemma'.
[22] Cf. Rev 2.17; Jn 10.3.

individual authors. Perhaps one should make no bones about conceding that inspiration is not limited to the Bible: the single movement of grace, which shapes the development of all religious cultures and leads to the composition of their scriptures, Jewish, Christian and pagan, deserves the name of inspiration. There are, however, two ways in which the Christian scriptures are unique. First, only the New Testament is the explicit expression of a unique series of events, the incarnation, death and resurrection of God the Son, who, being his Father's Word, is the embodiment of all revelation. Secondly, as Karl Rahner emphasizes, the Christian scriptures belong to the unique Church, and are its foundation-documents. They are therefore unique not only in the fuller truth they contain, but in the practical function they have to serve. For these reasons there is no need to suppose the infusion of ideas into the authors' minds in order to account for the uniqueness of the Christian scriptures.

Inerrancy

There is, however, a third reason which might seem to demand the acceptance of the theory of implanted ideas: the inerrancy of scripture. Granted that God can reveal his truth to the human race by his general providence and his gifts of grace, how does he ensure that what is proclaimed will be nothing but the truth? [23]

The difficulty would be removed if, like certain post-reformation writers, we identified inspiration with canonicity. If an inspired book is simply one which the Church has chosen to adopt as the foundation of its faith, freedom from error is then simply one of the criteria by which *after* the composition, the Church selects its scriptures. This theory might be caricatured as one of natural selection from random developments:

---

[23] A similar problem arises concerning the truth of the Church's defined statements of faith. I have said something on this question in a short article, 'The Charism of Providential Teaching', *The Month*, Nov. 1971, pp. 134-141. I return briefly to the point at the end of this chapter, 148-9.

we have turned from a Marxist to a Darwinian model. But the theory has a serious defect: it makes inspiration have nothing to do with the *composition* of scripture. The word of scripture becomes the word of God only in the very tenuous sense in which an object chosen by an artist becomes the work of that artist.

The difficulty of accounting for inerrancy can be eased by several considerations. The reader must not interpret a figurative piece of writing as if it were meant as an exposition of literal fact. The Bible is not a treatise on history or natural science; we may without qualms admit that it contains factual errors on these subjects. The Bible is a source of *religious* truth, of what the Decree on Revelation of the Second Vatican Council calls 'saving truth', [24] the truth necessary for salvation, but the authors were not necessarily immune from the factual errors and prejudices of their contemporaries.

Nor is it necessary to conclude that the Bible is free from all error in matters of *religious* truth. It would in fact be surprising if the early books, or the books which are collections of writings spread over several hundred years and so representing an emerging religious consciousness, should be free from religious errors that could be avoided by those who interpreted life in the light of the developed tradition. A well-known example is afforded by the replacement of the theory of inherited guilt and punishment by the theory of individual responsibility. In the early, Yahwistic source of the Pentateuch, the decalogue contains the words: 'I, Yahweh your God, am a jealous God and I punish the father's fault in the sons, the grandsons and the great-grandsons of those who hate me' (Ex 20.5: Jerusalem Bible). But centuries later Ezekiel rejected this view and put forward instead a doctrine of individual guilt and punishment:

> What do you mean by repeating this proverb concerning the land of Israel, 'The fathers have eaten sour grapes, and the children's teeth are set on edge'? As I live, says the Lord God, this proverb shall no more be used by

[24] *Dei Verbum*, 7: *salutaris veritas*.

you in Israel. Behold, all souls are mine; the soul of the
father as well as the soul of the son is mine: the soul
that sins shall die (Ez 18.2-4). [25]

There seems here to be a clear example of the correction by a
later writing of a religious error contained in an earlier writing;
the only alternative — a most unacceptable one — seems to be
that God once followed but then abandoned the practice of
punishing descendants for the sins of their ancestors. Other
religious errors can be quoted: for example, the psalmist's
belief that the good always prosper in this life more than the
wicked; [26] or the apparent conviction in several writers of the
New Testament that the second coming of Christ is at hand. [27]

In the attempt to reconcile biblical inerrancy with the
existence of mistakes in particular religious matters, some
theologians maintain that the Bible itself provides the means
for correcting whatever religious errors there may be in particular passages. [28] Other theologians reach a similar conclusion
by a different approach. For them the guaranteed truth of the
Bible is not truth in the Western sense of a correspondence
with objective facts (*adequatio rei et intellectus*) but rather truth
in the sense of the biblical term *emeth*, which is not fidelity of
words to fact so much as the trustworthiness of God in his
utterances. To quote John Scullion again, 'the truth of the
Bible is the truth, steadfastness, constancy of God to himself,
to his people and to his creation'. We are brought back to the
phrase of Vatican II, '*saving* truth'. [29] The guaranteed truth of
the Bible is pragmatic; the words of scripture fulfil God's
purpose, they are the instrument that he has promised to use
in order to bring men to the knowledge and love of himself.
To draw upon another vocabulary, they are the means by which

[25] Cf. Deut 24.16: 'The fathers shall not be put to death for the
children, nor shall the children be put to death for the fathers;
every man shall be put to death for his own sin.'
[26] See especially Psalm 37.
[27] For example, Mk 14.62; 1 Cor 15.51-52; 1 Thess 4.15.
[28] Cf. Scullion, *op. cit.*, p. 90.
[29] See note 24. Scullion, *op. cit.*, p. 83.

the Christ-event is made present to us; no one who looks for such aid in scripture will search in vain. There may well be what the Warden of Keble calls 'erroneous, irrelevant, and even downright irresponsible statements in the Bible', [30] but God's *emeth* will function in scripture not only in spite of them, but through them. Of course, for the Bible to fulfil this saving function it must contain truth, even in the correspondence sense, about God and salvation. The Bible is not simply emotive, like music which touches the heart; it must also enlighten the mind, if salvation is to be relevant to our natural powers. The Bible can fulfil this end, despite some factual errors, because God has given us the means to correct them.

Revelation, as we saw earlier, is not only knowledge *about* God; it is knowledge *of* God. The revelation contained in the Bible takes the form of propositions, which the Christian believes on God's authority; but by them he knows God, not only as an object of study, but as a person. Such knowledge is quite different from the knowledge we gain about a person by reading his biography or his letters; no amount of biographical research will bridge the gap between knowing about a man and that mutual touching of minds which is a personal relationship. The implicit Christian can form a personal relationship with God without subscribing to the theoretical truth about him in the form of propositions; conversely, a man can give intellectual assent to propositions about God without being in a personal relationship with him. But when faith is explicit, knowledge about God in the form of propositions is the means by which we achieve the personal relationship with him. Even creeds are not only statements about God; they are prayers. Now propositional knowledge about God can still serve this purpose even if there is mixed in with it a proportion of religious error, just as my relationship with a person is not destroyed if I am mistaken concerning some of the facts about him; though I need to get many, perhaps most of my facts right, if a personal relationship of any depth is to be possible.

[30] D.E. Nineham, 'The Use of the Bible in Modern Theology', *John Rylands Bulletin*, 52 (1969), p. 186.

*

The inerrancy of scripture, then, implies two propositions: (1) God faithfully uses the scriptures throughout history as means of grace, as means by which he can lead men to knowledge and love of himself. (2) They contain sufficient factual truth about God and salvation to enable them to be such means, and to provide a corrective for whatever religious errors they may also contain. Neither proposition depends upon the supposition that God plants ideas directly into the author's mind.

If all of this is correct, it follows that there is no need to appeal to the infusion of ideas as the normal means of biblical inspiration. This is not to say that God *cannot* intervene directly in the development of the religious consciousness of a society by implanting ideas in the minds of certain individuals, nor that, though he can, he never in fact does this. Indeed, the scholastic theologians had much to say about the mental processes that would be needed for such divine intervention, and it would be valuable to have the question re-examined in the light of psychological and linguistic knowledge. My point is simply that there are no *a priori* reasons for stating either that God must have made use of this method of inspiration or that he could never have made use of it; if there are decisive considerations, it seems that they must be *a posteriori,* and restricted to the origin of particular ideas.

Further Queries and Corollaries

I am aware that I have left many questions unanswered. I will content myself with indicating five points which need further discussion; to attempt to answer them would upset the balance of this book, and would require in fact a new one.

The first point concerns the truth and falsehood of propositions about God. We can talk about God in two ways: either we can use a technical language specially designed to avoid misunderstanding, but with little relevance to ordinary life; or we can have recourse to analogies, metaphors, models which link up with our experience, but which can be applied to God only with great imprecision. [31] Because of this imprecision, most religious statements are true, but only partly true, if by truth we mean correspondence with the facts. [32] Therefore if we take the inerrancy of scripture or the infallibility of the Church to mean that the statements in question are factually true, we are making too low, not too high a claim, for the same could be said about almost any religious statement. If then we are to speak significantly about inerrancy and infallibility, we ought to concentrate on pragmatic rather than factual truth, insisting above all that God uses the statements of the Bible and the Church with *emeth*, with fidelity.

The second problem concerns the origins of the revelation contained in the Old and New Testaments. If I am right in suggesting that God did not need to implant ideas in the authors' minds, it follows that the essential ideas of the Old Testament could be derived from man's reflection on his own experience of grace. The same would be true of the New Testament, but with this difference: the experience includes the Incarnation. But even Jesus is not only the vehicle but also

[31] Cf. I. Ramsey, *Models and Mystery* (OUP, London, 1964). See also Ramsey's contribution to his own anthology *Words about God* (SCM, London, 1971): 'Theologians have far too often supposed, and mistakenly, that the most generalized doctrines were most free from all contamination (as it would have been judged) with metaphor, or as I would say, models. But none of us must ever despise the models whence our theological discourse is hewn, for without these we have no way to the cosmic disclosure and no way to relevance.' (pp. 216-217).

[32] 'An inevitable and essential aspect of the infallible teaching authority is precisely the right in a believing and teaching community to propose a regulation of language (which could in itself have been different) without determining the question of truth.' 'Every exercise of an infallible teaching authority is partly a regulation of language.' 'We have reached a situation in which a new definition can no longer be false', because 'the range of legitimate interpretation is so wide.' These quotations are from an article by K. Rahner (100 Jahre Unfehlbarkeitsdogma', *Stimmen der Zeit*, July 1970, pp. 27-29), and are cited in my article 'Charism' (see note 23).

the recipient of revelation. [33] In his own person, by his life, death and resurrection, he is the embodied revelation of the good news. 'He who has seen me has seen the Father' (Jn 14.9). But at the same time Jesus as man receives the revelation from the Father: 'The words that I say to you I do not speak on my own authority' (Jn 14.10). Jesus' teaching, based on the revelation he received, has of course been a decisive influence in the formation of the New Testament. But if my remarks in the fourth chapter about Jesus' psychology were correct, Jesus himself did not receive the revelation in the form of divinely implanted knowledge, but derived it from the same sources that would be available to a biblical author: religious experience and the traditional ideas he inherited from his milieu. Of course, his experience of God was unique, because he is the Son not by adoption but by nature. Still, it was the experience of a human mind, implicit revelation which he had to interpret in human words with the help of the explicit revelation available to him in the Old Testament. It is, I suppose, possible that when he appeared to the apostles after the resurrection he taught them new truths which he learned in his glorified state; but the gospel accounts suggest that he explained to them what they might have known before rather than that he added to what he had previously taught; [34] in the account of Acts, during the forty days he is still, as before, 'speaking of the kingdom of God' (Acts 1.3). Even the promise of the Spirit, made after the Resurrection in Luke and Acts, is made at the Last Supper in John. The one clearly new element seems to be the new mission entrusted to the apostles.

To test the theory I am proposing concerning the origin of the Christian revelation, it might be valuable to compare in detail the ideas of the Old and New Testaments to see if there are any which can only, or at least most plausibly, be explained on the supposition that they were implanted by God directly in the mind of Jesus, or of a biblical author, or of some

[33] See G. Moran, *Theology of Revelation* (Burns and Oates, London, 1966), pp. 63-71.
[34] Cf. Lk 24.25-27; 44-47.

other influential figure in the development of the tradition. Comparison of the Bible with the writings of other religions would be relevant to this inquiry.

The third question concerns the use that is made of scripture. If it is granted that scripture is the product of human experience under the influence of grace, and that it contains factual errors, and even some religious errors, how far can it be said to be normative? There is no problem here if one accepts the judgment of the Warden of Keble: 'Whatever may be said in theory, I do not believe the Church ever does, or ever can, settle its questions by reference to some allegedly external and objective norm.' [35] But there is a problem for those who believe in objective norms, not only fundamentalists, but also those who believe in the development of doctrine. The latter believe that the particular phrases of the Bible may not be definitive: they may need to be developed, that is to say, re-expressed in different categories; and these reformulations are not logical deductions from the biblical statements but a rethinking of those statements in different terms, perhaps with different presuppositions. [36] There is, of course, a problem of criteria here, as Newman saw: what reinterpretations are legitimate? But there is a more fundamental problem. Although the particular biblical form of words is not taken to be decisive, the underlying meaning is; but by what right are biblical teachings, even if reformulated, taken as norms for twentieth-

[35] D.E. Nineham, *op. cit.*, p. 198.

[36] 'The Object of religious veneration being unseen, and dissimilar from all that is seen, reason can but represent it in the medium of those ideas which the experience of life affords (as we see in the Scripture account, as far as it is addressed to the intellect); and unless these ideas, however inadequate, be correctly applied to it, they re-act upon the affections, and deprave the religious principle... Thus the systematic doctrine of the Trinity may be considered as the shadow, projected for the contemplation of the intellect, of the Object of scripturally-informed piety: a representation, economical; necessarily imperfect, as being exhibited in a foreign medium, and therefore involving apparent inconsistencies or mysteries' (J.H. Newman, *The Arians of the Fourth Century*, Pickering, London, 4th ed. 1876, pp. 144f). For this passage I thank Rev. A. Mead.

century thought and action, if the teachings are human religious judgments, which are liable to error? Is it sufficient once more to appeal simply to God's *emeth?*

This leads to the fourth question: what happens if one ceases to regard the Bible as the source of ethical norms? With regard to the status of the ethical teaching of the Bible, there are at least three possible positions. The first is that there are special obligations incumbent upon Christians, and these (or at least some of them) are to be discovered in the New Testament. The second is that, apart from liturgical and disciplinary rules, there are no special ethical obligations incumbent upon Christians which are not incumbent upon all human beings, but that the Bible provides infallible help towards recognizing what these general human obligations are. For example, what the New Testament has to say about the permanence of marriage applies to all marriages. The third position is that the ethical teachings contained in the New Testament, far from providing infallible guidance, simply reflect the moral insights of the first century; some may represent values which are proper to all humanity and are therefore immutable; but others may have no permanent validity. If this is so, what the New Testament teaches about the permanence of marriage may no longer apply in the twentieth century. If the first or second position is correct we have to explain how the New Testament authors learned the ethical principles which they teach with infallible authority; perhaps the source is the insight into human nature which Jesus possessed. If on the other hand the third position is correct, the appeal to the Bible has no validity; all Christian rules of conduct are subject to the same critical checks as natural ethical principles. What would the Christian response be if it were claimed that statistics proved that the possibility of divorce made for happier and more stable marriages and for less psychological disturbance among children? The problem would be one of nerve: am I prepared to put Christian ethics at the mercy of secular criticism by renouncing the let-out of saying: 'I don't care what the sociologists or the psychologists say. This is what the Bible (or the Church) teaches.' ? And even if we accept the first or second positions, how do we distinguish between the immutable ethical principles and the changeable disciplinary rules? Not by an appeal to the Bible, for the Bible contains them both; ultimately the distinction is made by subjecting biblical prescriptions to the criticism of rational judgment. [37]

The fifth and last problem concerns the mechanics of inspiration. I have been suggesting that the scriptures are God's word because he enlightens the author's mind in two ways: by his providence and by his grace. This presupposes that an appeal to these two modes of divine action is more credible than the hypothesis that God implants all the ideas in the author's mind. I have indicated that the communication of grace requires no new activity on God's part; it is the consequence of the indwelling of the Holy Spirit which engenders in man the new life of habitual grace. But I have left unexplained the means by which God's providence controls the course of human history. That God does exercise control over the events in this world seems to follow from the New Testament's repeated commendation of petitionary prayer. But whether God exercised this control once for all in sowing the seeds of the universe at the beginning, or whether he continues to shape the course of events moment by moment, it is outside the scope of this book to decide.

*   *   *

To sum up, after giving reasons for rejecting the view that grace and revelation are identical, I have gone on to consider the close connection between them. Although God *may* on occasion plant ideas directly in men's minds, I have suggested that inspiration can be more plausibly explained without recourse to this hypothesis. As in our consideration of redemption and Jesus' psychology, habitual grace has been at the heart

[37] Cf. G.J. Hughes, 'A Christian Basis for Ethics', *Heythrop Journal* 13 (1972), pp. 27-43.

of the explanation. Inspiration is an actual grace, a religious experience springing from the author's abiding habitual grace, and shaped by the cultural tradition in which the author lives. Inspiration is not a baboon whispering in the author's ear; it is the air which he breathes, the self to which he must be true.

CHAPTER 7

SACRAMENTS AND WORD

In what has been said so far, the emphasis has been on the individual, and God's self-communication to him which we call grace. This was true even when we were considering the doctrine that each person is redeemed by incorporation into the unity of Christ's body. For even in that context the emphasis was on the practical consequences for the individual of this solidarity with Christ. In this chapter I wish to consider some of the corporate aspects of grace by examining the individual's relationship with the Church.

It is a generally accepted principle of modern Roman Catholic ecclesiology that the Church is the basic or archetypal sacrament. [1] This statement itself depends upon another, namely that Christ is the basic and archetypal sacrament. I propose to examine these two theorems in reverse order.

Christ, the Basic or Archetypal Sacrament

In Chapter Four I put forward the view that the Christian's life of grace is a participation in the created grace of Jesus' humanity, from whose fullness we have all received. We receive the second gift — which in New Testament terms consists of rebirth, life, adoption as sons, the indwelling of the Holy Spirit,

[1] Cf. Vatican II's Decree on the Church (*Lumen Gentium*), 1, 9.

redemption — not only through Christ's merits and intercession
on our behalf before the Father, not only by faith in him who
is the Father's Word, but by abiding in him, [2] sharing his
humanized divine life, which is a divinised human life, becoming
in the phrase of Emile Mersch, *filii in Filio,* sons and daughters
of the Father *in* the Son. [3]

The word 'sacrament' is appropriate to describe this relationship with Christ, whether we think of the meaning it holds
in Christian theology, or whether, since 'sacramentum' is the
Latin translation of the Greek word *musterion,* we draw upon
the more primitive notion of a pagan mystery. In the Greek
and Roman mystery-initiations, the votary was put into mystic
communion with the deity through the contemplation of cult-
objects, and through taking an active part in the representation
of the God's sufferings and triumph. The purpose was the
communication of a religious experience (*pathein*), rather than
knowledge (*mathein*), as Aristotle put it. The experience was
intended to remain luminous in the initiate's consciousness as
an abiding sense of communion with the deity, giving him
serenity and prosperity in the present life, and the assurance of
a blessed immortality. [4] When St Paul used the word 'mystery'
he may have had the pagan sense in mind (e.g. Eph 1.9). It
is in fact not far removed from the more familiar Christian
understanding of a sacrament as a sign of grace which imparts
the grace which it signifies.

Both the pagan and the Christian contexts illuminate the
meaning of the statement that Christ is the basic sacrament.
Like the pagan initiate, the Christian shares in Christ's own
death and resurrection, but with a deeper kind of participation,
which consists not only in conscious imitation but in a communion of life. [5] The humanity of God the Son made man is the

[2] Cf. Jn 15.4.
[3] E. Mersch, *La Théologie du Corps Mystique* (Desclée de Brouwer,
Paris and L'Edition Universelle, Brussels, 1946), ch. 13.
[4] Cf. E.J. Yarnold, 'Baptism and the Pagan Mysteries', pp. 248-257.
[5] This truth was emphasised by Casel (cf. p. 82).

'mystery'; by experiencing it and entering into communion with it, men enter into communion with the divine. The same truth can be expressed by the analogy of a Christian sacrament: the humanity of God the Word is the point of contact, the sign which effects the union between the Christian and God the Father.

The Church, the Basic or Archetypal Sacrament

It would be reasonable to describe Christ as the sacrament because of what he has accomplished in the past: his incarnation, death and resurrection won us access to the Father, and his life and his teaching enlighten and inspire our own lives. These considerations would still be true if Christ's humanity had ceased after the Ascension; but God the Son is still incarnate, glorified as the Lamb who was slain; [6] it is God made man who is to come again, and who is the same yesterday, today and for ever. [7] Jesus in his humanity is still the sacrament of our salvation; and it is through the Church that he is so.

In so saying, one is clearly not speaking of an invisible, purely spiritual Church, the sum total of all who have charity and at least implicit faith; if the Church corporately is the sign and the cause of our salvation, it must be a visible Church with recognizable membership. Consequently I am not speaking either about the Church in an ideal or eschatological sense, as if it were God's will that his visible Church should be a means of salvation, but man's sin constantly prevented God from accomplishing his purpose; or as if the Church will be the sacrament of salvation only at the end of time, when Christ will 'present the Church to himself in splendour, without spot or wrinkle, . . . holy and without blemish' (Eph 5.27). By the Church I mean the universal Church as it exists on earth, united in 'one Body and one Spirit, . . . one Lord, one faith, one baptism, one God and Father of us all' (Eph 4.4-6); and I

[6] Cf. Rev 5.6.
[7] Cf. Heb 13.8. The entry of the humanity of Christ into the presence of his Father is a recurrent theme in this epistle.

would add, as an essential note of this visible Church, that it should be united under the guidance of one God-given ministry, so as to share the one eucharistic Bread. When there is schism or heresy, the power of the whole Church to be a sign and cause of grace is weakened; and every lack of holiness on the part of individual members weakens the whole Church in the same way. Nevertheless, despite heresy, schism and sin, the visible community of the baptized, divided though they are into separate denominations, form a single sacrament of salvation, through which the incarnate and risen Christ continues himself to be the sacrament of salvation.

The Fathers and later theologians frequently compared the relationship of Christ to his Church with the union between the human body and the soul. [8] Sometimes the comparison is made rather with the union of humanity and divinity in the incarnate Christ; [9] sometimes the application of this comparison is elaborated: in the words of the Second Vatican Council, it is Christ's own Spirit, the Holy Spirit, who 'vivifies' the 'communal structure of the Church'. [10] In other words, despite its spots and wrinkles, this divided Church of sinners, with its tares as well as its wheat, is the sacrament of salvation, the saving presence of Christ in the world, because Christ has poured out on his Church the Spirit by whose power he himself took flesh, who anointed him to preach the good news to the poor, and through whom he was himself raised from the dead by his Father. [11]

Sacrament and Word

If the Church is *the* Sacrament, it remains to show the function of the particular sacraments. Just as we experience the

[8] For example, St Thomas Aquinas: 'As the body is made a unity by its unity with the soul, so too the Church is made a unity by its unity with the Spirit.' (*In Col.*, 1.18, lect. v).
[9] Cf. Leo XIII, *Satis Cognitum* (DS 3301).
[10] *Lumen Gentium*, 8.
[11] Cf. Lk 1.35; 4.18; Rom 8.11.

saving presence of Christ in his Church, so too we experience the saving action of the Church only in its particular forms, namely the various sacraments and the word.

Sacraments and word are not distinct: sacraments are a particular class of word. God's word is related to his Word, who is his Son, in somewhat the same way as the Body of Christ is related to its Head. The word is not a thing, a collection of printed pages bound together to form the Bible, or a body of dogmatic formulas put together to form a creed. The word of God is a happening; it is the Spirit of Christ taking Christ's teaching and bringing it here and now to those who are listening in faith. The word is not brought to others by a person acting as an individual, nor does one discover it for oneself; the word is always the word of the Church. This is most clearly true when the scripture is read or a sermon is preached by the Church's commissioned minister; but it is also true, though less obviously so, when someone is moved by his private reading of the scriptures. For the Bible is the Church's book, the official expression of the faith of the apostles, who are the Church's foundation;[12] to read the scriptures with faith is to encounter Christ in his Church. Consequently the efficacy of the word proclaimed to a congregation does not depend ultimately upon the skill of the preacher or the reader; it rests on Christ's fidelity to his promise to give the Church his Spirit. The efficacy of the proclaimed word is *ex opere operato;*[13] that is to say, its effectiveness does not depend on man but on

[12] Cf. Eph 2.20.

[13] The expression *ex opere operato* (by virtue of the Church's action) is used in contrast with the expression *ex opere operantis* (by virtue of the person who performs the action). The former term is more usually applied to the Church's sacraments, as later in this chapter, in order to state that their fruitfulness does not come from the holiness of the minister or the recipient, but from the action of Christ in his Church. K. Rahner, however, also applies the term *ex opere operato* to the Church's ministry of the word (*The Church and the Sacraments,* Herder, Freiburg and Nelson, Edinburgh and London, 1963, p. 27). For the history of this terminology, see B. Leeming, *Principles of Sacramental Theology* (Longmans, London and Newman Press, Westminster, Maryland, 2nd ed. 1960), pp. 7-10.

160 THE SECOND GIFT

God's promise to offer his grace when his word is proclaimed. Of course, the hearer can put obstacles in the way of grace; but when the Church proclaims its word, even though the preacher is stupid, mumbling, misleading, negligent or domineering, Christ is present offering grace. Naturally the preacher may not presume upon the certainty of God's action so as to be careless in his preaching; other things being equal, a good sermon is a more effective proclamation of the word than a bad one; but in the ears of one who listens with faith, the Spirit can turn an incoherent mutter into the words of life.

Sacraments are also examples of the word, not only because words are spoken in their administration, but because they are signs. The immersion or pouring or sprinkling in baptism, the taking of bread and wine in the Eucharist, are instances of the Church's proclamation of the word. The difference between the sacraments and the other forms of the Church's proclamation is not as easy to define as theologians have often supposed. [14] It does not lie in the fact that sacraments confer grace *ex opere operato*, i.e. by virtue of Christ's promise which is attached to the sacramental sign, for, as I have just suggested, the same is true of all proclamation of the word. Nor does explicit institution by Jesus constitute the difference. Those who limit the use of the term to the two sacraments of baptism and Eucharist can make a stronger case than theologians who hold seven sacraments, for it is impossible to point with conviction to moments in Jesus' life when some of the other five were instituted. But whether there are two sacraments or seven, dominical institution alone cannot be the distinguishing mark of sacraments, for preaching was also commanded by Christ ('teach all nations'), [15] and the washing of feet seems to be enjoined no less explicitly than the celebration of baptism and the Eucharist ('You also ought to wash one another's feet. For I have given you an example, that you also should do as I have done to you'). [16]

[14] Cf. K. Rahner, *The Church and the Sacraments*, pp. 24-33.
[15] Mt 28.19.
[16] Jn 13.14-15

Karl Rahner suggests that the seven sacraments differ from the rest of the Church's proclamation of the word because only they are 'the word as the fullest actualization of the Church in its absolute commitment, and the word spoken in the decisive situations of human salvation'. [17] However, neither can these criteria account for the distinctiveness of the sacraments. For it is not evident that the celebration of the seven sacraments involves a fuller, more absolute commitment of the Church than preaching does. And though it is true that the seven sacraments mark decisive situations in a human life, there are other decisive moments in which the Church speaks God's word with full assurance that the divine promises will be fulfilled, but does not claim to be administering a sacrament: for example, the acceptance of the solemn vows of a religious, or the blessing of one whose husband or wife has just died. Perhaps in the last resort all that can be said is that such rites are not sacraments simply because the Church has not seen fit to call them sacraments. God's promise is as certainly fulfilled in them as in the sacraments themselves; but precisely because they are not distinguished by the name of sacrament, God's word is spoken, so to speak, less solemnly and with less emphasis. A sacrament is like a statement made on oath. If we regard the speaker to be trustworthy, we believe him utterly without the oath; what the oath adds is not credibility but a sense of the exceptional importance of the occasion.

Later in this chapter I shall discuss another possible distinguishing mark of sacraments, the fact that they establish the recipient in a new or deeper relationship with the Church. But the time has now come to turn to my main theme, the experience of grace in the sacraments of the Church.

The Experience of Grace in the Sacraments

In one sense the Church itself could be called a visible grace, a second gift God makes to man beyond man's natural endow-

[17] 'The Word and the Eucharist', *Theological Investigations,* iv.272.

ments, for it is the work of the Holy Spirit. The Church is a permanent gift of God, and might be described as an habitual grace, by analogy with the habitual grace of the individual. Just as the grace of the individual is not episodic, and does not consist of unconnected creative touches by God from the outside, but is an abiding internal transformation, a new life which makes the person capable of acts beyond his nature, so too the Church is the abiding, redemptive, visible presence of Christ in the world. The presence is visible, because it is incarnate, so to say, in human form. In addition to this 'habitual' grace of the Church, there are particular moments which might be called 'actual' graces, when the abiding presence of Christ in the Church becomes operative and perceptible through a sign. Such signs are the proclamation of the word, and above all the celebration of the sacraments.

However, although one could speak in this way of the visible or external 'habitual' and 'actual' grace of the Church as a whole, I am more concerned with the internal grace of the individual member. The grace conferred on the child by the sacrament of baptism is the beginning of habitual grace; the effect of the other sacraments can be described in terms of both kinds of grace, habitual and actual. When the sacramental sign is performed, the Christian's response to it in faith springs from the habitual grace which has already become part of him through the abiding presence of the Holy Spirit; and through this particular response in faith he grows in habitual grace. On the other hand it is possible to consider the grace of the sacrament as a particular, momentary activation of the habitual grace which is a permanent disposition to know and love God; in this sense the sacramental grace is an actual grace. A comparison may help to illustrate the point. Someone I love treats me with unexpected consideration and kindness — perhaps with extraordinary perceptiveness goes to some trouble to come along and say just the right thing to encourage me after a disappointment which I thought no one would have noticed; this corresponds to the external grace consisting of the sacramental sign which embodies God's promise made through his Church.

I respond to this act of sympathy by a feeling of grateful affection which I express in a few words of thanks. This response springs from my habitual love for my friend (which corresponds to habitual grace), which receives its immediate impulse (actual grace) from his particular expression of sympathy (sacramental sign); and in turn my response deepens my habitual relationship with him, just as by responding in faith to the sacrament we grow in habitual grace.

In the sacraments therefore there is an experience of grace involving two of the three levels that we are investigating: habitual grace, which is realized and experienced in actual grace. Can we also find in the sacraments an example of the third type of grace, extraordinary grace, in which God's grace is manifested without the normal preparation? Whenever a sacrament is the occasion on which grace is for the first time conferred upon, or is restored to, a person who has been totally devoid of it, grace is operative in this third way. However, the only clear example of this is infant baptism. At first sight it might appear that the sacraments of baptism and penance, when received by one in mortal sin, also provide examples; but it seems likely that normally the sinner will have been granted grace through repentance before he receives the sacrament. More generally, it might be thought that the word of God addressed to the recipient of any sacrament bears some of the features of extraordinary grace. For, though the sacraments are normal means by which God acts through his Church, and though the results are not normally spectacular, the sacramental sign, which is the cause of grace, is addressed to the Christian from outside. However, before attempting to answer this question, it may be helpful to consider at some length the way in which the sacraments cause grace.

The Sacraments as Causes of Grace

The problem of the nature of sacramental causality has occupied the attention of theologians since the middle ages.

L

Some speak of them as moral causes or occasions of grace: [18] through the sacraments the Church pleads before God the Father the merits of his Son, and so the Church's prayer that grace may be offered is unfailingly granted. Others advanced a theory of so-called 'physical' causality, and explained that the sacraments are the instruments which God uses in order to confer grace. [19] Both of these theories contain a considerable element of truth; but they miss the fundamental point, which is that sacraments are essentially signs. They are not simply signs that *accompany* 'moral' or 'physical' causality, but *as signs* they are the means by which God confers his grace; the grace is caused by being brought to our mind by the sign. [20]

A sacrament is a sign by which the Church expresses its pleading on our behalf to God; it is a sign of God's fidelity here and now to his promises; it is a sign of the recipient's faith; and it is a sign of the particular grace of the sacrament. To this sign the recipient responds in faith by virtue of the abiding presence in him of the Holy Spirit, filling him with the vital principle of habitual grace, so that this habitual grace unfolds in the particular actual grace of the sacrament, and itself grows under the stimulus of the sign. If this is correct, God does not so much confer grace by means of the sign, as use the sign to elicit an actuation and growth of the habitual grace already present. There are, of course, two exceptions: by baptism habitual grace may be conferred for the first time; by penance, and perhaps other sacraments, habitual grace, once lost, can be

---

[18] 'But some say that they [sacraments] are not a cause of grace by effecting some operation; but because God, when the sacraments are performed, produces grace in the soul. They put forward as an illustration the case of a man who, by royal decree, is given a hundred pounds in exchange for a lead token; the token cannot produce anything which makes it worth this amount of money; it is the king's wish alone which gives it this value.' (Aquinas, ST III.62.1). This view, which foreshadows the nominalistic theory of God's free acceptation (cf. Chapter 5, note 18), is attributed among others to St Bonaventure. (Cf. Leeming, *op. cit.*, pp. 287-288, 290-294).

[19] Cf. Leeming, *op. cit.*, pp. 288-290.

[20] Cf. K. Rahner, *op. cit.*, pp. 36-40.

restored. It is only in these two cases that grace is conferred from outside.

Sacraments as Signs

The connection between a sacrament and the grace it confers may be clarified by a brief consideration of the nature of signs. Some signs, such as a clock face, are designed to convey information; others, like the double yellow lines at the side of the road, convey a command or prohibition. These two classes of sign can be called respectively 'informative' and 'prescriptive'. There is a third class of sign, which might, to borrow J.L. Austin's term, be called 'performative'. [21] The essence of such a sign is that it does not essentially convey information or a prescription about an action: it *constitutes* an action. Thus the signs consisting of the words 'I apologize', or even in certain circumstances 'I'm sorry', are not necessarily the description of a feeling of regret or of an apology (as such they would be an informative sign); they actually *are* the apology. Austin illustrated the point drily, though he was not, of course, thinking in sacramental terms: 'When I say, before the registrar or altar . . . , "I do", I am not reporting on a marriage: I am indulging in it.' [22]

A performative sign can institute a new relationship between human beings, or restore an old one (such is the effect of an apology). A performative sign, as such, is neither true nor false, since its aim is not to convey information. To say 'I apologize' *is* to apologize; you can withdraw the apology later ('I didn't mean it'), or deny that you spoke the words; but you cannot say that the words were not true.

Sacraments are performative signs in three senses. First, they constitute God's promise here and now to confer grace on the recipient, just as in everyday speech the words 'I promise'

---

[21] J.L. Austin, *How to do Things with Words* (Clarendon Press, Oxford, 1962).

[22] *Ibid.*, p. 6.

are not a description of a promise but *are* a promise. Secondly, just as the words 'Arise, Sir Bedevere', as well as expressing an order, are performative because they make the man a knight, so too the sacramental sign, in many cases at least, establishes the recipient in a new position in the Church; by baptism, for example, one becomes a member of the Church; by holy order one becomes a minister; by the sacrament of penance one is restored to full communion within the Church.

There is a third sense in which sacraments might be considered as performative signs: they effect the grace which they signify. In this they differ from ordinary promises. The words 'I promise' are the promise, but they are not the keeping of the promise; the fulfilment is distinct from the act of promising. So too a sacramental sign is, as we have just seen, an act of promising and like all promises, it does not *constitute* what it promises, namely grace. However, unlike other promises, the sacramental sign, while not *constituting* the fulfilment of the promise, *effects* its fulfilment. Many an empty space on a book-shelf can testify to the difference between saying, 'I promise I shall let you have the book back next week', and actually giving it back; whereas the words 'I absolve you from your sins' themselves bring about the restoration of grace provided the penitent puts no obstacle in the way of their fulfilment.

There is another difference between sacraments and other performative signs. It does not much matter if a performative sign is apt, so long as it is understood. The custom attested in the book of Ruth of handing over one's sandal seems an odd way of making a contract; [23] but the sign presumably fulfilled its purpose perfectly adequately because it was understood by both sides. Now in so far as sacraments are performative signs by which God commits himself through his Church, or someone receives an appointment within the Church, it scarcely matters how appropriate the signs are. God could be committed to conferring grace, and a person could be admitted to the Church, when the priest daubed somebody's face with paint or

[23] Ruth 4.7.

stood him on his head. Nevertheless such ceremonies would not be suitable from another point of view: they would not adequately signify the grace they would be required to effect, namely purification from sin and new birth. A sacramental sign needs to be apt, because its effectiveness as a means of grace is connected with its effectiveness as a sign.

The distinction often drawn between signs and symbols is relevant here, though different writers draw the distinction in different ways. I propose to use the word 'symbol' for a particular kind of sign, namely one which has an emotive power. A symbol is designed to arouse in the beholder an affective attitude to the thing signified. Thus a status-symbol is not only an informative sign, announcing status, and a performative sign, constituting status; it is also a symbol, creating an aura of status. It may be the possession of something considered magnificent, like a colour-television set, or it may be the fact that one does not possess something which is regarded as a vulgar toy, like a colour-television set. In both cases the status-symbol is calculated to arouse feelings of admiration and envy in the less fortunate, and of respect among equals.

Now sacraments are symbols as well as signs. As informative signs they point to the grace of the sacrament; as prescriptive signs they enjoin appropriate conduct; as performative signs they constitute God's promise and his appointment. As symbols they are intended to arouse in the recipient a particular affective response. This was especially true of the sacraments of initiation in the early Church, which were carefully contrived to inspire awe, and were even described by contemporary preachers as 'hair-raising' or 'spine-chilling' rites. [24]

Every word and gesture of the celebrant contributes to the sacrament's effectiveness as a symbol, or else detracts from it: the same is true of the vestments he wears, the architecture and decoration of the church, and, of course, the part played by the

[24] Cf. E.J. Yarnold, 'Baptism and the Pagan Mysteries' in *The Awe-Inspiring Rites of Initiation: Baptismal Homilies of the Fourth Century* (St Paul Publications, Slough, 1972), p. 247.

congregation. The same sacrament can be celebrated at different times with a different symbolic emphasis: the Eucharist, for example, can be performed, at one extreme, in a cathedral in Latin with elaborate vestments, choral singing and incense; and, at the other end of the scale, in a private house round a dining-table in the vernacular with the simplest of vestments or none. In the first case the ceremonial is intended to convey a sense of mystery and adoration; in the second the informal setting is meant to arouse a sense of community and of Christ's entry into everyday life. Both types of liturgy have their value, and each, by its peculiar symbolism, elicits a different grace.

If I am right in suggesting that sacraments cause grace by producing a psychological effect in the mind of the recipient which stimulates a response springing from his abiding habitual grace, it is the effectiveness of the sacrament as a symbol which makes it effective as a means of grace. At very least, however inappropriate the symbol may be, it will have power to elicit a response because it embodies Christ's promise of grace; to read good news can make us happy even though it is printed in uneven type on dirty paper. Again, even though depression or distractions make us insensitive to sacramental symbolism, the fact that we come to receive the sacrament (provided we do not do so for an unworthy motive) is already a psychological response to the symbol. But the celebrant must do all that lies in his power to make the symbol speak as suggestively as possible.

The Ecclesial Effect of Sacraments

There is another point of sacramental theology which is relevant to the experience of grace: the theory that each sacrament modifies the recipient's relationship with the Church. It is commonly held nowadays by Roman Catholic theologians that the grace conferred on the individual is not the immediate effect of the sacrament: the immediate effect of each sacrament is to establish the Christian in a new, or a deeper, relationship with the Church, so that it is through this social effect that the

individual receives grace. This theory follows from the principle
that the Church is the basic or fundamental sacrament. In the
words of Otto Semmelroth:

> the sacramental Church joins itself to man in the individual
> sacraments and holds him in itself, in the Church as the
> fundamental sacrament, just as a man carries something
> in physical closeness within the clasp of his arms. All
> sacraments have the initial and direct effect of bringing
> man, for the first time or in a new way, into a living union
> with the Church itself. [25]

This is most clearly seen in the sacraments which are said
to confer a permanent character, namely baptism, confirmation
and holy order. The social effect of the first two is to initiate
the recipient into the Church; the social effect of holy order is
to confer the status of a minister within the Church. This
social effect is permanent; even if a man renounces membership
of the Church or his orders, the sacrament does not need to be
repeated for his membership or his orders to be restored.
According to the view we are considering, this character is the
immediate effect of the sacramental sign, and in its turn the
sign and the cause of the grace conferred on the recipient.
There are therefore three stages: first, the sacramental sign;
secondly, the reality signified, namely the new status within
the Church, which in its turn is the sign of the third stage,
which is the ultimate reality signified, the peculiar grace of
the sacrament. The three stages are traditionally called *sacramentum* (sign), *res et sacramentum* (immediate social reality
signified, which is itself a sign) and *res* (the final reality, i.e. the
grace of the sacrament). [26]

St Augustine put forward a form of this theory to explain
why the sacraments of baptism and order, when conferred by
heretics, though unable to confer grace (since the Spirit could
not work in this way outside the Church), did not need to be

[25] *Church and Sacrament* (ET Gill, Dublin, 1965), p. 85; cf. pp. 81-7.
[26] On the character and social effect, see Leeming, *op. cit.*, pp. 129-250;
on the term *res et sacramentum, ibid.*, pp. 251-265.

repeated, because they did confer the character. [27] Modern
Roman Catholic theologians apply the same three categories of
sacramentum, res et sacramentum and *res* to the other four
sacraments, which do not confer a character and a permanent
status within the Church. [28] For these four sacraments also
confer a status, though less obviously than baptism, confirmation and order. The sacrament of penance restores a sinner to
communion with the Church; by matrimony the couple accept
in the Church the married state. The sacrament of anointing
consecrates the sick so that, in the words of the second Vatican
Council, they 'contribute to the welfare of the whole people of
God by associating themselves freely with the passion and death
of Christ'. [29] Finally there is a clear connection between the
Eucharist and membership of the Church; for St Paul the link
was so close that he allowed the term 'Body of Christ' to slide
between the two senses of Eucharist and Church. [30] First
communion has long been seen as one of the sacraments of
initiation, and every subsequent communion deepens one's
membership of the Church.

Now it would be only part of the truth to say that the
sacraments each establish a person in a new or deeper relationship with the Church, and *also* confer grace upon him. For the
two effects are interconnected: the individual's grace is never
simply for the sake of the individual, but is a building up of
the Body of Christ; and conversely the grace which a sacrament
confers upon an individual issues from the new relationship
with the Church in which that same sacrament establishes him.

[27] Leeming, pp. 143-161. Augustine did not himself use the precise
term *res et sacramentum*. It is used in the 11th century in connection with the Eucharist during the Berengarian controversy
(Leeming, pp. 252-253), and by the 13th century of baptism, confirmation and order (Leeming, p. 262).

[28] On the application of these three categories to all seven sacraments,
see Leeming, pp. 251-265; Rahner, pp. 76-117; E. Schillebeeckx,
Christ the Sacrament (ET Sheed & Ward, London, 1963), pp.
190-219.

[29] *Lumen Gentium,* 11.

[30] Cf. 1 Cor 10.16-17; and perhaps 11.27, 29.

The baptized and confirmed receive new birth and the Spirit because they have become members of the Church, and in turn they are enabled to serve the Church. The married couple and the ordained minister not only receive grace *for* their new responsibilities, but receive grace as a consequence of them. The same is true of the anointed sick. The penitent receives grace through his reconciliation with the Church, and so is able once more to serve the Church. Holy Communion, which Aquinas called 'the sacrament of the Church's unity', [31] confers grace upon the individual by strengthening his links with Christ's Body, the Church, so that, having grown in grace, he is in turn more closely linked with his fellow-Christians.

What sort of entity is this *res et sacramentum*, the immediate, social effect of each sacrament? A children's catechism described the character as a 'mark or seal on the soul'; if this is true of the *res et sacramentum* of each of the seven sacraments, it seems to be a special kind of imperceptible, habitual grace which emerges into effect in actual graces. There is, however, a difficulty here. If this is a hidden entity, how can it be described as a 'mark or seal', as a sign (*sacramentum*) as well as a reality? Some theologians have sought to solve the difficulty by claiming that the sign is visible in its causes; [32] but a more plausible explanation lies to hand. The *res et sacramentum*, being a new

---

[31] ST III.82.2 ad 3. Theologians disagree about the most appropriate way of applying the category of *res et sacramentum* to the Eucharist. For Rahner (83-4) and Schillebeeckx (217-8), the *res et sacramentum* is the social effect, namely deeper incorporation into the Church; other effects flow from this. For Innocent III (DS 783) and Leeming (265), the *res et sacramentum* is not a social effect, but is the presence of the body and blood of Christ; the *res* is, according to Innocent, 'unity and charity'. (It is worth pointing out that the sacramental sign is not the appearance of bread and wine, but the eating and drinking of what appear to be bread and wine.) The Eucharist, from one point of view, is an obvious example of what we have called extraordinary grace: a gift from outside us. The Real Presence is like the sacramental word or sign spoken of on p. 162 — only here the word is the Word; but even this Word is ineffectual, unless we respond to it in faith by virtue of our habitual grace.

[32] For example, the thirteenth-century theologian Hugh of St Cher (Leeming, p. 262).

relationship with the Church, is not a mysterious, invisible entity, but is something visible, in the social order, precisely because the Church is a visible society. To be a member of the Church and to have a particular status in it is as palpable a fact as to belong to a Trades Union and to hold office in it.

The communal nature of sacramental grace fits in with some of the considerations which were put forward in earlier chapters. In Chapter One we saw that what later theologians chose to call grace is described in the New Testament partly in corporate terms: the covenant, the people of God, solidarity in Christ the last Adam, etc. In Chapters Four and Five we considered how we receive grace and are redeemed through union with Christ, the representative man. In the present chapter I have been suggesting that sacramental grace not only has a corporate origin in the *res et sacramentum*, the relationship with the Church; the grace itself is expressed in a social way, in particular actions for the building up of the Body of Christ.

Non-Christians and Baptized Babies

One last point remains to be discussed: how does what has been said about sacramental grace and membership of the Church apply to the two special cases of non-Christians and baptized babies?

In Chapter Six I tried to show that good non-Christians are not saved by some arbitrary act of God's mercy when they die; their salvation, like that of the Christian, is a growth from a life of grace in this world. That being so, have we to conclude that the grace they receive from the Christ they do not know comes to them, not through the Church, but directly from Christ? In that case, there would be two ways of salvation, one through the Church, the other, in fact for the majority, without reference to the Church. There are theologians today who take this view. [33] The decree *Lumen Gentium* of the second Vatican

[33] This question is discussed by E. Hillman, *The Wider Ecumenism* (Burns & Oates, London, 1968).

Council, however, saw the matter quite differently: the visible Church on earth is 'the universal sacrament of salvation', through which God 'communicates truth and justice to all'. [34] It might be possible to produce a modified form of the theory of the two ways of salvation, according to which all men can find complete fulfilment only in the Church, but in fact the majority receive grace from Christ outside the Church, even though this grace, again in the words of *Lumen Gentium*, possesses 'an inner dynamism towards Catholic unity'. [35] In other words, according to this view, the grace of unbelievers impels them towards the Church, but does not come from the Church.

But before trying to suggest ways in which grace comes to the unbeliever through the Church, it will be helpful to consider in what sense grace comes to believers through the Church. At least five ways can be suggested: (1) It is through baptism that the Christian is born again and receives habitual grace. (2) The other sacraments of the Church, especially the Eucharist, and the word proclaimed by the Church, foster the growth of the grace received at baptism. (3) A person learns the truth of the gospel not only from the formal proclamation of the Church, but, less formally, by reading and listening to the words of members of the Church. For example, a child usually first learns the Gospel from its parents. (4) All the other occasions of grace in life are occasions for the growth of the habitual life of grace which began at baptism. (5) Because the members of the communion of saints help one another by their holiness, any individual's grace owes something to the total holiness of the Church.

Only the last of these propositions can normally apply to unbelievers: they receive grace by some participation in the holiness of the members of the visible Church. However, one can perhaps go further. In the Epistle to the Ephesians, Christ

[34] Nn. 48, 8; cf. 9: '...that for each and all she may be the visible sacrament of this saving unity.'
[35] N. 8.

is described as the head and the spouse of the Church; he 'loved the Church and gave himself up for her' (Eph 5.25). These words imply not only that grace comes from the Church and has a dynamism towards the Church, but also that Christ won grace by his death and resurrection *for the sake of* the Church. And though unbelievers are still the majority, and the visible Church is still a relatively 'little flock', [36] the extraordinary way of salvation is that of the majority, because they participate incompletely in an economy of salvation which is Christ's gift to his Church. But the human experiences which are the occasion of the unbeliever's growth in grace come to him not from the visible Church, but from the culture and society to which he belongs, including the non-Christian faith of which he is a member.

Karl Rahner takes a further step. [37] The visible, organized Church can exist, he maintains, only because there is a logically prior unity of the whole human race in Christ, who is the last Adam, through whom and for whom all things were made, and by whom God wills to save all men. Rahner calls this unity 'the people of God'. The salvation of the unbeliever, he holds, comes, and comes visibly, from his membership of this total humanity in Christ, which is not the visible Church, but is the foundation of it.

The position of baptized babies is in some respects the reverse of that of good unbelievers. The baptized baby is a member of the visible Church; the good unbeliever is not. The good unbeliever makes moral choices under the influence of grace; the baptized baby does not. However, the normal presupposition of infant baptism is that the baby receives through the sacrament new birth in Christ, and therefore, like the good unbeliever, is in a state of habitual grace.

But what sense does it make to say that a baby, who is

---

[36] Lk 12.32.
[37] 'Membership of the Church according to the teaching of Pius XII's Encyclical "Mystici Corporis Christi",' *Theological Investigations,* ii.76-87.

presumably incapable of any moral act, is in a state of grace?
If created grace is the capacity to know and love God, [38] how
can the child be said to be in a state of grace at an age when it
seems incapable of knowing and loving anyone? At least it can
be said that the baby through its baptism is brought into a
particular covenant-relationship with God which an unbaptized
child does not yet share. This relationship can be described in
terms of uncreated grace as the presence of the Holy Spirit,
a presence which will transform the child, as he grows, into
whatever degree of created grace he is capable of receiving at a
particular age. A baptized child is already 'called' a son of God
(uncreated grace); but whether or not from the moment of
baptism he receives that transformation which makes him 'be'
a son of God (created grace) seems to me uncertain. [39] It seems
possible that, just as a child begins very soon to know and love
its mother in a rudimentary way, so too by virtue of created
grace there can be an inchoate, unarticulated knowledge and
love of God even in a very small child.

*   *   *

In this chapter we have been examining the ways in which
grace is experienced through the Church. A sacrament (when
it is received by one who is capable of understanding) is God's
word addressed in a perceptible form by the Church to a human
being. To hear this word is a normal psychological experience,
but a man can respond to it in grace, by virtue of the grace
already in him. [40] Moreover, each sacrament in a perceptible

---

[38] Cf. p. 68.

[39] Cf. 1 Jn 3.1: 'See what love the Father has given us, that we
should be called children of God; and so we are.'

[40] The purpose of the sacraments of baptism and penance is to confer
habitual grace on those who have never received it or who have
lost it. When an adult is baptized or recovers grace through the
sacrament of penance, one of two things will happen. (1) He will
have already reached a state of grace through faith and charity
before receiving the sacrament, by virtue of what scholastic theologians call a *votum* (desire, explicit or implicit) of the sacrament;

way establishes the Christian in a new visible relationship with the visible Church. This new social reality, like the sacramental ceremony itself, is a visible sign to which the Christian can respond in grace, by virtue of the grace already in him. A sacrament is therefore an experience by which Christ through the Church stimulates in the recipient a growth in habitual grace.

---

it is then open to dispute whether this state of grace granted before the sacrament should be regarded as an anticipatory effect of the sacrament. (2) He is not in a state of grace before receiving the sacrament, but enters this state through the sacramental sign, which helps him to acquire the dispositions necessary for him to receive the sacrament fruitfully. I would conjecture that it is nearly always the first alternative which is true, for he will probably already be an implicit Christian (cf. pp. 132-136).

CHAPTER 8

THE FIRST FRUITS OF THE SPIRIT

In this last chapter I wish to consider the two intensest forms
of the experience of grace: the fulfilment of the second gift in
heaven, and the experience of grace in prayer.

Heaven

The transformation of man after death is a subject to which
St Paul constantly returns. It is most prominent in the Corin-
thian epistles. ' "What no eye has seen, nor ear heard, nor the
heart of man conceived, what God has prepared for those who
love him", God has revealed to us through the Spirit' (1 Cor
2.9-10). At the resurrection of the dead, the body is raised in
glory and power, imperishable and spiritual; 'we shall all be
changed, in a moment, in the twinkling of an eye' (1 Cor. 15.51-2).

> Here indeed we groan, and long to put on our heavenly
> dwelling, so that by putting it on we may not be found
> naked... Not that we would be unclothed, but that we
> would be further clothed, so that what is mortal may be
> swallowed up by life. [1]

St John writes in the same strain in his first epistle:

> Beloved, we are God's children now; it does not yet

---

[1] 2 Cor 5.2-4. For the continuity between this life and the next, cf.
M. Simpson, *Death and Eternal Life* (Mercier, Cork, 1971).

appear what we shall be, but we know that when he
appears we shall be like him, for we shall see him as
he is. [2]

Each of these passages in its own way expresses the belief that
heaven is a second gift: what God has prepared, the change
in the body, the new clothes that we put on, the likeness with
God that comes from seeing him.

The New Testament writers see the beginning of this
second gift already in this world. 'Blessed are the dead who
die in the Lord . . . , for their deeds follow them' (Rev 14.13).
Although, in St Paul's strange mixed metaphor, we put on a
new dwelling in heaven, we do not put it on over nakedness;
the achievements of grace in this life are not first stripped
away. This imagery is in sharp contrast with that of the
Gnostics, for whom a symbolic nakedness is the ideal: in
Gnostic teaching the spirit of man in this life is imprisoned in
hostile matter; heaven is the escape from life in the world, not
the crowning of it. So in the apocryphal Gospel of Thomas,
Jesus, when asked, 'What are your disciples like?', replies:

They are like little children
who dwell in a field which is not theirs.
When the masters of the field come,
they will say, Leave our field to us.
They are naked before their eyes,
as they leave it to them and give them their field. [3]

---

[2] 1 Jn 3.2.

[3] *The Secret Sayings of Jesus,* ed. R.M. Grant (Doubleday, New
York, 1960), [21], pp. 140-141. Cf. [38], p. 152:

His disciples said:
On what day will you appear to us,
and on what day will we see you?
Jesus said:
When you undress yourselves and are not ashamed
and take your clothing
and lay them under your feet,
like little children,
and tread on them;
then [you will become] sons of the Living One
and you will have no fear.

For St Paul, on the other hand, though prophecy, tongues and knowledge pass away, there are some activities of the present which will not be discarded in the future life: we do already see, though dimly; faith, hope and charity will abide in heaven. [4] The Spirit already reveals what God has prepared. [5] Already 'we all with unveiled face, reflecting (or 'beholding') the glory of the Lord, are being changed into his likeness from one degree of glory to another' (2 Cor 3.18). 'We are God's children *now*' (1 Jn 3.2). The second gift, inaugurated in this life, perfected in the next, is the Spirit himself, who is the first fruits, the guarantee, the Spirit of promise. [6]

It follows that this life is both continuous and discontinuous with the life of heaven. Discontinuous: 'we shall all be changed' (1 Cor 15.51); 'here we have no abiding city, but we seek the city which is to come' (Heb 13.14); 'our commonwealth is in heaven, and from it we await a Saviour, the Lord Jesus Christ, who will change our lowly body to be like his glorious body' (Phil 3.20-1). Yet continuous, for we have already received the first fruits. Our eschatology must be both future and proleptic; we receive a foretaste of the future for which we are preparing. For Socrates in the *Phaedo*, [7] a pure life is a constant rehearsal for death; and Ladislaus Boros sees life as the preparation for the final decision which will irrevocably determine a man's eternal state. [8] But it would be truer to say that this life is a rehearsal and a preparation, not so much for death, as for eternal life itself. The New Testament writers often spoke of the next life as a reward; and it was in these terms above all

---

Hippolytus (*Ref.* V.viii.44; GCS p. 97) quotes a gnostic saying that only the spiritual (*pneumatikoi*) can enter the house of God; they must 'throw away their clothes, and all become bridegrooms who have become male through the virgin Spirit.'

[4] 1 Cor 13.8-13.
[5] Cf. 1 Cor 2.9-10.
[6] Cf. Rom 8.23; 2 Cor 1.22; Eph 1.13.
[7] 80E-81A: *meletē thanatou.*
[8] *The Moment of Truth: Mysterium Mortis* (Burns & Oates, London, 2nd ed. 1969), esp. pp. 86-99.

that the nominalist theologians conceived the connection between this life and the next. [9] But though heaven is a reward, it is not an arbitrary one. A life lived in the Spirit is not only the qualification for the reward; the reward itself is already present there in germ. For this reason a Christian is concerned for the quality of human life as much as any humanist; for the degree of a man's glory in heaven is necessarily determined by the level of his development in grace as a person in this life.

This is not to say that there can be no growth in heaven; it may be that even in eternity love cannot reach a limit. Nor is it to deny the possibility after death of purification, of a purgatorial state consisting in the resolution of inconsistencies of character, the integration of the personality round a level of moral achievement already attained at the deepest level of decision, and the straightening out of the distorting habits and effects of sin. But the growth will be the growth of a personality at a level already determined in this life; the purgation will be the crystallization of a character round a centre formed in this life. 'Now is the acceptable time' (2 Cor 6.2).

Old Age and Sickness

Here we are brought up against the problem of old age and sickness. Such experiences can bring a perceptible growth in the personality of the old or the sick; one who has been impatient, inconsiderate and self-centred can blossom in his

---

[9] Cf. Mt 6.4; 2 Tim 4.8. The language of reward or merit becomes Pelagian if it implies that man of his own powers deserves the reward; it becomes nominalist if it implies that the reward is arbitrary, depending on God's 'acceptance' (cf. ch. 5, note 18). John Staupitz sometimes (but not always) took the second view: 'If, then, God decreed to give himself as reward for such works, this is grace and not justice' (from the *Libellus de executione eternae praedestinationis,* Nuremberg, 1517, trans. P. Nyhus, in *Forerunners of the Reformation,* ed. H. Oberman, Lutterworth Press, London, 1967, p. 184). Catholic theology came to hold a middle position: God's grace so transforms man as to endow him with the power to merit, as a matter of justice, (or, as I prefer to put it, the power to grow into the kind of person who can receive) eternal life.

trials, and become a serene, considerate, unselfish man. But only too often it is the opposite which appears to be true. Many will have known the pain of seeing one whom we loved and admired as a humorous and generous person of vigorous mind, becoming through illness permanently testy, indifferent to others, complaining, lethargic. The cause may of course be totally physical; the onset of the sickness can gradually and irretrievably damage the cells of the brain. Now perhaps as we watch our friend's character falling apart, we may seek comfort in the thought that the deterioration is only superficial, that beneath the surface there is a conscious personality that is untouched by these ravages. We may imagine that the real friend we know and love is struggling to force his way out of his involuntary disguise, like Cyril Connolly's thin man trying to get out from the fat man who contains him. We may hope vaguely that, with his old self, he is aware of his new handicaps; that, like a stammerer, he tries, always unsuccessfully, to overcome them, and, if he accepts them without bitterness or self-pity, he is matured and purified by them. But the trouble is that in many cases there is no evidence that there is a 'real' self thinking in this way at all. From the point of view of medical science, in some cases such an intact self cannot exist; the damage to the brain has not just driven the old way of thinking underground; it has made it impossible. The materialist would simply say that, with the destruction of the tissues, there is no other self to survive intact.

I suggest that neither of these views is correct, though the first view is nearer to the truth than the second. On the one hand, we are not entitled to assume that, although the old qualities of mind can no longer find expression, they remain in the sick man's consciousness. For he is not, say, a patient man who is forced despite himself to go through the motions of impatience; he has become an impatient man. On the other hand, a Christian cannot accept that old age and disease are pure loss; indeed these experiences must be, on balance, a gain. For if the ravages of old age and sickness necessarily reduced the personality even at its deepest level, they would make a person less, not more, ready to see God face to face. Such an inescapable degeneration in the moral powers of man would be inconsistent with the fidelity and the wisdom of God.

It seems necessary therefore to conclude that there exists a centre of the personality, traditionally called the soul, which is unharmed and even enriched by the damage to the body and the more superficial layers of the self. In the words of Teilhard de Chardin:

> The great victory of the Creator and Redeemer, in the Christian vision, is to have transformed what is in itself a universal power of diminishment and extinction into an essentially life-giving factor. God must, in some way or other, make room for himself, hollowing us out and emptying us, if he is finally to penetrate into us. [10]

It is true that sometimes the familiar personality is inevitably changed for the worse, not simply masked. The sick man may not retain either internally or externally his old virtues of patience, humour and so on. But the centre of the personality, which, in Teilhard's phrase, is penetrated by God through suffering, is something deeper. This centre, must, however, impinge upon the conscious level in some way, though not necessarily in a form that is recognizable to the observer or even to the sick man himself. [11] Only on such a supposition, it seems, can the diminutions that Teilhard speaks of be fruitful.

I am not, of course, speaking of someone in a complete coma. I am speaking most of all of one who can talk and understand, but is changed in character. But the same considerations apply to one who, though retaining some consciousness, cannot converse, and shows no evidence of understanding,

---

[10] *Le Milieu Divin* (ET Collins, London, 1960), p. 68 (Fontana, pp. 88-89).

[11] The situation is different in Rom 7.15-23 ('... it is no longer I that do it, but sin which dwells in me...'). I have, like St Paul, spoken of a centre of the personality, a 'real me', of which my acts and attitudes are unrepresentative; but St Paul is clearly aware of his inconsistency; the sick man in my discussion is not.

apart perhaps from small gestures with the hands and eyes, and the occasional fragment of speech. In such a one, rightly or wrongly, it seems easier to detect evidence of acceptance than in the querulous patient; the process of 'hollowing out and emptying' may be very near completion.

In this purified centre of the self there is grace — habitual grace realized in actual grace as a dimension of each moral experience, but now in an almost totally hidden way. As St Paul declared in his great hymn of hope: 'In all these things we are more than conquerors through him who loved us. For I am sure that neither death nor life ... nor anything else in all creation', — neither depression nor imbecility, nor senility, nor paralysis — 'will be able to separate us from the love of God in Christ Jesus our Lord' (Rom 8.37-9).

The Religious Life

The Christian is bidden to regard heaven as his city, his commonwealth, his home.[12] 'If then you have been raised with Christ, seek the things that are above, where Christ is, seated at the right hand of God. Set your minds on things that are above, not on things that are on earth' (Col 3.1-2). From the early days there have always been people in the Church who renounced ordinary human values in order to devote themselves to the search for the things that are above. It was such a spirit which encouraged many of the martyrs to accept torture and death. It was the same spirit which, even before the days of persecution had ceased, drove men out from the company of their more earthly-minded fellows into the hermitages and monasteries. This other-worldly spirit, however, is not peculiar to the martyr or the monk; it should be a characteristic of every Christian. But the Church needs individuals who will reveal this other-worldly spirit in a more concentrated and recognizable form, and so constantly remind other Christians of the duty that all have in common, and show to the world where a Christian's

[12] Cf. Heb 13.14; Phil 3.20; Jn 14.2.

real treasure lies. Men and women who take the vows of religious life are committed to giving witness of this way of life.

Yet, although St Paul told the Colossians, 'set your minds on the things that are above', the angel seemed to give the Eleven different advice on Ascension Day: 'Men of Galilee, why do you stand looking into heaven?' (Acts 1.11). And Jesus prayed to his Father: 'As thou didst send me into the world, so I have sent them into the world.' [13] There are, then, two quite distinct emphases in Christian spirituality, one on renunciation and other-worldliness, the other on the duty to transform the world according to Christian values. These are not two alternative types of Christian spirituality; each individual Christian needs to exhibit both aspects, though in some people one aspect will dominate more than the other. Moreover, the renunciation itself will not be effective as a sign of the world to come unless men can see something to admire in it. Not all forms of renunciation, therefore, will serve in this way as an eschatological sign, but only forms which, while rejecting one human value, exhibit another, more precious one. To quote Teilhard again, man

> has not the right to diminish himself for the sake of diminishing himself. Voluntary mutilation, even when conceived as a method of inward liberation, is a crime against being, and Christianity has always explicitly condemned it. [14]

Renunciation which does nothing but violence to human nature is neither for the good of the one who makes the renunciation, nor a sign which can beckon others upwards to heaven.

Prayer

I wish to turn now to the experience of grace in prayer. Certainly it is impossible to pray without grace. 'No one can say "Jesus is Lord" except by the Holy Spirit' (1 Cor 12.3). 'When we cry, "Abba! Father!", it is the Spirit himself bearing

[13] Jn 17.18. Christians should be not 'of the world' but 'sent into the world'.

[14] *Op. cit.,* p. 81 (Fontana, p. 98).

witness with our spirit that we are children of God' (Rom 8.15-16).

Prayer can take many forms. As a child one learns to pray in words which other people have composed; then one learns to pray sometimes in one's own words too. One may find also that singing and the performing of ritual actions can also be ways of lifting up the heart to God. So too can silent consideration be; above all reading and listening to God's word, but also listening to sacred music, watching sacred ceremonies (and, when incense is used, even smelling them), provided always that one does not remain a disinterested spectator, but enters at heart into the movement of the worship.

There is another kind of prayer that ascetical writers speak of, which is commonly described in terms of darkness. St Gregory of Nyssa seems to have been the first to apply to contemplation the images of darkness and cloud, images which he borrowed from the biblical accounts of Moses' experiences in the presence of God on Sinai. [15] Colin McLeod has argued plausibly that the contemplation which Gregory had in mind was the intellectual contemplation of God; for God so far transcends our nature that he is 'separated on all sides by incomprehensibility as by a darkness'. [16] Later writers, on the other hand, apply the image of darkness to certain experiences in prayer. For example, the author of the anonymous fourteenth-century English treatise entitled *The Cloud of Unknowing* tells his reader that, if he can withdraw his desires from created things,

> thou findest but a darkness and as it were a *cloud of unknowing*, thou knowest not what, saving that thou feelest in thy will a naked intent unto God. This darkness and this cloud ... hindereth thee, so that thou mayest neither see him clearly by light of understanding in thy reason, nor feel him in sweetness of love in thine affection. [17]

[15] *Life of Moses,* SC ii.162-9 (Jaeger vii.86-9; PG 44.376-380).
[16] *Ibid.,* ii.163 (PG 377). McLeod: JTS 22(1971) pp. 362-79.
[17] Ed. J. McCann (Burns, Oates and Washbourne, London, 5th ed. 1947), ch. 3.

Two hundred years later in Spain St John of the Cross applied the imagery in a similar way. He spoke in fact of two dark nights, both of which consist in a state in which one seems unable to pray, but in fact one is not only praying, but even experiencing through this apparent inability an advance in prayer. [18] The first night is the night of sense, which is the state of one who gives himself seriously to living a Christian life, practising self-denial and regular mental prayer, but finds that he has lost all the contentment and facility in prayer that he used to enjoy. Now when he tries to pray, no thoughts will come except distractions; joy and contentment are replaced by heaviness and emptiness. It sometimes happens that, although he has an insistent urge to pray, and when he is not formally praying the thought of God comes readily, the moment he tries to enter expressly into prayer, it is as if a fog descended on the mind. [19] This first night has been said to centre round the emotional life of the Christian; the second night, which St John of the Cross calls the night of spirit, reaches down to 'the mind and will, or deepest self, in man'. [20] It is experienced sometimes as a sense of emptiness, a feeling of loss of faith in one for whom this loss is the greatest pain conceivable. Both of these nights are periods of purgation, when the Christian learns to seek God, not for the sake of his consolations, but simply for himself.

But the dark nights are not only purifying experiences to be lived through; they are periods of what the author of the *Cloud* called 'naked intent unto God'; that is to say, of naked prayer. We were considering earlier how prayer can take a variety of forms. These different forms of prayer are not so much the various species of a common genus of prayer; they are rather different forms in which a common element is cast. Under the

---

[18] See *The Dark Night of the Soul* in *The Complete Work of St John of the Cross,* trans. and ed. E. Allison Peers, vol. i (Burns, Oates & Washbourne, London, 2nd ed. 1953).

[19] 'This darkness and this cloud ... is betwixt thee and thy God, and hindereth thee.' (*Cloud,* ch. 3).

[20] J. Dalrymple, *The Theology of the Spiritual Life* (Mercier, Cork, 1970), p. 85.

guise of different forms of activity, there is a single basic operation going on, which is the raising up of the mind and heart
to God, [21] the children of God crying 'Abba! Father!', the
Spirit coming to our aid in our weakness and praying with
sighs too deep for words. [22] In the dark nights, however, the
palpable forms are absent, or scarcely present; deep calls to the
deep. [23] C.H. Dodd says of the verse from Romans just referred
to, 'This inarticulate aspiration is the deepest form of prayer,
and it is itself the work of the Spirit within.' [24] St John of the
Cross explains the second night by referring to pseudo-
Dionysius:

> ... when this Divine light of contemplation assails the
> soul which is not yet wholly enlightened, it causes spiritual
> darkness in it; for not only does it overcome it, but like-
> wise it overwhelms it and darkens that act of its natural
> intelligence. For this reason Saint Dionysius and other
> mystical theologians call this infused contemplation a ray
> of darkness — that is to say, for the soul that is not
> enlightened and purged — for the natural strength of the
> intellect is transcended and overwhelmed by its great
> supernatural light. [25]

In such experiences of the dark nights of prayer, according
to the theory I have been putting forward in these pages, grace
is felt as a dimension of our experience; but as the familiar psychological faculties play very little part in this dark prayer, the
experience is not easily recognized. There seem in fact to be
three possible ways in which the experience of grace in the
prayer of darkness can be explained: first, the natural faculties
are still operative, though very faintly, and grace is perceptible
equally faintly only as a transcendental dimension of them;

---

[21] This is the definition of prayer given in *A Catechism of Christian
Doctrine* (Catholic Truth Society, London, revised ed. 1971), qu.
141: but it has a much longer pedigree.

[22] Cf. Rom 8.15, 26.

[23] Cf. Ps 42.7.

[24] *The Epistle of Paul to the Romans* (Collins, Fontana, London and
Glasgow, 1959), p. 150, on Rom 8.26.

[25] *The Dark Night of the Soul*, II.v.3.

N

second, that what we experience is only a psychological by-product of an operation which is essentially imperceptible, namely the movement of the self in its habitual grace towards the source of grace; third, that such prayer is not an actual grace issuing from habitual grace, but is an extraordinary grace, a word spoken by God coming from outside, and bringing with it the faint psychological experience which has been described as darkness.

Of these three possibilities, it seems that the second can be eliminated at once. For, since habitual grace is the capacity to know and love God, actual graces cannot be imperceptible; acts of knowledge and love can be unarticulated and unrecognized, but they cannot be totally hidden. Such a view would imply a Platonic conception of man: the real self is seen as the spiritual soul, to which the bodily and lower psychological functions are an irrelevance or a hindrance.

The term 'infused contemplation' which St John of the Cross applies to the both dark nights [26] seems to support the third hypothesis, namely that such prayer is a gift coming directly from God, and not the consequence of habitual grace. Some writers, in fact, like A. Poulain, [27] make such a clear-cut division between mystical and ordinary prayer as to imply that ordinary prayer does not contain 'the least germ of the mystic state'. Both ordinary prayer and mystical prayer, he admits, are supernatural; but while ordinary prayer, though supernatural, is always at our disposal, because the grace is never refused, we cannot produce mystical prayer, Poulain maintains, by our own choice even 'in a *low degree or momentarily*'. [28] Thus St Teresa of Avila reserves to this form of prayer the term 'supernatural'; [29] and the editor of Abbot Chapman's *Spiritual Letters* echoes the

[26] *Ibid.*, I.x.6; II.v.3.
[27] A. Poulain, *The Graces of Interior Prayer* (ET Routledge & Kegan Paul, London, 1950), p. 213.
[28] *Ibid.*, p. 2.
[29] Relation V, *Complete Works*, trans. and ed. E. Allison Peers (Sheed & Ward, London, 1946), vol. i, p. 327.

same idea when he defines the highest stages of prayer as ' "extraordinary", and only to be reached by means of a special grace from God unobtainable by any human efforts'. [30] In other words, if ordinary prayer is part of the second gift, mystical prayer is a third.

Dr Urs von Balthasar, on the other hand, while agreeing that the ways of the dark nights 'depend on vocation and a special mission', maintains that 'fundamentally' it is 'grace as election, calling, justification by God the Father' (what I have called 'habitual grace') which makes us capable of any form of prayer. [31] On this view, mystical prayer seems to be an actual grace springing from the particular form of habitual grace with which God chooses to endow certain members of Christ's body. This explanation has the advantage that it allots more importance to the transforming power of the grace by which all Christians become adopted children of God through the Spirit who prays within them. On the other hand, to maintain, as some writers do, that the prayer of the contemplative differs only in degree from ordinary Christian prayer does not allow sufficiently for the fact that as experiences, at least, they are poles apart. To maintain that a few prayers repeated by heart in the last weary moments of a busy day are, as experiences, the same sort of thing as St John of the Cross's 'living flame of love' is to turn one's back on the facts. Perhaps the only safe course is to assert both aspects of the truth, as Professor David Knowles does in consecutive sentences in his book *What is Mysticism?* [32] First, that

> the mystical way differs in degree and in kind from the common life of Christian practice, and . . . the raising of a soul from one to the other is an uncovenanted gift of God.

[30] *Spiritual Letters of Dom John Chapman, O.S.B.,* ed. R. Huddleston (Sheed & Ward, London, 1944), p. 328 note.

[31] H. U. von Balthasar, *Prayer* (ET G. Chapman, London, 1961), pp. 113, 42.

[32] Burns & Oates, London, 1967, pp. 44-45. The first sentence quoted ends one chapter, the second begins the next.

Secondly,

> In these pages the mystical life has been presented as a
> full expansion of the Christian life of grace... Its goal
> is the goal of all serious Christian endeavour, that is, the
> love of God without measure, the perfect fulfilment of
> the commands of Christ, and of the spirit, at least, of his
> counsels, and the union of will with him.

Knowles resolves the paradox by appealing to God's freedom
in making his gifts. 'God has willed this variety, this inequality,
from all eternity, though we know not why he has willed it.'
The Spirit blows where he wills. In other words, the 'infused'
contemplation of the mystic and the snatched prayers of the
man immersed in the cares of his work and his family are both
the flowering of habitual grace.

This fits in with the first of the three hypotheses I listed:
mystical prayer is the fruit of habitual grace; in it actual grace
is felt as a transcendental underneath psychological activity.
But what is the psychological activity in the prayer of darkness?
If grace is the power to know and love God, it seems that there
must be an element of knowledge of God in the prayer, even
though this knowledge is obscure and inarticulate. The existence
of love is easier to maintain, as writers often speak of a deep
desire of God as the most positive element in such prayer. And
at least we can point to the sheer slog of it, the trust and the
faith involved: at least under these humdrum experiences the
knowledge and love of God lurk as a transcendental.

If this first hypothesis is correct, the habitual capacity for
mystical prayer, i.e. for knowing and loving God in the way
peculiar to the mystics, derives from habitual grace. But to say
this is not to deny that God sometimes may, by an extraordinary
grace, speak to this capacity of the mystic, so that his contemplation ceases to be dark. On to these highest levels of Mount
Carmel, however, I shall not intrude.

But in the 'naked entry unto God' the knowledge and love
of God are so unarticulated that they are often unrecognized.
The Christian who experiences such dark prayer for the first

time is almost certain to think that he is not praying at all, however much he may have read about it. The good unbeliever, whom I have called the implicit Christian, also shares a dark (because unrecognized) experience of God; [33] and it is perhaps at the same inarticulate level that the sick man preserves his integrity despite the dissolution of the more superficial levels of his character. Mystical writers have given a variety of names to this core of the personality where sighs are too deep for words: for Proclus it is the 'flower of the soul', [34] for St Augustine the 'spirit of the mind', [35] for St Teresa the 'interior castle', [36] and for other writers the 'fine point of the soul'. [37]

Mystical and Charismatic Phenomena

Even so short a treatment of mystical experience as this one must pay some attention to the more palpable forms of mystical phenomena. They range from 'the delicate sense of the divine presence' that St Francis of Sales [38] speaks of, to levitations, visions, voices, the gift of tongues, the stigmata, and even, according to St John of the Cross, 'dislocation of the bones'. [39] Are we to regard them as experiences of grace?

According to the great mystics there is only one answer to be given: external phenomena are unimportant, irrelevant, even an obstacle to the true mystical grace. In the *Ascent of Mount Carmel*, [40] St John of the Cross speaks of visions of saints and

---

[33] See pp. 133-6.

[34] *In Alcib.*, (ed. Cousin, col. 519.37).

[35] *De Trin.*, xiv.16 (CC 50A.451-3; PL 42.1053), quoting Eph 4.23.

[36] Or rather, the 'chiefest mansion' in the centre of the castle, 'where the most secret things pass between God and the soul'. (*Interior Castle, Works*, ed. Peers, vol. ii, p. 202).

[37] *Fine pointe de l'âme, acies mentis, acumen mentis*. Cf. L. Reypens, 'Ame', *Dict. Spir.*, i.443. The term originally seems to mean the 'eye' rather than the 'point' of the soul.

[38] *Treatise on the Love of God* (ET Burns & Oates, London, 1884), VI.viii. 255.

[39] *Dark Night*, II.i.2.

[40] *Works*, (ed. Peers, vol. i), II.xi.1.

angels, of 'certain lights and brightnesses of an extraordinary
kind'; words may be heard, sometimes spoken by a visible
figure; there may be a sweet scent or taste; 'and as to the touch
they experience great delight — sometimes to such a degree
that it is as though all the bones and the marrow rejoice and
sing [*literally* 'blossom'] and are bathed in delight.' St John
simply shows no interest in the origin of these phenomena; his
advice is practical:

> Although all these things may happen to the bodily senses
> in the way of God, we must never rely upon them or accept
> them, but must always fly from them, without trying to
> ascertain whether they be good or evil; for, the more
> completely exterior and corporeal they are, the less
> certainly are they of God. For it is more proper and
> habitual to God to communicate himself to the spirit,
> wherein there is more security and profit for the soul,
> than to sense, wherein there is ordinarily much danger
> and deception. . . For the bodily sense is as ignorant of
> spiritual things as is a beast of rational things, and even
> more so. [41]

St John of the Cross is speaking here of 'spiritual persons',
that is, people so far advanced in prayer as to be in the second
night of the soul. However, one might perhaps give a different
verdict with regard to extraordinary manifestations in the prayer
of the less advanced; I am thinking above all of the gift of
tongues in prayer of the Pentecostal type. The excessive emphasis
which the Pentecostal tradition has tended to place on this
extraordinary phenomenon is avoided in some recent treatments
of the subject by Roman Catholic writers, like Simon Tugwell, [42]
who maintain that the gift of tongues cannot be described as
'baptism in the Spirit' without doing violence to the New

[41] *Ibid.*, II.xi.2. This is one of the chief differences between Christian
mysticism and nature- or drug-mysticism. Christian mysticism is
never simply a search for an experience. R.C. Zaehner discusses the
question in many of his works; e.g., *Mysticism Sacred and Profane*
(Clarendon Press, Oxford, 1957).

[42] 'Reflections on "Baptism in the Spirit": I', *Heythrop Journal*, 13
(1972), pp. 268-281.

Testament, and risking the devaluation of the sacraments of baptism and confirmation, which together form the essential source of the Spirit for Christians. The Spirit can be given without tongues; what the gift of tongues can do is to provide an assurance of the gift of the Spirit, and a palpable form of shared prayer. This form of prayer appears particularly helpful to some who are emotionally disturbed, or trying to overcome some habit like drug-taking; this is not of course to deny that balanced people also find help in it. [43] Experiences and judgments vary: some find that speaking in tongues is on each occasion a gift apparently from outside; others find it a releasing and joyous form of prayer that they can sometimes adopt at will. Perhaps one might suggest that the gift of tongues can be a means by which, as by a sacramental sign, God gives grace; the experience of the sign is the cause of the growth in habitual grace. Whether the phenomenon is an extraordinary gift coming directly from God I shall not attempt to decide; according to one view held within the movement, the gift can be the fulfilment of the Spirit already given [44] — which is to say that it is the manifestation of habitual grace.

It seems to be true that an intense religious experience can naturally and genuinely express itself in the senses of the body, and tends to do so in the bodily form which one expects. In the sixteenth century religious experience led frequently to the gift of tears, because that is what was expected; in the eighteenth and nineteenth centuries to the deeply-felt experience of conversion, often with the physical accompaniments mentioned in the fifth chapter: [45] in certain cultures a religious crisis can

---

[43] Michael Ivens says of the Catholic Pentecostal Movement that it 'has borne fruit in a vigorous sense of human community. It has enabled people to find deep peace in a disturbed world and an untidy Church. It has restored to many the true sense of their married, priestly or religious vocation.' ('The Dimensions of Group Prayer', *The Way*, Suppl. 16, 1972, p. 74). There are, of course, other forms of group prayer, which can be helpful to those who would not feel at ease in prayer of the charismatic type.

[44] Cf. S. Tugwell, *op. cit.*, and 'Reflections on "Baptism in the Spirit": II', *Heythrop Journal*, 13 (1972), p. 407.

[45] p. 108.

result in visions and the hearing of voices. All these phenomena can be projected apparently from a genuinely religious internal experience, and presumably God can turn them to means of further grace.

Private Revelations

There is another class of representation which can accompany a mystical experience and which may be caused directly by God — the experience which is called a private revelation. The feature of such a revelation is that the visionary appears to be entrusted by God with a mission or message for the good of the people or the Church, like St Joan of Arc, St Margaret Mary Alacoque, with her visions of the Sacred Heart of Jesus, and St Bernadette Soubirous, who saw the Blessed Virgin Mary. Even if the mission these saints received was given them by God, it is possible, even likely, that their experience was fundamentally more internal, less visible or audible, than the form in which they describe it, and that the vision and the words which they relate are the articulation of the internal manifestation into the terms of the saint's own familiar ways of thinking and imagining. It may even sometimes be true that, just as dreams fade so quickly that what we remember is our memory or account of the dream rather than the dream itself, so too what remains impressed on the memory of the visionary is their interpretation of the experience rather than the experience itself. So St Bernadette reported the Virgin's words in a form which confused the abstract with the concrete: 'I am the Immaculate Conception'; [46] and frequently when mystics

[46] Bernadette, however, insisted that she had never heard the words before and did not understand them: cf. R. Laurentin, B. Billet and P. Galland, *Lourdes. Documents Authentiques*, tome vi (Lethielleux, Paris, 1961), p. 143 (the saint's *relation* to the Bishop of Tarbes in December 1860). The apparitions took place in 1858; the dogma of the Immaculate Conception was defined in 1854. It seems likely that Bernadette had heard the term mentioned in a sermon or conversation, even though by 1858 she no longer had any recollection of it.

try to describe their experience they begin with the warning that the experience was indescribable.

*   *   *

All of this discussion of mysticism will perhaps have seemed a wrong-headed attempt to analyse in dead categories the most intense activity of the human spirit. The reason for attempting it was to investigate the extent to which even this 'living flame of love' is the fullest flowering of the grace of sonship which every Christian shares through baptism. Each 'divine touch' (to use Ruysbroeck's term) is an occasion when the mystic is aware of grace as a dimension of the faint or intense experience we have been considering; but the same awareness underlies, though more obscurely, each attempt to pray by the most harried and unmystical of God's people. It is not for anyone to say whether the rapt love of the contemplative is greater than the courageous love of the martyr or the enduring love of one whose whole life is a sacrifice. The ways of God are inscrutable, and mystical prayer has never been considered a necessary qualification for the canonization of a saint. But the mystic experiences the intensest love; and with St Paul's description of the experience I shall end:

> I know a man in Christ who fourteen years ago was caught up to the third heaven — whether in the body or out of the body I do not know, God knows. And I know that this man was caught up into Paradise — whether in the body or out of the body I do not know, God knows — and he heard things that cannot be told, which man may not utter. [47]

[47] 2 Cor 12.2-4.

CONCLUSION

One of the reasons which led me to attempt this investigation was the suspicion that many people speak about grace with only the vaguest idea of what it is. It is often conceived as a help God gives us to do what otherwise we would find impossible or difficult; but it appeared to me that people had no conception at all of the form that help takes. I have tried, therefore, in this book to work out a systematic answer to the questions 'What is grace?' and 'How does it impinge upon our experience?' It may be helpful to the reader if I now provide a summary of my argument.

The sign-post that I chose to follow I found in Athanasius, that grace is God's second gift, creation being the first: and I tried to follow where that sign pointed through the two Testaments and the Fathers. The second gift is expressed in the Old Testament mainly as God's choice of a people from all the peoples of the earth; in the New Testament this idea is centred on the Incarnation, death and resurrection of God's Son, which enable men to be reborn as sons, to be renewed, to rise again, to share the divine nature, to live in Christ, to be members of his Body, temples of his Spirit, to be reconciled to the Father and to gain eternal life; the Fathers add the concepts of divinisation and the image of God. I went on to examine different models that later theologians employed to express the same truth: the supernatural, the covenant and evolution.

In the third chapter I tried to establish three principles on which the rest of the investigation into the second gift would

be based. The first principle was that the second gift is not
only the presence of the Holy Spirit, but is his transforming
presence; we become children of God, and are not merely
called so; this new creation that the Spirit works in us I called
by the traditional name of created grace. Secondly, created
grace does not identify us with God, but it is not to be regarded
either as a thing imparted to us: rather it is a permanent
relationship with the Trinity consisting of the power to know
and love God. Thirdly, I made use of the traditional distinction
between habitual and actual grace, taking habitual grace to be
the disposition to know and love God, and actual grace to be
the realization of that disposition for a particular act of knowledge and love at a particular moment of time.

This brought us to the question of the experience of grace.
For grace must be related to experience; otherwise grace is
irrelevant to this life, and this life irrelevant to the union with
God in heaven. Grace is in fact related to experience precisely
because it is a capacity to know and love God: and it is man's
capacity to know and love created objects which makes him
capable of receiving this second gift of the capacity to know
and love God. I suggested that this second gift can be related
to experience at the three levels of habitual, actual and extraordinary grace. Habitual grace, being a disposition, is not itself
experienced. Actual grace, the particular realization of habitual
grace, we experience not only in explicit acts of knowledge and
love of God, but implicitly, as a transcendental, as a dimension
underlying all our moral activity. Extraordinary grace is an
interruption in the smooth continuity of that self-communication
of God which leads to created grace; such grace is recognized
as a miracle of grace when a person reveals a goodness which
is dramatically discontinuous with his previous spiritual
development.

In the remaining chapters I considered particular examples
of these experiences of grace. I first examined Jesus' own
experience of grace, which must be comparable with ours, as
it is the source of ours. In particular I suggested that his

experience of actual grace contributed to his growing awareness
of his divine relationship with his Father and of his mission.

Next I turned to the redemptive aspect of grace in Chapter
Five. Grace is first received as conversion at least from original
sin. This first grace, the beginning of habitual grace, can be
called an extraordinary grace, as there is nothing in man to
prepare for it. The habitual grace of reconciliation with God
can be totally lost through sin, in which case it can be restored
only as an extraordinary grace. By lesser sin the habitual capacity
to relate with God is weakened, but it still remains and is
realized in every truly reconciling act in our lives.

In the next chapter I tried to show that revelation can be
explained without postulating extraordinary graces to enlighten
the biblical authors by some form of infusion of ideas. I
suggested that biblical inspiration is an actual grace, a realization
of the author's habitual grace, which leads him to interpret
the religious traditions of his society in his own way, and to
hand on this interpretation to posterity.

The sacraments I conceived in Chapter Seven as essentially
signs by which Christ promises his help to the Christian
through the Church; the recipient, by virtue of habitual grace,
the dynamic presence of the Holy Spirit transforming him,
responds to the sign in actual grace, so that his habitual relationship with God and his particular relationship with Christ
in his Church are deepened.

In Chapter Eight I considered habitual grace as the first-
fruits, the inchoate form, of the glory of heaven. The gift of
mystical prayer, I suggested, is a privileged form of the habitual
grace by which all true followers of Christ are enabled to know
and love God; the 'divine touches' by which God communicates
with the mystic may be extraordinary graces, but the mystic's
power to receive this communication consists simply of his
habitual grace.

The key to the whole of this account has been habitual grace.
The particular movements of actual grace are not disconnected

episodes in my relationship with God, still less are they experiences injected into me from outside myself. They are the
expressions of myself, which is a self transformed and reborn
by the life of Christ which has become my life through the
gift of his Spirit. 'It is no longer I who live, but Christ who
lives in me' (Gal 2.20).

BIBLIOGRAPHY

The following are the modern works to which I have referred in the text and notes of this book:

Anglican/Roman Catholic International Commission, *An Agreed Statement on Eucharistic Doctrine*. SPCK, London, 1972.

Anon., *A Catechism of Christian Doctrine*. Catholic Truth Society, London, revised ed., 1971.

J. Ashton, 'Theological Trends: The Consciousness of Christ'. *The Way*, 10 (1970) pp. 59-71, 147-157, 250-259.
— 'The Imitation of Christ'. *The Way*, Suppl. 16 (1972) pp. 28-45.

M. Argyle, *The Psychology of Interpersonal Behaviour*. Penguin Books, Harmondsworth, 1967.

J. Aulén, (ET) *Christus Victor*. SPCK, London, 1965.

J.L. Austin, *How to do Things with Words*. Clarendon Press, Oxford, 1962.

H.U. von Balthasar, (ET) *Prayer*. G. Chapman, London, 1961; SPCK, London, 1973.

L.W. Barnard, *Justin Martyr, His Life and Thought*. CUP, Cambridge, 1967.

K. Barth, (ET) *Church Dogmatics*. T. and T. Clark, Edinburgh, 1936-69.

C. Bigg, *The Christian Platonists of Alexandria*. Clarendon Press, Oxford, 1913.

J. Bligh, *Galatians*, St Paul Publications, Slough, 1969.

D. Bonhoeffer, (ET) *The Cost of Discipleship*. SCM, London, 1964.

L. Boros, (ET) *The Moment of Truth: Mysterium Mortis*. Burns and Oates, London, 2nd ed., 1969.

J.B. Bossuet, *Oeuvres Oratoires*, ed. J. Lebarq. Hachette, Paris, 1890-1921.

J.T. Burtchaell, *Catholic Theories of Biblical Inspiration since 1810*. CUP, Cambridge, 1969.

R. Butterworth, 'A New Edition of Theophilus of Antioch'. *Heythrop Journal*, 12 (1971) pp. 425-430.

O. Casel, (ET) *The Mystery of Christian Worship*. Newman Press, Westminster and Darton, Longman and Todd, London, 1962.

H. Chadwick, 'Philo and the Beginnings of Christian Thought'. *The Cambridge History of Later Greek and Early Medieval Philosophy* (ed. A.H. Armstrong). CUP, Cambridge, 1967.

J. Chapman, *The Spiritual Letters of Dom John Chapman, O.S.B.*, ed. R. Huddleston. Sheed and Ward, London, 1944.

R.E. Clements, *Abraham and David*. SCM, London, 1967.

R.G. Collingwood, *The Idea of History*. Clarendon Press, Oxford, 1946.

F.C. Copleston, *A History of Philosophy*, vol. 1. Burns and Oates, London, 1946.

E. Coreth, (ET) *Metaphysics*. Herder and Herder, New York, 1968.

A. Cowley, *Aramaic Papyri of the Fifth Century B.C.* Clarendon Press, Oxford, 1923.

F.L. Cross (ed.), *Athanasius de Incarnatione: an Edition of the Greek Text*. SPCK, London, 1939.

R. Cudworth, *A Sermon Preached before the Honourable the House of Commons on March 31st 1647*. Rivingtons, London, 1812.

J. Dalrymple, *The Theology of the Spiritual Life*. Mercier, Cork, 1970.

W.D. Davies, *Paul and Rabbinic Judaism*. SPCK, London, 2nd ed., 1955.

C. Davis, *Liturgy and Doctrine*. Sheed and Ward, London, 1960.

F.W. Dillistone, *The Christian Understanding of Atonement*. James Nisbet, Welwyn, 1968.

C.H. Dodd, *The Epistle of Paul to the Romans*. Collins, Fontana, London and Glasgow, 1959.

A. Dulles, *A History of Apologetics*. Hutchinson, London and Corpus, New York, 1971.

C. Ernst, *St Thomas Aquinas: Summa Theologiae*, vol. 30, *The Gospel of Grace*. Eyre and Spottiswood, London and McGraw-Hill, New York, 1972.

R.F. Evans, *Pelagius: Inquiries and Reappraisals*. A. and C. Black, London, 1968.

P. Fransen, (ET) *The New Life of Grace*. G. Chapman, London, 1969.

J.B. Franzelin, *De Divina Traditione et Scriptura*. Typographia Polyglotta, S.C. de Prop. Fide, Rome, 3rd ed., 1882.

C. Gore, *Belief in Christ*. John Murray, London, 1922.
— *Dissertations on Subjects Connected with the Incarnation*. John Murray, London, 2nd ed., 1896.
— *The Incarnation of the Son of God*. John Murray, London, 1891.

R.M. Grant, *Theophilus of Antioch ad Autolycum*. Clarendon Press, Oxford, 1970.
— (ed.), *The Secret Sayings of Jesus*. Doubleday, New York, 1960.

A. Grillmeier, *Christ in Christian Tradition*. Mowbray, London, 1965.

A. von Harnack, (ET) *History of Dogma*. Williams and Norgate, London, 1894-9.

E. Hillman, *The Wider Ecumenism*. Burns and Oates, London, 1968.

G.J. Hughes, 'A Christian Basis for Ethics'. *Heythrop Journal,* 13 (1972) pp. 27-43.

A. Hulsbosch, (ET) *God's Creation*. Sheed and Ward, London, 1965.

M. Ivens, 'The Dimensions of Group Prayer'. *The Way,* Suppl. 16 (1972) pp. 67-79.

W. James, *The Varieties of Religious Experience*. Longmans Green, London, 1st ed., 1902.

J.N.D. Kelly, *Early Christian Doctrines*. A. and C. Black, London, 4th ed., 1968.

J.P. Kenny, *The Supernatural*. Alba House, Staten Island, 1972.

J. Kirchmeyer, 'Grecque (Eglise)'. *Dictionnaire de Spiritualité,* vol. 6, coll. 813-822.

M.D. Knowles, *What is Mysticism?* Burns and Oates, London, 1967.

M.J. Lagrange, (ET) *Historical Criticism and the Old Testament*. Catholic Truth Society, London, 1905.

R. Laurentin, B. Billet and P. Galland, *Lourdes, Documents Authentiques,* vol. vi. Lethielleux, Paris, 1961.

B. Leeming, *Principles of Sacramental Theology*. Longmans, London and Newman Press, Westminster, 2nd ed., 1960.

C.S. Lewis, *Mere Christianity*. Fontana, Collins, London, 1955.

H.P. Liddon, *The Divinity of Our Lord and Saviour Jesus Christ*. Longmans Green, London, 14th ed., 1890.

S.R.C. Lilla, *Clement of Alexandria*. OUP, London, 1971.

B. Lonergan, *Collection*. Darton, Longman and Todd, London, 1967.

H. de Lubac, (ET) *Augustinianism and Modern Theology*. G. Chapman, London, 1969.

— (ET) *The Mystery of the Supernatural*. G. Chapman, London, 1967.

— *Surnaturel*. Aubier, Paris, 1946.

S. Lyonnet and L. Sebourin, *Sin, Redemption and Sacrifice*. Analecta Biblica 48, Biblical Institute Press, Rome, 1970.

J. McCann (ed.), *The Cloud of Unknowing*. Burns Oates and Washbourne, London, 5th ed., 1947.

D.J. McCarthy, 'Personality, Society and Inspiration'. *Theological Studies,* 24 (1963) pp. 553-576.

J.L. McKenzie, *Myths and Realities: Studies in Biblical Theology*. G. Chapman, London and Bruce, Milwaukee, 1963.

J.P. Mackey, *Life and Grace*. Gill, Dublin, 1966.

C. McLeod, *Allegory and Mysticism in Origen and Gregory of Nyssa*. JTS 22 (1971) pp. 362-79.

H. du Manoir, *Maria,* vol. 3. Beauchesne, Paris, 1954.

o

J. Maréchal, *Le Point de Départ de la Métaphysique*. Museum Lessianum, Louvain and F. Alcan, Paris, 1st ed., 1922-6.

E.L. Mascall, *Christ, the Christian and the Church*. Longmans Green, London, 1946.
— *The Openness of Being, Natural Theology Today*. Darton, Longman and Todd, London, 1971.
— *Via Media*. Longmans Green, London, 1956.

E. Mersch, *La Théologie du Corps Mystique*. Desclée de Brouwer, Paris and L'Edition Universelle, Brussels, 1946.

J. Meyendorff, (ET) *A Study of Gregory Palamas*. Faith Press, London, 1964.

C. Moeller and G. Philips, (ET) *The Theology of Grace and the Ecumenical Movement*. Mowbray, London, 1961; St Anthony Guild Press, Paterson N.J., 1969.

C.F. Mooney, *Teilhard de Chardin and the Mystery of Christ*. Collins, London, 1966.

G. Moran, *Theology of Revelation*. Burns and Oates, London, 1966.

I. Murdoch, *The Sovereignty of Good Over Other Concepts*. CUP, Cambridge, 1967.
— *The Sovereignty of Good*. Routledge and Kegan Paul, London, 1970.

H. Musurillo (ed.), *The Acts of the Christian Martyrs*. Clarendon Press, Oxford, 1972.

J.H. Newman, *The Arians of the Fourth Century,* Pickering, London, 4th ed., 1876.

D.E. Nineham, 'The Use of the Bible in Modern Theology'. *John Rylands Bulletin,* 52 (1969) pp. 178-199.

R.A. Norris, *Manhood and Christ*. Clarendon Press, Oxford, 1963.

H. Oberman, *Forerunners of the Reformation*. Lutterworth Press, London, 1967.
— *The Harvest of Medieval Theology*. Harvard University Press, Cambridge, Mass., 1963.

J. Oman, *The Natural and the Supernatural*. CUP, Cambridge, 1931.

A.R. Peacocke, *Science and the Christian Experiment*. OUP, London, 1971.

E. Allison Peers (ed.), *The Complete Works of St John of the Cross*. Burns, Oates and Washbourne, London, 2nd ed., 1953.
— (ed.), *St Teresa, Complete Works*. Sheed and Ward, London, 1946.

A. Poulain, (ET) *The Graces of Interior Prayer*. Routledge and Kegan Paul, London, 1950.

G.L. Prestige, *Fathers and Heretics*. SPCK, London, 1940.

H. Rahner, (ET) 'The Beginnings of the Devotion [to the Sacred

Heart] in Patristic Times'. *Heart of the Saviour* (ed. J. Stierli). Nelson, Edinburgh and London and Herder and Herder, New York, 1958.

K.   Rahner, (ET) 'Christianity and the Non-Christian Religions'. *Theological Investigations,* vol. 5, Darton Longman and Todd, London and Helicon, Baltimore, 1966.
— (ET) *The Church and the Sacraments,* Herder, Freiburg and Nelson, Edinburgh and London, 1963.
— (ET) 'Dogmatic Reflections on the Knowledge and Self-Consciousness of Christ'. *Theological Investigations,* vol. 5, 1966.
— (ET) *Inspiration in the Bible.* Herder, Freiburg and Nelson, Edinburgh and London, 1961.
— '100 Jahre Unfehlbarkeitsdogma'. *Stimmen der Zeit,* July 1970.
— (ET) 'Membership of the Church according to the teaching of Pius XII's Encyclical "Mystici Corporis Christi" '. *Theological Investigations,* vol. 2, 1963.
— (ET) *Nature and Grace.* Sheed and Ward, London, 1963. (Also included in *Theological Investigations,* vol. 4, 1966.)
— (ET) 'Revelation: I B. Theological Interpretation'. *Sacramentum Mundi,* Burns and Oates, London and Herder and Herder, New York, 1970.
— (ET) 'Reflections on the Experience of Grace'. *Theological Investigations,* vol. 3, 1967.
— (ET) 'Some Implications of the Scholastic Concept of Uncreated Grace'. *Theological Investigations,* vol. 1, 1961.
— (ET) *The Trinity.* Burns and Oates, London and Herder and Herder, New York, 1970.
— (ET) 'The Word and the Eucharist'. *Theological Investigations,* vol. 4, 1966.

A.M. Ramsey, *From Gore to Temple.* Longmans, London, 1960.

I.T. Ramsey, *Models and Mystery.* OUP, London, 1964.
— (ed.), *Words about God.* SCM, London, 1971.

L. Reypens, 'Ame'. *Dictionnaire de Spiritualité,* vol. 1, coll. 433-469.

L. Richard, (ET) *The Mystery of the Redemption.* Helicon Press, Baltimore, 1965.

J.A.T. Robinson, *The Body.* SCM, London, 1952.

H. Rondet, (ET) *The Grace of Christ.* Newman Press, Westminster, 1967.

I.F. Sagüés, 'De Deo Creante et Elevante'. *Sacrae Theologiae Summa,* vol. 2, Biblioteca de Autores Cristianos, Madrid, 1958.

E. Schillebeeckx, (ET) *Christ the Sacrament.* Sheed and Ward, London, 1963.

P. Schoonenberg, (ET) *The Christ.* Sheed and Ward, London, 1972.
— (ET) *Covenant and Creation.* Sheed and Ward, London, 1968.

E. Schweizer, (ET) 'Sōma'. *Theological Dictionary of the New Testament* (ed. G. Kittel, G. Friedrich, G.W. Bromiley), vol. 7, W.B. Eerdmans, Grand Rapids, 1971.

J.J. Scullion, *The Theology of Inspiration*. Mercier Press, Cork, 1971.

O. Semmelroth, (ET) *Church and Sacrament*. Gill, Dublin, 1965.

M. Simpson, *Death and Eternal Life*. Mercier, Cork, 1971.

A. Solignac, 'Image et Ressemblance'. *Dictionnaire de Spiritualité*, vol. 7, coll. 1406-1425.

W.B. Stanford and R.B. McDowell, *Mahaffy: A Biography of an Irishman*. Routledge and Kegan Paul, London, 1971.

J. Stierli, (ET) 'Devotion to the Sacred Heart from the end of patristic times down to St Margaret Mary'. *Heart of the Saviour* (ed. Stierli), Nelson, Edinburgh and London and Herder and Herder, New York, 1958.

M. de la Taille, 'Actuation Créée par Acte Incréé'. *Recherches de Science Religieuse*, 18 (1928) pp. 253-268.

P. Teilhard de Chardin, (ET) *Christianity and Evolution*. Collins, London, 1971.
— (ET) *The Future of Man*. Collins, London, 1964.
— (ET) *Le Milieu Divin*. Collins, London, 1960; Fontana, London, 1964.
— (ET) *The Phenomenon of Man*. Collins, London, 1959.

H. Thurston, 'Anima Christi'. *Dictionnaire de Spiritualité*, vol. 1, coll. 670-672.

E.J. Tinsley, *The Imitation of God in Christ*. SCM, London, 1960.

S. Tugwell, 'Reflections on the Pentecostal Doctrine of "Baptism in the Holy Spirit"'. *Heythrop Journal*, 13 (1972) pp. 268-281, 402-414.

G. Tyrrell, *Christianity at the Crossroads*. Longmans Green, London, 1909.

E. Waugh, *A Little Learning: the First Volume of an Autobiography*. Chapman and Hall, London, 1964.

E.J. Yarnold, *The Awe-Inspiring Rites of Initiation: Baptismal Homilies of the Fourth Century*. St Paul Publications, Slough, 1972.
— 'Baptism and the Pagan Mysteries in the Fourth Century'. *Heythrop Journal*, 13 (1972) pp. 247-267.
— 'The Charism of Providential Teaching'. *The Month*, November 1971, pp. 131-141.
— *The Theology of Original Sin*. Mercier, Cork, 1971.

R.C. Zaehner, *Mysticism Sacred and Profane*. Clarendon Press, Oxford, 1957.

Two other works deserve mention, though they were published after this book had gone to the press:

C. Ernst, *The Theology of Grace*. Mercier, Cork, 1974.

B. Häring, (ET) *Sin in the Secular Age*. St Paul Publications, Slough, 1974.

Ascension of 11, 157, 184
authority of 104f
beatific vision of 92f
body of, *see* body of Christ
death of 13, 58, 62, 80, 82,
   91, 103, 114, 117, 118,
   122, 132, 156f, 174, 196
divinity of 1f, 23, 66f, 79,
   85, 90f, 95, 99, 101,
   105, 118, 158
non-verbal knowledge of
   101f
grace of, *see* grace of Christ
Heart of 85-9
historical knowledge about,
   83f, 103
ignorance of 93-6, 98f
imitation of 83-5, 92, 156
Incarnation of 22, 28, 45f,
   64, 65-7, 78f, 89-91, 96,
   98, 100, 102, 113, 115f,
   144, 149, 157f, 196
infallibility of 96-7
knowledge possessed by 92f,
   97f, *see* Christ, psychology of
Logos, *see* Word
manhood of 23, 66f, 79,
   81, 83, 85, 87, 90f,
   94-6, 113f, 118f, 127,
   156-8
mediator 80f, 114, 133
miracles of, *see* miracles
obedience of 104f, 111, 117
one subject of 101
prayer of 94-6
psychology of 23, 77, 87,
   89-106, 150, 153
representative man 20, 81,
   118, 172
Resurrection of 13f, 24, 58,
   62, 80, 82, 104, 115,
   117f, 132, 150, 156-8,
   174, 196
Sacrament of God 155-7
sacrifice of 109, 111, 113,
   115, 118f, 123
side of 86-8
temptations of 103f
two operations and wills of
   100

virgin birth of 91
Christian, implicit ('anonymous')
   17, 133-7, 176n, 191
Chrysostom, *see* John Chrysos-
   tom, St
Church, and sacraments, *see*
   sacraments, ecclesial effect of
   as sacrament 155-8, 162,
      169, 173f
   holiness of 157f
   membership of 157f, 170-5
   unity of 158
Clement of Alexandria 17n, 22
Clements, R.E. 3n
Cloud of Unknowing 185f
Collingwood, R.G. 2
communion of saints 173
confirmation 82, 169-71, 193
Connolly, C. 181
contrition 129
conversion 128, 193, 198
Copleston, F.C. 17n
Coreth, E. 73n
Councils, Carthage (416) 23
   Chalcedon 66f, 91, 100
   Florence 65
   Trent 32, 56f, 64n, 108,
      128, 134
   Vatican I 32, 138
   Vatican II 132, 145f, 155n,
      158, 170, 172f
covenant 3-8, 9, 41-4, 172, 175,
   196
Cowley, A. 5n
creation 2-4, 16, 21, 23f, 32f,
   40, 42-9, 63-6, 196
   new 12, 24, 36, 58f, 62, 68,
      127, 132, 197
Cudworth, R. 130, 132
Cyril of Alexandria, St 32

Dalrymple, J. 186n
darkness, experience of 123, 125,
   185-191
Davies, W.D. 118n
Davis, C. 82n
death 179, *see* immortality
desire of God, natural 34f, 49,
   58, 69
development of doctrine 151
devil 104, 110f, 115, 119

212

Samuel, Books of 141
salvation, *see* redemption
sanctification, *see* justification
Satan, *see* devil
Schillebeeckx, E.   170n, 171n
schism 158
Schleiermacher, F.   115
Schoonenberg, P.   43f, 49, 74,
    139n, 143
Schweitzer, E.   9n
Scotus, Duns   57n, 114n, 121
Scripture, and Church   141, 144,
    159
    canon of   144f
    inspiration of   137-54, 198
    inerrancy of   144-9, 152
    non-Christian and
        non-Jewish   143f
    normative value of   151-3
    social inspiration of   140-3
Scullion, J.J.   138, 141, 146
seal, *see* sacraments, 'character'
    of
Semmelroth, O.   169
sex 22
Shaw, G.B.   39
sickness   170f, 180-3, 191
sign, *see* sacraments as signs
Simpson, M.   177n
sin   7, 15, 19-21, 23, 38, 40,
    43f, 50-2, 60, 97, 107-129,
    137, 157f, 170, 182n, 198,
    see redemption
    mortal/venial   129, 163
    personal/original   128f, 198
    sense of   121
social nature of man   74, 123
Socrates 179
solidarity of man, *see* Christ,
    representative man
Solignac, A.   19n
sons of God, *see* adoption
Soto, D.   37
Spirit of God   5f, 9-14, 19-21,
    23f, 33, 36, 50, 52-5, 57f,
    60-2, 65-7, 69, 78, 81, 85f,
    88, 103, 106, 125, 127-9,
    132-4, 137f, 150, 153, 155,
    157-60, 162, 164, 169, 171,
    175, 179f, 184, 187, 189f,
    192f, 196-9.

and charity   53
Starbuck, E.D.   108
Staupitz, J.   180n
Stierli, J.   86n, 87
Stoics   9, 16, 17n
supernatural/natural   20f, 26-41,
    46-8, 55f, 58, 61, 69, 188,
    196
    different senses of   17-30
symbols, *see* sacraments as signs

de la Taille, M.   64-7
Tatian   18-20
Teilhard de Chardin, P.   45-7,
    49, 182, 184
Teresa of Avila, St   188, 191
Tertullian   71, 86f
Theodore of Mopsuestia   119
Theophilus of Antioch, St   18-9,
    22
Thomas, Gospel of   178
Thomas Aquinas, St   32, 34-8,
    54f, 57, 70f, 78f, 81, 92f,
    111, 135n, 158n, 164n, 171
Thurston, H.   87n
Tinsley, E.J.   83f
Toletus 37
tongues, gift of, *see glossolalia,*
    Pentecostalism
Toplady, A.M.   85
tradition   140-3
transcendental experience of
    grace   74, 90, 125f, 136,
    187, 190, 197
Transcendental Method   73f
Trinity   24, 46, 62, 65-7, 85, 90,
    102, 137, 151n, 197, *see*
    God, personal relationship
    with
Tugwell, S.   192f
Tyrrell, G.   83

Universals   118

Vicarious punishment   111f
vicarious satisfaction   111
Vignaux, P.   121
de Vio, T., *see* Cajetan
vision of God   34f, 49, 60, 92f,
    134, 178
vocation, *see* call

213

Waugh, E. 29
Wesley, J. 107
Whitehead, A.N. 28
Windsor Statement 82
Word of God 2f, 16-8, 21f, 24,
  45, 52, 63, 101, 105, 113,
  116, 118f, 132, 144, 157,
  159, 171n

and sacrament, *see* sacraments and word
works, salvation by 113

Yahwist 145
Yarnold, E.J. 82n, 128n, 144n,
  156n, 167n

BIBLICAL INDEX

215